Daniel Webster and
the Unfinished Constitution

AMERICAN POLITICAL THOUGHT

Jeremy D. Bailey and Susan McWilliams Brandt
Series Editors

Wilson Carey McWilliams and Lance Banning
Founding Editors

Daniel Webster and
the Unfinished Constitution

Peter Charles Hoffer

University Press of Kansas

Published by the University Press of Kansas (Lawrence, Kansas 66045), which
was organized by the Kansas Board of Regents and is operated and funded by
Emporia State University, Fort Hays State University, Kansas State University,
Pittsburg State University, the University of Kansas, and Wichita State
University.

Library of Congress Cataloging-in-Publication Data

Names: Hoffer, Peter Charles, 1944– author.
Title: Daniel Webster and the unfinished Constitution / Peter Charles Hoffer.
Description: Lawrence : University Press of Kansas, [2021] | Series:
    American political thought | Includes index.
Identifiers: LCCN 2020040388
    ISBN 9780700632008 (cloth)
    ISBN 9780700632015 (epub)
Subjects: LCSH: Webster, Daniel, 1782–1852. | Constitutional law—United
States—Interpretation and construction. | Federal government—United
States—History. | Constitutional history—United States.
Classification: LCC KF4550 .H624 2021 | DDC 342.7302/9—dc23
LC record available at https://lccn.loc.gov/2020040388.

British Library Cataloguing-in-Publication Data is available.

Printed in the United States of America

10 9 8 7 6 5 4 3 2 1

The paper used in this publication is recycled and contains 30 percent
postconsumer waste. It is acid free and meets the minimum requirements of
the American National Standard for Permanence of Paper for Printed Library
Materials Z39.48-1992.

Contents

Preface

Daniel Webster was the foremost constitutional lawyer of his day, the first choice for litigants (who could afford his fee) when their claim was grounded in the federal Constitution. He did not come from elite or even comfortable circumstances like many of his compatriots in the antebellum bar. Instead, as his contemporary and rival New Hampshire lawyer Joel Parker conceded, "no man ever rose more rapidly to distinction by his unaided efforts" than Webster. Not just a practitioner, Webster was an innovative jurist. While Chief Justice John Marshall gets credit for much of our early constitutional jurisprudence, in fact in a series of key cases Marshall simply borrowed Webster's oral and written arguments.

For antebellum lawyers and judges, professions of adherence to the Constitution were universal. Yet they knew that the Constitution could not be fixed in time; that its text had to be read in light of changing circumstances or it would become irrelevant. As Chief Justice Marshall explained in *Bank of the United States v. Deveaux* (1809): "a constitution, from its nature, deals in generals, not in detail. Its framers cannot perceive minute distinctions which arise in the progress of the nation, and therefore confine it to the establishment of broad and general principles."

But were these broad and general principles themselves fixed? Or were they, like the changing circumstances in which they were examined, subject to reinterpretation? "Which arise" was the key phrase. To this day, the explication of the Constitution's meaning remains an unfinished project. As judge Richard Posner explained, the Constitution still contains "major gaps," which is "the nature of our, or perhaps any, written Constitution." It becomes the job of each generation of jurists "to plug at least the most glaring gaps."

Gaps—silences—abound in constitutional texts. The documents cannot cover every exigency or new question. Hence lawyers and judges strive to fill the silence with their own voices. Think if you will of the Constitution as a textual landscape and the jurisprudent as a surveyor. There are landmarks of course. For Webster, one of these was the Contracts Clause. Another was the Commerce Clause. But for him there were spaces in the landscape that were unmarked. This book tries to follow Webster's level staff and surveyor's chains as he set out to map the constitutional terrain.

For him three of these open spaces were (and for us remain) vast and yet crucial to the survey of our constitutional order. The first is the relationship between the federal government and the existing states. This is the familiar issue of "federalism." Hotly contested in Webster's time, still a matter of controversy today, this boundary is not and perhaps cannot be precisely charted. The second is the boundary between public interest and private right. Across the entire scope of law, from arbitration to zoning, this boundary remains a dark and bloody ground. The third is the relationship between law and ordinary partisan politics, sometimes conceptualized as the relationship between courts and legislatures, court-made law and legislative enactment. In a system designed with checks and balances in mind, this relationship was and still is contentious.

Webster was also a politician, ambitious for high office and remuneration therefrom. The interplay of his public politics and his lawyering made his life complex, and in the end, tragic. That too is part of his jurisprudential contribution and a subject of this book. But I make no claims for Webster as an original political thinker. His distinction, and his contributions, lay in the realm of law.

I am once again indebted to my long-time collaborators N. E. H. Hull and Williamjames Hull Hoffer for their comments on the manuscript. The members of the American Founding Group at the University of Georgia provided helpful insights on this and our other, related, readings. I am especially grateful to Keith Dougherty for his incisive comments. Among the students in my legal history seminar here, I am grateful to Imani Carter, Christian Choe, Megan Copelan, Morgan Geiser, Valerie McLaurin, Nathan Rothenbaum, and Alexandra Velez for their input. Daniel Walker Howe and H. Robert Baker, readers for the University Press of Kansas, were generous and constructive critics. Jeremy Bailey and Susan McWilliams Barndt, editors of the American Political Thought series at the press, graciously agreed to include the book in the series and made valuable suggestions for revision. David Congdon, editor at the press, guided the manuscript through to publication. My thanks to him are heartfelt.

Daniel Webster and
the Unfinished Constitution

Introduction:
The Incomplete Constitution

As the time in which it was crafted receded into a distant past, the federal Constitution became part of a founding mythos, given as a blessing to the people by what Thomas Jefferson half-jokingly called an assembly of demigods. The document, preserved under glass at the National Archives in Washington, DC, has gained in the popular mind a completeness and canonical authority. In fact, this near worship of an immutable founding text, though widely promoted to hold together a diverse and often raucous public sphere, is not historically accurate. The meaning of the Constitution has always been a subject of contention among jurists.[1]

Indeed, the framers expected their words to be viewed differently over time. Edmund Randolph's "Draft Sketch" of the Constitution on July 26, 1787, proposed "to insert essential principles only; lest the operations of government should be clogged by rendering those provisions permanent and unalterable, which ought to be accommodated to times and events." James Madison too understood that the Constitution must be open to changing interpretations. "All new laws, though penned with the greatest technical skill, and passed on the fullest and most mature deliberation, are considered as more or less obscure and equivocal, until their meaning be liquidated and ascertained by a series of particular discussions and adjudications." He conceded that the new frame of government was "by necessity and design" imperfect. Time, experience, and the wisdom of legislators and jurists would improve what the drafters offered, he argued.[2]

The second generation of American judicial leaders, lacking the cachet of the framers, and facing fierce political party factionalism unanticipated by the framers, introduced the rhetoric of immutability. For example, in his *A General View of the Origin and Nature of the Constitution and Government of the United States* (1837), US Supreme Court justice Henry Baldwin insisted that Constitution exhibited "safe principles . . . these principles are few and simple." His colleague on the bench, Joseph Story, concurred in the concluding passage of his monumental *Commentaries on the Constitution* (1833), "The seal of eternity is upon it. The wisdom, which it has displayed, and the blessings, which it has bestowed, cannot be obscured; neither can they be debased by

human folly, or human infirmity." Baldwin and Story occupied opposing positions on many issues, Baldwin a Jacksonian Democrat and Story a Whig, but
on the immutability of the Constitution they agreed.[3]

The reason for the introduction of fixity was obvious to all who sat on
the High Court in the 1830s and those who practiced before it in the period
between 1815 and 1850. Then, contending political factions of Democratic
Republicans and National Republicans, followed by Democrats and Whigs,
sought the cachet of the Constitution for their programs. As Story himself
warned, such politicians "reverenced power more in its high abuses . . . than in
its calm and constitutional energy." The true guardians of the law felt real "solicitude both for the virtue and permanence of our republic." The greater the
factions' search for support in the fundamental law, the greater Story thought
the need to characterize the Constitution as fixed and immutable.[4]

It was in this context that Daniel Webster began his storied practice before the
High Court. Seen from the perspective of those like Webster who inherited
the new system of federal self-government, three unanswered questions in the
new Constitution recurred. All three interacted with the political quarrels of
the day. The first was what later scholarship would call the problem of federalism. What exactly was the relationship of the new federal government to the
states? The compromises that comprised "dual sovereignty" were brilliant and
innovative ones, but the details were few in the document itself. What were the
enumerated powers of the new government? What powers were explicitly delegated to the states? Which powers could be exercised by both governments,
without trampling on enumerated or delegated powers? In a general way, the
Supremacy Clause of Article VI (clause 2) addressed the question, but it raised
as many questions as it may have answered. "This Constitution, and the Laws
of the United States which shall be made in Pursuance thereof; and all Treaties
made, or which shall be made, under the Authority of the United States, shall
be the supreme Law of the Land; and the Judges in every State shall be bound
thereby, any Thing in the Constitution or Laws of any State to the Contrary
notwithstanding."

Citing the Supremacy Clause's vague and terse quality as the basis for federal authority did little to settle anything when states claimed the primary allegiance of their citizenry. For example, did enumeration of interstate commerce in Article I bar states from regulating commerce on internal waterways?

Did the guarantee of republican form of government for each state in Article IV mean that the federal government could intervene in states' constitutional disputes? Did the Supremacy Clause apply to state legislation? Did state governors, as opposed to judges, have to bow to federal law? In other words, what was constitutional law, such that all the branches of state governments must obey it? A hasty and itself unclear amendment to the Constitution that became the Tenth offered, "The powers not delegated to the United States by the Constitution, nor prohibited by it to the States, are reserved to the States respectively, or to the people." Alas, like the Supremacy Clause, the Tenth Amendment's reach far exceeded its grasp. It was both vague and overbroad. What powers were there that the people could exercise outside the federal and state governments, or, in the alternative, to check the federal and state governments?[5]

The second incompleteness Webster tackled was the absence of a clear boundary between the public weal and private rights. This too overlapped sharp contemporary political divisions. When did a taking of some or all private property for a public purpose impermissibly incise private ownership rights? To be sure, different answers to the question had played into the American Revolution. There was no such distinction in earlier times in England and the colonies—that is, there were no truly private property or personal rights. Despite treatises and protests to the contrary by everyone from Diggers, Levellers, and Ranters to learned lawyers and men of affairs, everything one owned or did was a privilege granted by crown—and later by crown in Parliament—and could be rescinded. Much-vaunted "English Liberty," aka private property, was itself the gift of the government. Although the American colonists from the inception of the Atlantic Empire claimed fee simple rights of land ownership, these were subject to quit rents and the rescinding of colonial charters. Property was the basis of Anglo-American imperial commerce, but again Parliament claimed the authority to regulate and tax this commerce. Once this liberty was rooted in American law, the framers regarded it as a right rather than a gift, but the boundary between this individual right and the public interest remained undefined in the federal Constitution. As legal historian Morton Horwitz concluded, "At the turn of the century there still existed a perhaps dominant body of opinion maintaining that individuals held their property at the sufferance of the state."[6]

In *Federalist*, no. 10, Madison recognized the fuzziness of the public/private boundary along with its explosive political potential. "The diversity of the faculties of men from which the rights of property originate, is not less an insuperable obstacle to an uniformity of interests." Men of property were the authors of the Constitution, and their interests were, like Madison's (a very rich man himself), "the first object of government. From the protection of different and unequal faculties of acquiring property, the possession of different degrees and kinds of property immediately results: and from the influence of these on the sentiments and views of the respective proprietors, ensures a division of the society into different interests and parties." In short, the reach of public interest was and always would be a contest of factions.[7]

Madison believed that one of the great accomplishments of the American Revolution was to impose a distinction between public interest and private rights in the form of bills of rights. The original federal Constitution included prohibitions on both the federal and the state governments abusing certain rights but relied on the varieties of state constitutions for other basic protections. The demand for a federal bill of rights was a centerpiece of antifederalist objections to the Constitution, and Congress, led by Madison, drafted a bill of rights in the first session. Federal courts would enforce these rights. As Madison wrote to fellow Virginian Edmund Pendleton near the end of the first session of the Congress, a bill of rights would take from the antifederalists their most potent objection to lower courts.[8]

The language of the new Bill of Rights passed by both houses of Congress in 1789 and ratified in 1791 was supposed to define the boundary between what the federal government could do in the public interest and what rights an individual could assert against the government. The sweeping language of the amendments was in many ways just as vague as the language of the parent document, however. Each amendment could and in time would give rise to competing interpretations. The Ninth Amendment seemed to address the public interest/private rights question: "The enumeration in the Constitution, of certain rights, shall not be construed to deny or disparage others retained by the people." What those rights might be was left to later generations to liquidate. The inclusion of this language, however, only demonstrated that the framers understood how important the line between public power and private right was. They just could not draw it.[9]

The last of the three missing pieces in the Constitution may well have been the most important: the document did not draw a boundary between law and ordinary politics. Politicians wrote the Constitution. All of the delegates had or were currently occupying some position in state or national governance. They were public men doing a political duty.

To deny that the Constitution was in some sense a political document, or at least a compromise among partisan factions, is to ignore the history of its drafting and ratification. As historian Jack Rakove has explained, "the interplay between politics and political thought" was also the interplay between the realms of politics and law. But the document itself said nothing about politics, save that the federal government could guarantee a republican form of governance to the states in Article IV: "The United States shall guarantee to every State in this Union Republican Form of Government, and shall protect each of them against Invasion; and on Application of the Legislature, or of the Executive (when the Legislature cannot be convened), against domestic Violence."[10]

The new federal government itself had three branches, separated by checks and balances. The separation was intended, in part, to prevent any particular partisan group from dominating the federal government. Which among the branches had the final word when it came to the constitutionality of any law was not clear. One of the branches was popularly elected (given the limitations of the franchise at that time). If it had the final say, then surely the line between everyday politics and law would be drawn far toward the former. The president was elected by a college of electors, apportioned among the states according to their representation in Congress. If he decided where to draw the line, perhaps it would be on the side of law—but this did not anticipate the rise of the political parties, and the consequent politicization of the executive office. The judiciary was independent of direct election, being appointed by the president with the advice and consent of the Senate. Surely it would draw the line far closer to the law as text or as judicial decisions than as the contest of parties in the legislature. But what if the federal judiciary itself became a handmaiden of one of the major parties? As Justice Stephen Breyer put it plainly, "The Constitution does not directly answer the who question or the limits question." Nor did the system of checks and balances between the legislative, or overtly political, and the judicial branches bridge the politics/law divide.[11]

One hopeful observation was and remains that the judicial branch is sufficiently insulated from ordinary politics and would exhibit impartiality in

politically charged questions. Were these judges and justices then above political allegiances? Hardly. In fact, from the inception of the federal bench, federal
judges were overwhelmingly chosen from the president's political party. All
of the members of the first federal judiciary were Federalists, selected with
that criterion in mind by George Washington. During the Alien and Sedition
Acts crisis of 1798–1800, the Federalist federal judiciary followed the party line.
When the Republican Party gained control of the federal executive and Senate
in 1801, all of the appointments to the federal courts went to Republicans. It
must have seemed to contemporary observers, as it does to some court watchers today, that the federal courts were little more than miniature legislatures
dominated by whichever party appointed the judges. (The state court high
judges were almost everywhere appointed by elected officials. States did not
switch to election of high court judges until the 1820s. Although almost all
were lawyers by training, almost all were also political figures before they as-
cended the bench.)[12]

Perhaps this silence over the part that party politics was to play under the
Constitution was due to the fact that the first decade under the new federal
government was a time of partisanship largely unanticipated in the 1787–1789
period. In the maelstrom of partisan politics, Madison's proposed "liquidation" of vexing constitutional questions was difficult. Party allegiance rather
than considered legalism dictated hasty and self-interested answers. The
rise of the two-party system played havoc with the project of constitutional
elucidation.[13]

The Federalist-Antifederalist debates of 1787–1788 were milk and water
things by comparison with the party wars of the 1790s. Former allies like Alexander Hamilton and James Madison offered such disparate interpretations
of the treaty provisions, the Necessary and Proper Clause, and freedom of the
press according to the First Amendment that one would think the Constitution was two entirely different documents. Who would settle the increasingly
vexing conundrum, who could draw the line between constitutional law and
the struggle for power among political factions under the Constitution in a
clear and convincing way? Put in other terms, insofar as the courts were the
branch charged with legal matters and the legislatures given to political decisions, which of the branches was to have the last word on the meaning and
implementation of the Constitution?[14]

At first, the federal courts and Congress, dominated by the Federalist Party,
seemed to be in accord. But by the beginning of the nineteenth century, when

Webster started to practice law, the federal courts, still staffed by Federalists, and the national legislature, now dominated by Jeffersonian Republicans, were at odds. The newly elected Republican majority in Congress dumped the Judiciary Act of 1801, forcing the Supreme Court justices to resume circuit riding. The Republicans in the House of Representatives began a campaign of impeaching vulnerable members of the federal judiciary. If anything, the separation between law and politics, federal courts and Congress, was closing, if not already gone.[15]

One way to resolve the law/politics debate was to concede that the Constitution was a political document. It apportioned and limited federal power, hence it had to be political. Did that mean it had to be partisan? Was law then simply a creature of whichever party governed? Webster never conceded this, however. For it would follow that courts must defer to legislatures, especially nonelected courts like those created by the Constitution.[16]

Webster's view, explored in the following chapters, accorded with that of former chief justice John Jay. In 1801 Jay wrote to John Adams, when both men had departed federal office,

> Such was the temper of the times [in the 1790s], that the Act to establish the Judicial Courts of the United States was in some respects more accommodated to certain prejudices and sensibilities, than to the great and obvious principles of sound policy. Expectations were nevertheless entertained that it would be amended as the public mind became more composed and better informed; but those expectations have not been realized, nor have we hitherto seen convincing indications of a disposition in Congress to realize them. On the contrary, the efforts repeatedly made to place the judicial department on a proper footing have proved fruitless.

It seemed to Jay, whose experience with the virulent politics of the 1790s included vilification for concluding the treaty with Britain bearing his name, that politics in Congress had swallowed law and the Supreme Court. Ironically, Thomas Jefferson, formerly secretary of state, was one of those whose negative opinion of the Jay Treaty led to the crisis that Jay lamented, blamed the politicization of the government on "the court lawyers, & courtly judges, & would-be ambassadors," in short, on Jay and his ilk. Politics as usual—exactly what Jay and Adams feared.[17]

In the final analysis it may be true, as one historian has recently concluded, that "the irony of the endless search for the original Constitution is that such an inquiry will never reveal a fixed document." Such academic relativism would have been lost on the generation that followed the framers, however. They were determined to prove—or improve—the work of their fathers. Indeed, they believed that the effort was vital if the Constitution, and the nation for which it stood, was to survive intact.[18]

Nothing in the forgoing, except for the occasional quotation from a modern jurist, would have surprised Webster. Well-to-do clients hired him to litigate a series of Article I claims about contracts, banks, and commerce in federal court because he knew all about the Constitution's missing parts. They were not paying him to engage in theoretical jurisprudential asides, but he did. Famous for oral argument that went on for hours, in them he ranged far beyond business enterprise and commercial questions. He used the facts of cases to launch into sweeping analyses of the unanswered questions of law and politics. In his most famous senatorial addresses, he did the same, rising above the motion at hand to offer the members a coherent reading of government powers and private rights.[19]

Let us return now to why Webster's constitutionalism was so important. Judges go to school on counsel's briefs. So should scholars. Acknowledged by Rufus Choate, a colleague, coworker, and eminent lawyer himself, Webster was "the leader of the American bar" in his time. Webster took great pains with his presentations, and with the law in them. As those who remembered him throughout his career would say in his eulogies, "The serious, earnest attitude toward the duties before him that mark the youth abode with him till his work was done." But this was not just true of Webster's briefs. As Suzanna Sherry wrote in a classic law review article, "I rely not only on judicial opinions, but also on the arguments made by lawyers. Although made in an adversarial context, these advocates' positions provide evidence of the types of arguments considered legitimate and within the bounds of the legal culture of the period. In many instances, the advocates' position was ultimately adopted by the court." This was particularly true in the early years of the federal courts; as historian Maurice Baxter put it, "These years were a formative era of constitutional law . . . and counsel enjoyed the freedom of pioneers."[20]

Legal practitioners know all about the impact of lawyers on constitutional interpretation. Antifederalists recognized the role that lawyers would have in bringing the Constitution to life, although some among them (who were not lawyers) feared the "sly art of sophistry" and "false glosses" of lawyers, those "scribes and Pharisees" whose arcane arts alone would enable them to "interpret and give [the Constitution] meaning." What the Antifederalists excoriated, the Federalists celebrated. Indeed, when the convention in Philadelphia needed a final revision of the draft Constitution, it turned to a Committee on Style and Arrangement, including Gouverneur Morris, of Pennsylvania; Rufus King, of New York; William Samuel Johnson, of Connecticut; and Alexander Hamilton—all lawyers.[21]

That it was true in the case of Daniel Webster is beyond dispute. For thirty-eight years, from 1814 to 1852, he had a remarkable impact on federal constitutionalism. Following Webster into the courtroom, standing beside him, and listening to him, one can focus on his arguments rather than the opinions of the judges. True, as precedent this impact was filtered through the opinions of Chief Justice John Marshall, and, to a much lesser extent, Chief Justice Roger Taney, with the result that the credit for novelty and vision has gone to the justice rather than the advocate.[22]

On seven occasions Webster attempted to traverse and map three largely uncharted spaces that the framers had left in the Constitution. Four of those occasions arose in the course of his legal practice. In arguments Webster made in representing clients before the Supreme Court, the *Dartmouth College* case (1819), *M'Culloch v. Maryland* (1819), *Gibbons v. Ogden* (1824), and the *Charles River Bridge* case (1837), he addressed issues of politics v. law, public interest v. private rights, and federal power v. state sovereignty left unexplored at the constitutional convention. Two further occasions for Webster to survey what the framers left unmapped occurred in the course of debates in the Senate. The first was an exchange at the end of January 1830 between Webster and Robert V. Hayne of South Carolina concerning the expansion of slavery to the West. The second again took place on the Senate floor, in March 1850, during which Webster joined in general debate on the fugitive slave bill. The final episode occurred when Webster served as President John Tyler's secretary of state and required Webster to apply his jurisprudence to a series of diplomatic crises.

I do not mean to say that Webster set out from the beginning of his career in front of the High Court bench to resolve ambiguities and survey the unmapped regions in the Constitutional text. But as he prepared arguments for his clients, that is exactly what he did. In other words, he was never just a litigator, changing his arguments to fit the occasion. There was a whole-ness in them, a set of recurring themes, that amounted to a constitutional jurisprudence.[23]

How original was Webster's thinking on the three questions? Of course he was not the only antebellum lawyer/politician to face them in court or in Congress, nor the only one to think and write about them. Compared to the other great litigators of his day—William Wirt, Joseph Hopkinson, and Henry Clay—however, he was the only one to engage in deep consideration of them. A comparison of his briefs with his co-counsel's and opposing counsel's reaffirms what the *New York Daily Times* obituary of Daniel Webster concluded: "If mighty interests were at stake, or new and interesting questions involved, or if causes depended upon constitutional construction, the services were invoked of this Goliath of the North."[24]

What was Webster's motivation in assaying what were, even for his time, such extended briefs and oral arguments? One answer thus far missing from the literature on Webster is his combative nature. He was an intellectual brawler. Not only did he hate to lose in a court case or a legislative debate, but he wanted his victory to be a memorable one. In law, that kind of triumph takes a unique form. One's argument becomes precedent. That means that one has convinced the bench to adopt one's reasoning. Webster did not always attain or even seek such triumphs. Sometimes he simply went through the motions. In the following episodes, I believe, it was the quality or influence of his opponent that drove his own efforts: In *Dartmouth College* it was New Hampshire chief justice William Richardson's opinion. In *M'Culloch* it was the arguments of opposing counsel Joseph Hopkinson. In *Gibbons* it was Chancellor James Kent's opinion. In the *Charles River Bridge* case, it was Chief Justice Roger Taney. In the 1830 Senate debates with Robert Hayne, it was the gray eminence literally sitting at the front of the chamber, John C. Calhoun, the same sparring partner as in the famous March 7, 1850, address.

A second reason for the length of Webster's briefs (and the integration of his jurisprudential thinking from one case to another) was that Webster was a pedant. He read widely and took notes profusely, not only in legal matters but in history and political theory as well. He tried to master the classical literature and philosophy. He liked publicly to display his learning. While his public addresses were the prime occasions for this pedantry, it made its way into his oral court presentations.[25]

A final thought: a compelling speaker, Webster was not an elegant writer.

He repeated himself and belabored the obvious. He engaged in long, rhetorical asides. Something like this was necessary in an era when much pleading in court rested on the judges' real-time note taking. He gave them time to write down the essentials. Written reports of Webster's addresses to the justices can thus be tedious reading. With this in mind, I have tried to listen to his words, rather than just reading them, re-creating the "lexicon of aurality" of lawyers from the scribal record.[26]

1. A New England Man

Most Americans know Daniel Webster as a politician first and lawyer second. To his political opponents, there seemed something shifty about Webster's career in politics. He went from populist defender of the yeoman farmer to free trade advocate of the overseas merchants to spokesman for tariff protection for New England manufacturing. Was it political ambition that drove him; Webster looking for a popular stance to propel him from Congress to the presidency? If so, with all due respect to his actual achievements, he had no clue. He took unpopular positions, New England positions, when the region was increasingly atypical of the rest of the country. Admired as a political advocate and for a time certain of reelection to Congress, he never quite got the hang of what the mass of voters wanted. In the end, he seemed out of place—a crotchety defender of older values when successful presidential candidates spoke for more popular positions in a democratic vernacular.

Did he do it all for lucre? He was certainly not averse to charging fees equal to anyone's in the legal profession. Yet comparing his fees against the hours he put into each case, the hourly rate was hardly exorbitant. Money seemed to seep through his hands, however. He died in debt, having burdened his estate with loans he could not repay. He owed mortgage repayments on Elm Farm in Franklin, New Hampshire, formerly Salisbury; Green Harbor, in Marshfield, Massachusetts, on the south coast; and a four-story mansion on the corner of High and Summer Streets in Boston. He furnished all of them elegantly. Growing up with ten siblings in a rustic farmhouse/tavern, he remembered being house poor. He also remembered how important the tavern was to his father's political standing, and Daniel entertained lavishly and often. His first, frugal, wife Grace Fletcher passed away in 1828, and the next year Daniel married a New York socialite, Caroline Le Roy. He underwrote his second wife's expensive tastes.[1]

Going into debt was almost too easy for those who devoted lives to public service. Jefferson died in debt. So did Alexander Hamilton, Aaron Burr, James Wilson, and Robert Morris. Morris, the financier of the American Revolution, spent some time in debtors' prison. Creditors pursued Wilson on his Supreme Court circuit rounds. Webster had the same penchant for overinvesting in land schemes as the previous generation of political leaders. Had Webster, who in the 1820s earned $20,000 a year for his legal work (about half a million dollars in modern terms), simply devoted himself to it, building a bigger firm, seeking out remunerative cases, and leaving politics behind, he would not have died in debt. But speculation, like politics, was his passion.[2]

Perhaps insecurity drove Webster to excess? His arguments in court were excruciatingly long and detailed. His speeches in Congress were similarly exhaustive. He repeated himself, a sign that he was not always sure of his influence. Before he acted on an issue, he had his speeches on that issue printed and sent to influential clients, political allies, and members of the legal fraternity. He needed their approval. He longed for public respectability. He never quite departed that rough country start, working for but not sitting at the head table with the entrepreneurs, although in no way was he a "country lawyer." He loved applause and sought it; and oratory was something that he could control. No outside influence save illness could stop him from preparing and delivering an oration. The words were his; the pauses, intonations, pace, and meter were his. If oratory was the only thing in his life he could control, perhaps that was enough. Galvanizing audiences in Congress with his oratory, he nevertheless was not invited to the back room where the party moguls determined who would be president. One cannot entirely separate Webster's career as a politician from his career as a lawyer, but the latter reveals a different and more interesting Webster.

Daniel Webster was born five years before the federal Constitutional Convention met, and his entire adult and professional life was played out in its shadow. Unlike the members of the New Hampshire delegation to Philadelphia, Nicholas Gilman and John Langdon (both men were later US senators), Webster did not come from an already prominent family. His origins lay in the self-sufficient yeomanry of New Hampshire. His ancestors had migrated to the new colony in the 1630s, and his family were small landowners, farmers, tavern keepers, and local officials. Like many of their kin, his father fought in the French and Indian War and the American Revolution. Again, like many who farmed the land, his father had other occupations—tavern keeper, town clerk, coroner, and local judge. The family was large, like most farm households.

Daniel, who arrived on January 18, 1782, was one of ten children (five from his father's former marriage). Never much of a fan of hard physical labor, he was sickly in his childhood, though he grew to a solid nearly six-foot height. Extraordinarily bookish, he was home tutored—an expense for his father but one that Daniel used to great advantage. At fourteen, he entered Phillips Exeter Academy, and a year he later enrolled at Dartmouth College, in Hanover, New Hampshire. There he developed his oratorical skills and joined the Federalist Party. In later years, he would recall his attachment to the college.[3]

Rhetoric, including public speaking, was one of the classic college subjects. Its instruction aimed to assist those students in future legal and ministerial careers. Webster already excelled at oratory because he was long used to entertain customers in his father's tavern with recitation of bible passages from memory. Little "Black Dan" (like his father, Daniel's complexion was dark, and that is how he introduced himself when he stood for entrance to Dartmouth), seemed a born orator. Whether innate or learned, he honed his abilities in public speaking in college. It was a heady time for oratory in the nation, changing from an exercise in "decorum, rational persuasion, and controlled appeals to the sentiments" to emotional excess. Law students especially absorbed the new canon of energy and expressiveness.[4]

Speaking in public, "Godlike Daniel" could shift rhythms, tones, and vocabulary so effortlessly that listeners did not perceive the many hours he put into the preparation of each oration. In maturity, Webster's voice was described as rich and deep, always controlled, "majestic, almost superhuman." Compared to some of his congressional and courtroom peers, he spoke slowly, and that may have enabled him to go on for hours, sometimes for days (although he could not match Thomas Hart Benton in the Senate or William Pinkney in the Court). There was a dark side to the voice too, a fierceness that was almost out of place in public discourse.

Not quite attractive, but muscular, with a Roman brow, dark hair and eyes, and imposing features, his face "could show disgust, and contempt, smiling in ridicule" even as his "voice rose with eloquence." Galleries in the Senate and seats in the Supreme Court chamber below filled with visitors when Webster was scheduled to speak. One thinks of the mythical giant Golem, or some other being whose presence is so riveting that one cannot take one's eyes off them.[5]

At Dartmouth College Webster's interest in politics was indefatigable. His interest in law was not. The road to political office led through public speaking and civic activity. This was also a road to a legal career, however. The connection between the two was well known. Famous Roman public speakers included notable lawyer/politicians like Cicero and Cato. Lawyering in the Roman Republic was largely reliant on swaying listeners with speeches. Law and oratory seemed to move in opposite directions in the era of Justinian, when precedent and code were reduced to writing, but in the English common law tradition, the ability to plead for a client was once again vitalized. Lawyers like Patrick Henry and Alexander Hamilton could mesmerize a jury for hours. They were the epigones of Cicero and Demosthenes—the orator statesmen of the republic.[6]

The power of persuasive speaking was a skill that could translate into political office when the auditory was the electorate. "It was a sound-conscious" political culture, the effect of which "was a stirrer primarily of common sentiments between a speaker and a listener." If strong at the beginning of the century, the power of oratory in the public imagination only grew as the decades passed, in what one scholar has called "an atmosphere of debate" in which "oratorical wishes" became "legal documents."[7]

Webster graduated Dartmouth College in 1800, a year of electoral turmoil. During Webster's college years, president John Adams and vice president Thomas Jefferson, both lawyers, led opposing political parties, Adams (although he despised political parties) the Federalists, and Jefferson the Republicans. The Federalists, a pro-English, conservative, anti-French party, were the dominant political organization in New England, and during the later 1790s, party rivalry between the Federalists and the Jefferson Republicans heated to fever pitch.

The Federalist majority in Congress passed a series of acts, including a sedition law to criminalize criticism of the government (truth was a defense, but who could prove a political opinion true?), and under it successfully prosecuted over a dozen Republican editors and political writers. Was that law, or partisanship masquerading as law? Was Congress taking onto itself the role of courts? Did the law politicize criminal procedure in the federal courts? Hamilton, no mean partisan himself, warned that the seditious libel law went too far—that is, it was no longer law but partisanship. Both Jefferson and James Madison authored protests against the seditious libel law, arguing that it was a violation of Congress's enumerated powers in the Constitution. The essence of their resolves was that the law had impermissibly moved the boundary between private rights (in this case freedom of the press) and government power in the direction of the latter.[8]

The 1800 presidential election itself was chaotic, with two Republican candidates, Jefferson and New York's Aaron Burr, receiving the same number of electoral votes. The Constitution sent the choice to the House of Representatives. Here again the law did not determine a result, however. Instead, the constitutional provision led to intense politicking in the House of Representatives. New Hampshire's congressional delegation voted for Burr, the Federalists' preferred candidate, although Burr's rival in New York politics, Alexander Hamilton, convinced Federalists in other delegations to abstain, throwing the vote (by state delegation) to Jefferson, ten to four. Webster surely took note of these proceedings and of the way that both the public/private and the political/legal questions were not addressed in the Constitution itself.[9]

The sedition law expired in 1801, and with the victory of the Jeffersonian Republicans in the 1800 elections, the time of the Federalist domination of the federal government was coming to an end—with one exception. President John Adams, with the aid of the lame duck Federalist majority in Congress and secretary of state John Marshall of Virginia, managed to find federal judicial offices for Federalists leaving Congress. Marshall himself was appointed and confirmed as the new chief justice of the US Supreme Court, joining other Federalists on the bench. The district courts, sitting in each state over which a district judge presided; circuit courts, created by the Judiciary Act of 1801, in which a newly named corps of circuit judges sat; and the Supreme Court, consisting of seven justices, were entirely Federalist in character. Had the line between law and politics been redrawn, or was the staffing of the federal courts with tried and true Federalists a proof that law and politics were never separable? Republican majorities in the House and Senate repealed the Judiciary Act of 1801 in 1802, shortly after the new Congress met. The Constitution had no answer to that question, and neither did the politicians or the lawyers.[10]

In 1801, once more in Salisbury, Webster decided to read law in the office of Thomas Thompson. Webster had political ambitions, but there were few hints in his correspondence that he was already thinking about the places where the two realms overlapped. For reading law was literally that—memorizing passages in books, talking about cases, copying documents. Webster, given to bouts of depression, wrote to one correspondent, "The language of the law is dry, hard, and stubborn as an old maid." The English cases in abridgements and manuals of forms dominated legal education. For Thompson and others of the revolutionary generation of lawyers, the emphasis was on pleading a case, that is, on the forms of action (grounds for bringing or defending a suit). By the beginning of the nineteenth century, a new concept of law, and consequently in legal education, was making its influence felt: the idea of categories of substantive law. Instead of the writs of trover, conversion, covenant, and the like, one learned about contracts for sale and purchase of property. Still, one had to read the classic English treatises on law, Edward Coke's *Institutes*, William Blackstone's *Commentaries*, organize rules and principles of the various categories of law, and then help perform the onerous duty of preparing cases for trial.[11]

Thompson was Boston bred, educated at Harvard, but removed to Salisbury, near to the Webster family homestead. Courtly and polished, he was different from Webster's neighbors and the Dartmouth crowd. Whether this rubbed off on Webster, or his rough country ways had already been polished by his time at Dartmouth, observers noticed that he was beginning to show something of the tastes of a gentleman. He was also learning something fundamental about lawyering that would, many years after his passing, mislead his biographers. They seemed to agree that he was inconsistent, if not outright duplicitous, in his politics, because he would shift from a pro-agrarian, free trade stance to a protectionist, pro-manufacturing position in Congress. Even in these early years of his practice, fellow lawyers knew that Webster was a consummate advocate for his clients' interests. As those clients changed, so did his epitomization of the public good.[12]

New Hampshire had abolished slavery during the revolution. No former slave owners in New Hampshire brought suit against Great Britain for wartime runaway slaves. Portsmouth ship owners did engage in the overseas slave trade, but they could not bring slaves back into the state. Webster rarely defended a slave owner, trader, or slavery itself in court. His law practice showed that the nation could thrive without slavery. In 1804, taking time from his clerking duties, he published a newspaper piece denouncing the Three-Fifths Clause of the Constitution. At the outset of the controversy over the admission of Missouri as a slave state, Webster drafted a memorial from Boston calling the institution a "great evil" and demanded that it not be extended into the West. A year later, in 1820, Webster interrupted his address commemorating the arrival of the Pilgrims with concluding remarks on slavery:

> In the sight of our law, the African slave-trader is a pirate and a felon; and in the sight of Heaven, an offender beyond the ordinary depth of human guilt. There is no brighter page of our history, than that which records the measures which have been adopted by the government at an early day, and at different times since, for the suppression of this traffic; and I would call on all the true sons of New England to cooperate with the laws of man, and the justice of Heaven. If there be, within the extent of our knowledge or influence, any participation in this traffic, let us pledge ourselves here, upon the rock of Plymouth, to extirpate and destroy it. It is not fit that the land of the Pilgrims should bear the shame longer. I hear the sound of the hammer, I see the smoke of the furnaces where manacles and fetters are still forged for human limbs. I see the visages of those who by stealth and at midnight labor in this work of hell, foul and dark, as may become the artificers of such instruments of misery and torture. Let that spot be purified, or let it cease to be of New England. Let it be purified, or let it be set aside from the Christian world; let it be put out of the circle of human sympathies and human regards, and let civilized man henceforth have no communion with it.

He added, "I care not of what complexion, white or brown" when he extolled the virtues of New Englanders. The printed version of the oration was widely disseminated in the North and widely admired. Webster was never an abolitionist; he preferred voluntary colonization. In 1822, joined by the attorney general of the United States, Webster argued that the slave trade was piracy under international law and congressional acts. In 1847, near the end of his life, he responded to opposing counsel in the Passenger Cases (1847) on the issue of slaves taken into the port of Boston. He was reported to have said, in an aside, that slavery was a "peculiar institution, the existence of which was recognized by the constitution of the United States. There it was placed by those who favored its existence, and he did not wish to disrobe it, nor should he lift his finger to do so. It belonged not to him, but to those alone who had power over it." It was clear as well that he believed, as did most New Englanders, in white supremacy.[13]

Though unenthusiastic about studying the details of book law, Webster believed that becoming a lawyer would allow him to "live comfortably" and avoid the poverty that periodically visited yeomen families. As for choices, he "fell into a law office," he later recalled. His father, now old and enfeebled by years of toil, was immersed in debt (sending Daniel and his brother Ezekiel to college had not helped) and needed Daniel's assistance. Webster even set aside his legal studies for a short time (six months was all he could manage) to teach school at Fryeburg Academy in Maine.[14]

In 1804 he resumed his course of studies, this time in Boston with Christopher Gore. Gore was a bon vivant who had traveled widely and whose practice was wider than Thompson's, including subjects like international commerce. In time, that would become part of Webster's own practice. Webster moved to Boston and was admitted to the state bar in 1805. He had also ingratiated himself with the Federalist political machine in the state. But there was little room for a New Hampshire farm boy in Massachusetts politics or legal business, and Webster returned to New Hampshire.

Setting up practice in Boscawen, in Merrimack County, a rural market town (the county seat was Concord), in effect Webster had come home. There he mixed local politics with the drudgery of pursuing deadbeat debtors—ironically, men like his father. Webster won almost 90 percent of his cases, usually representing the plaintiff, and was much in demand. Nevertheless, Webster's political ambition was already evident. He knew high political office and great wealth would not come to a country lawyer, so after his father died in 1806, Webster moved to Portsmouth, New Hampshire, a mercantile town on the Atlantic Coast. There, another mentor helped Webster learn the art of pleading to a jury: Jeremiah Mason. Mason was a Federalist and would become one of Webster's closest and most admired friends. Webster made enemies too. William Plumer, like Mason a lawyer and US senator, observed Webster from a less admiring standpoint: "As a speaker merely he is perhaps the best at the bar. His language is correct, his gestures good, and his delivery slow, articulate, and distinct. He excels in the statement of facts. But he is not thought to be a deep read lawyer." Webster's upbringing in hardscrabble rural New Hampshire was also evident to the more polished Plumer. "His manners are not pleasing—being cold, haughty, and overbearing." In 1849 Webster offered a more generous eulogy of Plumer, "a man of learning and of talent . . . he has lived a life of study and attainment." Webster did not add that Plumer was one of the staunchest defenders of religious liberty, a stance that Webster shared. From 1806 to 1815, Webster lived in Portsmouth, handled over 1,700 cases, often vying with Plumer, served on a commission to revise and reform the state's criminal laws, and campaigned for Federalist state and national candidates.[15]

The New Hampshire practice was neither remunerative nor intellectually stimulating. A typical case was *Lewis v. McGregor*. New Hampshire woodland was a major source of timber for ships, house construction, fencing, carpentry, and other related industries and crafts. Timber was also a major export crop. In 1807 Webster brought suit on behalf of Moses Lewis for logs allegedly delivered by him to Robert McGregor's sawmill, for which McGregor did not pay. There followed a series of writs, pleas, an attachment of McGregor's property, a losing decision in the court of common pleas, permission to bring an appeal to the state supreme court (under New Hampshire law a way to get a fresh trial), and another "count" (charge)—that Lewis had delivered the logs, but McGregor had them and converted them to his own use. Webster kept increasing the damages sought for the breach of contract, but both the logger and the miller knew something that the lawyers did not: it was never entirely clear who actually owned cut logs. They bore the marks of their owners, but the marks were often damaged on the way to the mills. Sometimes, once milled, the marks disappeared (something like disputed cattle brands in rustling cases). Webster and opposing counsel nevertheless took depositions (questions and answers under oath) from the parties. Imagine a witness for McGregor sitting opposite Webster, fixed in Webster's deep, dark eyes, his Roman brow wrinkling at the presumption of anyone telling him what he did not want to hear. In any case, it all came down to whose witnesses' evidence was believable. The two men settled the suit. Webster, as usual, was poorly compensated for his labors. He was always on the edge of bankruptcy during these days. As he wrote to his brother on December 12, 1807, "When you come to Court I hope you will be able to bring some needful. The cash I paid to Mr. Reid was appropriate to another purpose, and I am now sadly straitened for it. From my debts [i.e., what was owed to him] or some other resource, I hope you will bring it to me." The answer was a return to Portsmouth and its more remunerative clients.[16]

The Napoleonic Wars of the 1800s were troubled times for merchants sailing out of Portsmouth and other New England harbors. The merchants' major markets were in Europe. The rise of Napoleonic rule in France, and the resumption of war between England and France in 1803, imperiled New England shipping. The Royal Navy stopped New England ships at sea, impressed sailors who allegedly deserted from the Royal Navy, and grabbed cargoes it claimed as contraband. In retaliation, the French seized New England vessels and cargos that reached French ports. President Jefferson's diplomatic efforts failed, and a short-lived embargo on outgoing shipping hurt New England even more. Under his successor, James Madison, New England mercantile interests fared no better, and in 1812, Madison requested and Congress passed a declaration of war against Great Britain. The war devastated what remained of New England's overseas trade.[17]

Webster did not hold public office before the war (Portsmouth was a Republican town in a Federalist state), but he wrote and spoke in opposition to the war. In 1812 he was elected to the House of Representatives as an anti-war candidate. The Federalist Party was in the minority in Congress during Webster's two terms, and with the end of the war, Federalist prospects were dim because they held a convention in Hartford in 1814 to oppose the war (an effort in which Webster joined). In Congress, Webster opposed wartime measures, while despite setbacks on the battlefield (including the British burning of federal buildings in the District of Columbia), the Republicans successfully cast the struggle as a second war for independence. It helped their case that after the terms of peace had been negotiated, a British invasion of New Orleans was turned back by Andrew Jackson–led militia and US troops. After the war men like Webster saw that the Federalist Party as a political entity had no future, and they began to drift into the Republican camp.[18]

In this time of so-called good feelings and one-party government, new sets of political and economic issues gave Webster a chance to combine his legal talents and his political ambition. He was not a staunch conservative, as some thought him, nor a nationalist, as he would become, but still absorbing information, ideas, and tropes for expressing himself. He was a man on the make, to be sure, and if still rough in manners, astute when it came to judging local political currents. In this, law was never a distant, arcane, intellectualized subject for Webster. It was part of the weft and warp of life—mixed with business, politics, and personal aims. Law was a higher good. As he told the Washington Benevolent Society on the eve of the War of 1812, "Resistance and insurrection form no part of our creed. . . . If we are taxed, to carry on this war, we shall pay. If our personal services are required, we shall yield them to the precise extent of our constitutional liability." Conviction must be tempered with loyalty, and interest moderated by patriotic sentiment. It was a balancing act, cutting corners across the divide that should have separated law and politics (after all, he was now a politician), the public and the private (though he still represented private clients he was also an officer of the government), and, finally, the federal government and the states.[19]

In 1813, newly elected to the House of Representatives, Webster had journeyed to Washington, DC. There he lived in a boardinghouse with other New England Federalists, all of whom opposed the war effort. In the House chamber he met two other young members, both Republicans: Kentucky's Henry Clay and South Carolina's John C. Calhoun. Both were blessed with good looks and the bearing of gentlemen, something that Webster lacked. Both were lawyers, but unlike Webster, whose public addresses were deep voiced and slow paced, they spoke quickly and sharply in favor of wartime measures for a land-hungry South and West. In contrast to their eager and aggressive nationalism, Webster remained the advocate of a New England distressed by the war and opposed to new taxes to support it.

In 1816 with the fiscal chaos of the War of 1812 fresh in his mind, Madison agreed to the recharter of the Bank of the United States. The bank, like its ill-fated forerunner, was a private corporation into which the federal government poured its revenue. The bank then managed the many state and local bank currencies, supposedly imposing a manner of fiscal responsibility on other banks. Clay and Calhoun supported this, along with a program of publicly funded highways and a mildly protective tariff. Webster, in Congress from New Hampshire, opposed these measures, though he thought a national bank and some tariffs were permissible. He represented merchants, not manufacturers, and the agrarian interests of rural New England. His objections to the measures Madison proposed were complex, and he failed to prevent their passage. Here, as in his opposition to the war, he had marginalized himself, falling back into technical objections.

Another explanation presents itself. Think of Webster as an intellectual. Young Webster longed for the time to read the classics. While immersed in his legal studies, he wrote to friends how much he missed disinterested intellectual inquiry. Between 1805 and 1808, just as his practice was beginning, he wrote four essays for a Boston literary anthology, the first a book review "filled with literary allusions." The next three pieces were, according to Webster's legal papers editors, more narrowly legal. But they conclude that the essays "reflect in part Webster's anxiety over his loss of direct contact with Boston society." Insofar as the three great conundrums of the Constitution can be seen as intellectual conundrums as well as legal and political questions, Webster's lifelong interest in them may explain something consistent in his otherwise shifting politics. His answers to them infuse his oral arguments before the Court and his orations, often appearing as irrelevant asides or self-preoccupied excursions. Moving them to the center of his thinking, seeing how his views on the three evolved, reveals that they were not tangential parts of his work at all.[20]

His progress as a legislative rainmaker blocked during the war, Webster returned his attention to his legal business and relocated to Boston. He had already pled his first case before the Supreme Court, in 1814, and it established a pattern of regular peregrination—Boston to Washington, DC, and back again. It was an expensive program and a trying one for his wife Grace, who remained behind with his growing family. He did not have to ride circuit with the justices, however, providing some relief in his busy schedule. Thwarted for a time by the rise of the Republicans in Congress and the election of James Monroe, a Republican, Webster found fame of a sort as an appellate lawyer. Indeed, he was one of the first of these specialists, bringing his talents to the Supreme Court. Most lawyers practiced in all the courts—local, state, and federal, and most of their business involved preparing legal papers, filing writs with the court clerks, handling criminal cases, and other trial court matters. Webster, although he did not shun ordinary legal work for fees (states had fee schedules providing fixed compensation for every paper filed and pled), he developed a system of soliciting retainers from litigious businessmen and setting his own fee for representing them when their cases came to the courts of appeal. These were the state supreme courts and the US Supreme Court (although the federal circuit courts had some appellate jurisdiction, for example, in equity cases). Webster had thus taken a step toward the modern law practice in two ways—billable hours remuneration (he sent bills to clients for varying amounts, depending on how much time he put into their cases), and specialization in appellate pleading.

It did not hurt Webster's federal appellate practice that he shared something of Chief Justice John Marshall's ideology and personal preferences. Both men entered politics as Federalists. Both understood the importance of the judiciary in the new system of checks and balances. Both recognized that the federal government must be the final voice in contests between the states and the federal branches. Both were conservative in their tastes, moderate in their social views, and devoted to their wives (in a time when others were not so faithful). Neither man was deeply pious, although for much of this period the "second great awakening" of religious fervor was sweeping the country. When Webster first came to Washington as a congressman, he boarded at the same inn as Marshall. In addition, both men were capable of great charm. They had known and appreciated each other across the dinner table before they met across the bench, as Webster reported to his brother Ezekiel shortly after the judge and the advocate met.[21]

Webster would find another friendly face when he stood before the justices. This was Joseph Story. Story and Marshall were allies and friends on the court, Story the junior partner in some ways, though more learned than Marshall, in what historian R. Kent Newmyer has called the "Heroic Age" of the Court. But Webster's attachment to Story was even stronger than Story's with the chief justice. Story and Webster traveled back and forth to Massachusetts together; their wives were close; and Webster and Story out of Court perhaps crossed over the line of legal ethics that barred counsel and judge from discussing cases in which they were involved. In any event, according to Newmyer, "The alliance was one of the most extraordinary in American law and politics." Story was encyclopedic in his knowledge of law, Webster shrewd in his understanding of politics. "The two men consulted" when Webster prepared his major speeches, and Webster leaned on Story for advice in Supreme Court advocacy. "The two men thought as one," Newmyer states.[22]

Until 1861, when it moved into the old Senate Chamber, the Supreme Court sat in a drafty, mildewed basement room in the Capitol. When Webster and Marshall first met there, on January 14, 1814, winter had brought its chill into the room. The seven justices, robed as much for warmth as for dignity, sat behind a long, raised bench. Opposite the bench sat counsels' tables and the area for spectators and guests. The room was small and dimly lit, with poor acoustics and sightlines. It was perfect for Webster's oratory, however, as his voice could fill all its corners.[23]

Webster's first arguments before the Supreme Court, beginning in 1814, concerned shipping. This was natural, as his clients were Portsmouth merchants and the issues revolved around privateering during the War of 1812. In short, these were "prize cases" heard in the federal district courts, then appealed to the circuit courts (at that time these were trial courts held by the district court judge sitting in that state and a Supreme Court justice riding that circuit). Prizes were ships and cargos seized at sea, usually by private American armed vessels and brought into American ports. Then the privateer's owners and the owners of the ship and cargo captured at sea argued about everything. In the meantime, the flour rotted in the barrels and the wine leaked from the kegs.

Using admiralty law more or less adopted from the English courts, the American judges reached a wide variety of decisions. Ordinarily, even if the vessel were American owned and American merchants had paid for the cargo, ships carrying goods from ports of enemy combatants or goods that were considered contraband of war would be liable to confiscation and sale for the benefit of the privateers. In all eight of the cases of this nature, Webster's argument rested in part on admiralty law but even more so on the validity of witness testimony. Impeaching the testimony of witnesses apparently was common at the time in appellate court hearings. His practice featured a procedural win on a writ of error case (the decision for Webster's client read by Justice Story); another win on a customs duty case, Webster representing the importer against the United States (a second decision in Webster's favor by Justice Story); and finally a win on a diversity land ownership suit, the appeal being denied in a Marshall opinion.[24]

Webster was a busy and successful advocate in other courts, but his big breakthrough was his defense of the corporate rights of the trustees of Dartmouth College. By linking the grant of a private charter to general ideas of private property, Webster made his first major contribution to constitutional law, and a first step to drawing the boundary lines in the three unchartered spaces of the framers' federal Constitution.

2. "Impairing the Obligation of Contracts": *Dartmouth College v. Woodward* (1819)

Webster's reputation as a litigator was well established when he agreed to represent the trustees of his alma mater, Dartmouth College. In 1818 he joined more senior New Hampshire counsel US senator Jeremiah Mason and former chief justice Jeremiah Smith as plaintiffs' lawyers. Every branch of the New Hampshire government had already weighed in on the suit, along with the college's trustees, faculty, and graduates. It seemed that everyone who was anyone in New Hampshire had a stake in the case. The case was thus as much political—a Republican governor, majority in New Hampshire legislature, and state bench versus Federalists on the board of trustees of the college—as purely legal.

As Webster framed it, the case also included questions of state sovereignty versus federal supremacy and public interest versus private vested rights. In short, it presented Webster with the occasion to discourse on the three constitutional issues left unfinished in the framers' Constitution. That opportunity, more than the dispute over the precise nature of the college charter, made the case so important for him and for later constitutional jurisprudence.

For others involved in the litigation, however, the issue in the case seemed simpler. Did abrogation of the charter of the college by the New Hampshire legislature violate the Contracts Clause (aka Obligations Clause) of the federal Constitution? Buried in Article I, section 10, clause 1, was an omnibus prohibition on certain state activities: "No State shall enter into any Treaty, Alliance, or Confederation; grant *Letters of Marque and Reprisal*; coin Money; emit *Bills of Credit*; make any Thing but gold and silver Coin a *Tender* in Payment of Debts; pass any *Bill of Attainder*, *ex post facto Law*, or Law impairing the Obligation of Contracts, or grant any Title of *Nobility*." Taken together, these were a blow to claims of states' rights, for a truly independent sovereignty can do all of the activities forbidden in the clause. What was more, the clause seemed to offer a glimpse, if not a clear vision, of a line between private property and public purpose that a state could not cross—unless politics choices outweighed legal rules.

Given the nationalist potency of the Contracts Clause, and, contra, the solicitude so many of the delegates had for their states' sovereignty, it is surprising that the clause did not arouse much debate at the Constitutional Convention in Philadelphia. Introduced very late in the meeting, on August 28, by Rufus King, a New York lawyer whose business included land grant contracts, it tracked a similar provision in Article II of the Northwest Ordinance of 1787. The text of that provision read, "No law ought ever to be made or have force in the said territory, that shall, in any manner whatever, interfere with or affect private contracts, or engagement, bona fide, and without fraud previously formed." In other words, if the particular contract was private, it was safe from state interference, but if based on a fraud, it could be overturned by a court of law or by a statute ("no law").

The debate on the draft clause that ensued concerned whether the ban was restricted to contracts already executed, a motion to which purpose then failed. Of course, a legislature in the Northwest Territory could outlaw certain kinds of contracts, for example, those concerning the sale or purchase of slaves, as slavery was barred from the territory. An attempt to drop the matter also failed. Protecting contracts from state interference was too important for the delegates, all men of property, to ignore. When the Committee on Style and Arrangement met at the very end of the convention to redact the document, the Contracts Clause was bundled together with the other restrictions on states. When the Committee on Style reported its work on September 12, the clause read "altering or impairing the obligation of contracts." On September 14, in one of its final acts before adjourning and sending the draft to the Congress in New York City, the convention members voted to drop the term "altering."

James Madison's notes on the debates did not record whether anyone thought a distinction should be made between private and public contracts, a distinction that was implicit in the Northwest Ordinance. (A public contract was a very different legal thing from a private contract, on which see more below.) Madison defended the clause in *Federalist*, no. 44, as a "constitutional bulwark in favor of personal security and private rights." Clearly he understood the need to draw some line between the public interest and private rights, and the Contracts Clause was one place to do so. At the Virginia ratification convention, Patrick Henry, a vigorous Antifederalist, feared that the clause, as written, included public as well as private contracts, as he too worried about the vagueness of the proposed Constitution on the public/

private law divide. Edmund Randolph, who now favored the Constitution as drafted (having previously declined to sign it), insisted that "virtue and justice required the clause," although he did not define how or what virtue applied. The line between legitimate public interests and inviolable private rights remained unclear.[1]

By the early 1800s, *contract* was a familiar term to counsel. It meant an agreement that could be enforced in a court of law. Nothing in the federal Constitution defined *obligations*. The word only appeared conjoined with contracts. Neither term appeared elsewhere in the document. Certain kinds of contracts entailed obligations, for example, a contract made to deliver goods or perform services in future. These were promises to perform. The idea of obligation was thus a forward-looking one. In this sense, the prohibition against impairing an obligation was confusing, for what did it mean to impair in the present something that was supposed to happen in the future? There would develop in contract law a delict called anticipatory repudiation, that is, the announced intention not to perform something that had been promised. Although a breach of contract had not yet occurred, the aggrieved party could sue for anticipated damages.[2]

Whether they understood the clause or not, states did not always obey the admonitions in the clause. They made agreements with one another, established state banks to emit bills of credit, arranged for payment of debts in a variety of ways, passed ex post facto laws, and prosecuted individuals with the equivalent of bills of attainder. Could they also impair the obligation of contracts in corporate grants they had made to individuals or groups? Arguing that many of these grants—for example, the creation of local governments and educational institutions—were public rather than private, states assumed they had the power to unmake corporate grants. But was the charter of the college a private contract, or a public one? That was the facial question in *Dartmouth College v. Woodward* (1819), but a lot more was at stake.

Webster was familiar with common law notions of private contracts. The law regarding these agreements had come into the state from colonial law, according to the state constitution of 1776: "all Writs, Processes & Proceedings in Law, and in any of the Courts of Justice in this Colony, which have been used or Accustomed, or by any Laws of this Colony, are Required to be issued, used or practiced in Law, and in any of the Courts of Justice" in the state were still in force, with any reference to the crown or parliament excised. The statute was later repealed, but the core idea that contracts were to be regarded in light of common law never departed. They were part of the basic education of lawyers. They arose in many failed business deals between private parties. Webster dealt with defaulting private contractors in his Boscawen, Portsmouth, and Boston practices. The questions contested in court in private contract suits were whether the contract was actually agreed to, and whether one of the parties had failed to fulfill his or her obligations under the contract.[3]

What constituted evidence that a contract had been made (as opposed to a promise that could not be performed or an offer without an acceptance)? This was called *consideration*—not care, but something of value. The terms of private contracts were still full of abstractions, which was good for lawyers, who mastered the intricacies of commercial transaction law, but bewildering for parties to a contract who were not expert in the law. The simple exchange, a barter or a book debt, remained the staple of ordinary people's business, but more and more of the serious financial dealings of merchants required rethinking of the older forms of action, and more business for lawyers, even in the local courts. Contracts were the answer.[4]

The private contract was a private matter. It only became public knowledge when one or both of the parties failed to resolve a dispute about it among themselves and filed a lawsuit. The law made a distinction between a private contract, whose purpose was a benefit to the parties involved, and a public grant or charter from a legislature to private parties whose beneficiary was the public as a whole. Some corporate grants, acts of the legislature creating a legal entity, were nevertheless regarded as private when the purpose of the incorporation was the benefit of the group that sought the corporate charter. Businesses, charitable organizations, and most educational institutions fell into this category, although its boundaries were never entirely clear. These charters, while not perpetual, could not be changed by the legislature before their time had ended without evidence of wrongdoing by the grantees or their successors. By contrast, grants of charters to public institutions, for example municipalities, could be altered in the public interest by the legislature at any time, so long as the legislature followed its own due process.[5]

The English North American colonies began with charters, sometimes called *letters patent*, that were essentially contracts between the crown and a joint stock company or a group of settlers. The charter granted certain privileges to the company or the settlers, in return for which they were to fulfill certain obligations to the crown. These charters were a form of public contract, much as the grants of self-government to duchies and boroughs in England. Although the grantees benefited, the purpose of the charter was the expansion and protection of the British Empire. Thus the charters could be rescinded or modified through a process called *quo warranto* pursued through the royal courts. In a number of cases—for example, Massachusetts, the Jerseys, Pennsylvania, and the Carolinas—that is exactly what happened. New charters were then issued. Were these new charters a public, or a private, contract? That was one of the issues in the crisis following the American Revolution, with lawyers on both sides arguing whether the charters conferred inalienable rights or merely privileges.[6]

The revision or quashing of old and new charters in the new nation involved a challenge to the operation of the state legislatures. After 1788, the imposition of federal judicial supervision via the Contracts Clause itself became a hotly contested issue. This took two forms. First, it pit courts against legislatures. On the one hand, legislatures made law, but the assumption of the framers was that political considerations were the ground on which legislative acts stood. In this sense, statute law was political. Succeeding legislative majorities could change that law as the will of the electorate changed. After all, legislatures were the representative branch of republican self-government. As James Madison wrote to Thomas Jefferson shortly after the new federal government began its operations, the very basis of private property was the legislature. "Unless such laws [granting property or paying debts] should be kept in force by new acts regularly anticipating the end of the term, all the rights depending on positive laws, that is, most of the rights of property would become absolutely defunct; and the most violent struggles be generated between those interested in reviving and those interested in new-modelling the former State of property."[7]

Courts, on the other hand, were supposed to be above politics, and courts' interpretation of laws reflected not shifting popular majorities but fixed principles of law. As Hamilton wrote about Article III courts in his *Federalist*, no. 78, "They ought to regulate their decisions by the fundamental laws, rather than by those which are not fundamental [i.e., statute]." This was particularly true of the federal courts, as their judges and justices were not elected. They were appointed and held office during good behavior. The public contracts cases lay precisely across this divide. Were contracts matters for courts to interpret, and disputes over contracts to be finally settled in court, or were contracts created by legislatures matters of public will, and left to the representatives of the public to interpret and enforce, or rescind? In other words, were the corporate grants of legislatures political, or were they subject to fixed principles of law?[8]

The fact that the federal courts were the fora to which the losers in the *Dartmouth College* cases appealed raised the second issue: that of federalism. To the extent that the states were sovereign, their courts were the final arbiters of corporate charter law. But the states' sovereignty was constrained under the Supremacy Clause, and this meant that the Contracts Clause applied to state corporate charters. Federal courts overruling a state court decision on a corporate charter granted by the state thus pit a state government against the federal government.

Finally, recourse in court to the Contracts Clause raised the issue of private property rights. Today Americans take the right to private property as a given, somehow attached to the regime of rights they inherently enjoy. In fact, the very idea of private property as a right was relatively new in Webster's time. Prior to the American Revolution, all property in the colonies belonged to the crown. The king could (and had) allowed colonists to hold property in land as a privilege, like the privilege of limited self-government in the charters. All privileges were held at the pleasure of the crown and could be rescinded by the royal or proprietary grantor.[9]

Radicals during the English civil wars announced that the land should belong to the people who worked it, but this was out of touch with common law precepts. John Locke's second *Treatise of Government* made a similar claim, but it was theoretical rather than real. The colonists had long resisted the concept that all land belonged to the sovereign. From the moment they arrived, they expected that the land granted them belonged to them. In similar fashion, when land changed hands, colonists assumed that the title and record in the deed book gave them possession "in fee simple." This was good against the claims of other colonists, but not against the claim of the crown. Thus when the colonists protested against Parliament in the 1760s and 1770s, they argued that the land belonged to Americans because they had improved it. This was a "labor theory of value" applied to small as well as large holdings, and even if not entirely articulated by farmers like Daniel Webster's father, it underlay their new world. What may seem to us the very foundation of conservative political economy was in its own day the revolutionary rejection of royal servitudes.[10]

But, and this is a very big but, for Webster the case was not just about the obligation of contracts. Had it been, he need only have spent an hour or so reminding the Court of its own precedents in *Fletcher v. Peck* (1810) and *New Jersey v. Wilson* (1812). In both of these cases the Court, speaking through Chief Justice Marshall, told the states that they could not violate the federal Constitution. Webster saw a lot more in *Dartmouth College*, worth hours of oral argument.

In *Fletcher v. Peck* (1810) the Marshall Court explored how the Contracts Clause might settle the issue of private versus public grants without addressing the politics/law question or private rights versus public policy. Instead, after much prancing about, Marshall resolved the case on the Obligations Clause. The case was collusive, Peck being a holder of Yazoo lands sold by Georgia, whose legislature later rescinded the sales for fraud. The sale created a vested right; the retraction was based on public interest. After he could not get Georgia to repay what he had paid, Peck turned to a lawsuit in federal court. In order to sue in federal court under the diversity provisions of the Judiciary Act, he needed another party to the suit to be a resident of a different state. (A second requirement was monetary, but the land was worth more than the $500 minimum.) He found Robert Fletcher, a New Hampshire real estate developer. Peck conveyed to Fletcher lands in the Yazoo sale for the price of $3,000. Filed in 1803 in the circuit court of Massachusetts, the suit was decided in 1807 in favor of Fletcher. In 1809, Peck appealed to the United States Supreme Court.[11]

The first time the case came to the Supreme Court, John Quincy Adams, recently resigned from the United States Senate, argued for Peck that the grant was a "contract executed" when the sale was made, and subsequent acts by the legislature could not extinguish Peck's title. Persuaded by Luther Martin, counsel for Fletcher, that there was a technical defect in the pleading, Chief Justice Marshall sent the case back to the circuit court, instructing it to consider that argument. Perhaps the justices were bothered by the manifest collusion of the parties, or perhaps they were stalling, hoping that Congress would step in and indemnify the Yazoo lands' purchasers. Congress had debated that proposition already. When the case returned to the Supreme Court on Fletcher's appeal, the argument made for the defendant in error (Peck), by his counsel

Joseph Story, was that "the legislature was forbidden by the constitution of the United States to pass any law impairing the obligation of contract. A grant is a contract executed, and it creates also an implied executory contract, which is, that the grantee shall continue to enjoy the thing granted according to the terms of the grant."

Chief Justice Marshall, writing for the Court, agreed with Story. Georgia could sell the lands. But the state constitution was not the only fundamental law in question. The federal Constitution also bore on the question of the constitutionality of rescinding the land sales. "The question, whether a law be void for its repugnancy to the constitution, is, at all times, a question of much delicacy, which ought seldom, if ever, to be decided in the affirmative, in a doubtful case." This was pure Marshall—first, show the gravity of the case and its difficulty. The Court did not jump to conclusions, particularly in such momentous cases. Next, assert the paramount role of the Court in deciding cases. "The court, when impelled by duty to render such a judgment, would be unworthy of its station, could it be unmindful of the solemn obligations which that station imposes." Then thrust the facts into the opinion, "But it is not on slight implication and vague conjecture that the legislature is to be pronounced to have transcended its powers, and its acts to be considered as void." Finally, he explained that the Court had reached the conclusion that "the opposition between the constitution and the [state] law should be such that the judge feels a clear and strong conviction of their incompatibility with each other."[12]

Georgia could also annul its own legislation. But here there was a third party, for Peck had purchased the land from an original grantee without knowledge of the fraud in the original grant. Fraud would set aside a land conveyance, "but the rights of third persons, who are purchasers without notice, for a valuable consideration, cannot be disregarded." As a matter of policy as well as of law, "Titles, which, according to every legal test, are perfect, are acquired with that confidence which is inspired by the opinion that the purchaser is safe. If there be any concealed defect, arising from the conduct of those who had held the property long before he acquired it, of which he had no notice, that concealed defect cannot be set up against him." Let the seller beware; the buyer is not at fault. "He has paid his money for a title good at law, he is innocent, whatever may be the guilt of others, and equity will not subject him to the penalties attached to that guilt." All titles would be insecure, and "the intercourse between man and man would be very seriously obstructed, if this principle be overturned."[13]

The state was not just any party to a contract, of course, but the state of Georgia was part of the federal union and so bound by the federal Constitution. "The validity of this rescinding act, then, might well be doubted, were Georgia a single sovereign power"—that is, if one regarded the Constitution as merely a compact among fully sovereign states. "But Georgia cannot be viewed as a single, unconnected, sovereign power, on whose legislature no other restrictions are imposed than may be found in its own constitution." More than Marshall's nationalism was on display here. For him, and for the unanimous Supreme Court, Georgia "is a part of a large empire; she is a member of the American union; and that union has a constitution the supremacy of which all acknowledge, and which imposes limits to the legislatures of the several states, which none claim a right to pass." It had not escaped his attention that when Georgia was called to account for its failure to pay a revolutionary war debt, in *Chisholm v. Georgia* (1793), the state did not even bother to send counsel to take part in the case. The strong, repetitive language of his opinion was as close to scolding as he would ever come. "The constitution of the United States declares that no state shall pass any bill of attainder, ex post facto law, or law impairing the obligation of contracts." The covenant (contract) had been breached by the state of Georgia, in violation of the Constitution.[14]

In *New Jersey v. Wilson* (1812) a purchaser of formerly Indian lands from the Indian possessor discovered that the tax exemption that went with title was void. The state had repealed the colonial act creating the tax exemption. The state courts upheld the rescission of the tax benefit, but Chief Justice Marshall, writing for the Supreme Court, reversed the state courts. The sales were private contracts between the Indians and the buyer, and the federal prohibition on impairment of the obligation of contracts, including the tax exemption granted by the state, applied.[15]

In *Dartmouth College*, Webster boldly strode where Marshall had tiptoed. In *Fletcher*, Marshall wrote as if there were no politics in the Yazoo lands scandal. But, like the Yazoo litigation, in which a change in the legislature's majority led to rescinding the Yazoo lands sales, politics were at the bottom of the *Dartmouth College* case. Webster recognized as much, and this led him to confront the politics/law conundrum. The political issue was straightforward. A Federalist board of trustees fought a Jeffersonian legislative majority, governor, and state supreme court. In 1815, with the embarrassment of the Hartford

Convention (a gathering of Federalists opposed to the War of 1812 pleaded that the Constitution be amended to prevent long-term embargoes on foreign trade and require two-thirds votes in Congress to declare war) undercutting their election efforts, the Federalists of New Hampshire watched the Republicans sweep the state offices. Out went Chief Justice Jeremiah Smith and, when his term ended two years later, US senator Jeremiah Mason followed. The state supreme court was reorganized, and its three new justices were all Republicans.

Another way to curb the pride and power of the Federalist elite running the college was to enlarge the board of Dartmouth, in effect taking away control from its co-opted conservative members and give that control to the elected state assembly. To ensure that the college policies (e.g., admissions) followed the Jeffersonian view of public education, a new board of overseers would set final policy, in effect making the private college into a state school. The trustees hired Mason and Smith to argue for them, and the two added Webster, although he did not prepare the initial arguments in the case.[16]

Webster knew much of the general story already and soon mastered the facts of the case. One of provincial New England's more colorful characters, the Reverend Eleazar Wheelock, believed in a divine mission to Christianize local native peoples in Connecticut. In furtherance, he opened a charity school with funds from a private donor (Joshua More) in Lebanon, Connecticut. No tuition or fees were imposed on the students, who had no way to pay in any case, which made running the school financially precarious. The first alumnus, Samson Occum, a Mohegan—by the 1760s an ordained minister himself—raised funds through personal solicitations and by gaining in 1769 a British crown charter to the trustees of Dartmouth College, named after Lord Dartmouth, a sponsor of the project. The royal charter gave to the trustees and the alumni shared governing responsibilities. Wheelock drafted it himself. The alumni elected the trustees, a common practice today among the private universities of New England. Wheelock needed a regular source of income, and not finding one in Connecticut, he turned to the governor of neighboring New Hampshire, John Wentworth. Wentworth provided a grant of land in the town of Hanover, on the Connecticut River border between New Hampshire and Vermont. Wentworth was no doubt aware that the frontier area was a volatile one, filled with difficult-to-manage settlers and sometimes hostile natives. A missionary school there might quiet matters. In any case, it was a popular step.[17]

In a controversial move of his own, Wheelock transformed the Indian school into a college for young gentlemen. The charter closely resembled the charter that the colony of New Jersey gave to the College of New Jersey, later Princeton (not Queens College, later Rutgers, whose charter came from the crown). It held that the trustees "shall be able, in and law capable, for the use of said Dartmouth College, to have, get acquire, purchase, receive, hold, possess and enjoy tenements, hereditaments, jurisdiction and franchise, for themselves and their successors, in fee-simple." In short, it was a closed corporation whose property and regulations "as they shall think needful and convenient, [were] for the use of said Dartmouth College."[18]

The charter rested on a grant from the English government. Were all such charters null and void as a result of independence, the result would have been chaos. Not only did Connecticut and Rhode Island retain their colonial charters as state constitutions, hundreds of enterprises, including colleges like William and Mary, the College of New Jersey, and Kings College, had charters granted either directly or indirectly by the crown. States could have annulled these and replaced them with state charters, of course, or modified the charter, but the state would have to assert that the charters were public corporations. In any case, independence did not dissolve the charters.[19]

In 1815, an eighty-eight-page anonymous pamphlet generally assumed to be the work of the president of the college, Wheelock's son John, accused the trustees of misappropriation of funds due the college. The work created a major stir, falling as it did at the beginning of an election year, and Wheelock followed it with an appeal to the legislature for assistance against the trustees. Webster, consulted by Wheelock, ultimately declined to represent him in a suit against the trustees, but the legislature agreed to investigate, and when in 1816 the Republicans won the governorship (returning William Plumer to the post) and control of the legislature, the issue became one of political partisanship rather than just personal animus. By this time, John Wheelock had died and the real party at interest was the state of New Hampshire. Plumer shared his desire to make the college public with Thomas Jefferson, whose University of Virginia, a public institution, may have been Plumer's model. Defenders of the trustees certainly saw it that way, one writing privately that "democracy wants to pour her poison into our fountains." Unmoved by the trustees' complaints, Plumer supported a Republican plan to revise the charter, and it passed the legislature on June 26, 1816. The trustees tried to oust William H. Woodward, an ally of the late John Wheelock's, from the treasurer's post, but he was too quick, and took with him the official records.[20]

The state did not renew the charter until it changed the terms of the charter in 1816. That was the basis of the writ of trover filed by the trustees against Woodward, who had taken the charter (the document) at the behest of Governor Plumer and his council. The writ, an old English form of action, or claim, sought the return of illegally taken goods. The trustees lost at a hearing before the superior court at Haverhill in May 1817. Smith and Mason argued for the trustees, Attorney General Sullivan for the state and Woodward. At the New Hampshire Supreme Court in September 1817, on appeal from the superior court finding, the issue was joined by Mason, Smith, and now Webster for the trustees, and George Sullivan and Ichabod Bartlett for the state of New Hampshire and Woodward. The question was whether an act of the state legislature of New Hampshire altering the charter, without the consent of the corporation, impaired the obligations in the charter and was thus unconstitutional and void. The New Hampshire Supreme Court delivered its opinion on these questions at the November 1817 session.[21]

Nathaniel Adams doubled as the clerk of the New Hampshire Supreme Court and the state court reporter. He did not include the briefs or oral arguments made at the session in his report of the case. His only text was Chief Justice William Richardson's opinion for the court. Richardson was born in Pelham, New Hampshire, graduated from Harvard College, and practiced law in Massachusetts, which state he served in the US House of Representatives until 1814, when he returned to Portsmouth as US attorney for New Hampshire. Two years later he was appointed to a place on the refashioned New Hampshire Supreme Court. He was a Republican in Congress and on the court, as the legislature's revision of the state courts ensured that they were staffed by Republicans.

It may be that Richardson goaded Webster's presentation in the US High Court. A short and colorless opinion by the New Hampshire chief justice upholding the trial court would have left little for Webster to contend, save the Contract Clause. But Richardson was intent on Republican posturing. He was well aware that a former New Hampshire chief justice, a current US senator, and a serving member of the House represented the trustees, all of whom were Federalists. His fulsome praise for appellees counsel was hollow. "This cause has been argued on both sides with uncommon learning and ability, and we have witnessed with pleasure and with pride a display of talents and eloquence upon this occasion in the highest degree honourable to the profession of the law in this state." For, "If the counsel of the plaintiffs have failed to convince us that the action can be maintained, it has not been owing to any want of diligence in research, or ingenuity in reasoning, but to a want of solid and substantial grounds on which to rest their arguments." So there.[22]

Richardson declined to consider whether the policy of the legislature was a good one or whether the trustees had acted unethically. "We must not for a moment forget, that the question submitted to our decision in such cases, is always one of mere constitutional right;—sitting here as judges, we have nothing to do with the policy or expediency of the acts of the legislature." In other words, Richardson rejected and resented any imputation or inference that he was acting as a politician or that the Republicans on the court were rubberstamping what the Republicans in the legislature and the executive had done. It was law, not politics, that he was doing—an attempt to draw a strict line between the two, as if anyone in the courtroom believed him.

Next came the chief justice's distinction between private corporations, companies for canals, turnpikes, and other business objects whose beneficiaries were the corporate grantees, and public corporations. The line between the public and the private was obvious to him: "*Public* corporations are those which are created for public purposes, and whose property is devoted to the objects for which they are created. The corporators have no private beneficial interest, either in their franchises or their property." For Richardson, this was a bright-line distinction between the public corporation and the grant of a private charter. In the former, holders of the grant are simply trustees for the public good. "Counties, towns, parishes, &c. considered as corporations, clearly fall within this description." By contrast, private corporate interests were meant to be enjoyed only by the members of that corporation, as a form of private property. Thus a grant of land, or provisions for the purchase of formerly publicly owned land, to a group for their own use was not a public corporation. For him Dartmouth College was a public corporation and a proper object of legislative concern, as it was founded to educate the Indians. It was thus an irrelevant question in law whether the private rights of the trustees were violated, as they had no private rights, no property, with respect to the grant. They merely saw to the proper operation of the college for the public good. The new trustees and the new board of overseers would simply be aiding the old trustees in their continuing duty to manage the college.[23]

Appellants' counsel had argued that the New Hampshire legislature had violated the Contracts Clause of the federal Constitution. Richardson was not persuaded. *Fletcher v. Peck* did not apply, because in that case the state of

Georgia had contracted with individuals to buy parcels in the Yazoo region. The buyers purchased land for their own use, not for the public good. The grant of land and other habiliments was a private contract. Thus, the final issue that the framers had left up in the air Richardson brought down to earth. In this area of law, the state's sovereignty was unchallengeable.

That should have settled the issue. But Richardson had a lot more to say. When judges go beyond what is necessary to decide the case, additional material is called *obiter dicta*. The first of these was Richardson's fulsome invocation of states' rights. Usually associated with the slave states' aversion to any federal action that imperiled their autonomy, the doctrine was more generally available, as Richardson's opinion demonstrated. "This clause was not intended to limit the power of the states, in relation to their own public officers and servants, or to their own civil institutions, and must not be construed to embrace contracts, which are in their nature, mere matters of civil institution; nor grants of power and authority, by a state to individuals, to be exercised for purposes merely public." In general, Federalists were advocates of a strong central government. The Jeffersonian Republicans, by contrast (read Jefferson's Kentucky Resolves of 1798, for example) advocated a weaker central government, confined to the letter of enumerated powers in the Constitution, hedged around by a robust state sovereignty. The passage on the power of the states herein was not necessary to resolve the suit. It was Richardson advocating states' rights.

The next set of obiter dicta involved a series of analogies. In common law, argument is often by analogy. Richardson offered some. Marriages were contracts. Did counsel mean that the state could not provide for divorce? What about the creation of townships and other inferior jurisdictions? "The legislature, both in this state and in *Massachusetts*, have always claimed and exercised the right of dividing towns; of enlarging or diminishing their territorial limits; of imposing new duties or limiting their powers and privileges, as the public good seemed to require; and this without their consent. Yet this right seems never to have been called in question, on the ground that their charters were contracts, within the meaning of this clause." Was the chief justice reminding Webster that their career paths were the reverse of one another's? Richardson represented Massachusetts in the House of Representatives, but then returned to New Hampshire and stayed there. Citing Massachusetts case law freely, when Webster never argued a case before the Massachusetts Supreme Judicial Court, was a swipe at Webster, who had left Portsmouth to live, work, and politic in Boston.

Richardson's final obiter dictum was a remonstrance at those (presumably Federalists) who felt that higher education in a republic belonged to an elite, or that a few men should tell the next generation what to study:

> I cannot bring myself to believe, that it would be consistent with sound policy, or ultimately with the true interests of literature itself, to place the great public institutions, in which all the young men, destined for the liberal professions, are to be educated, within the absolute control of a few individuals, and out of the control of the sovereign power—not consistent with sound policy, because it is a matter of too great moment, too intimately connected with the public welfare and prosperity, to be thus entrusted in the hands of a few.

Having in his first pages left politics at the courtroom door, he now brought politics back through the rear window. Indeed, despite his claims that the case offered bright-line distinctions between politics and law, public and private rights, and state and federal powers, Richardson blurred all three before he was done.[24]

The state of New Hampshire had spoken, faint praise for Webster and his cohorts hardly a balm for the stinging rejection of their claims. The trustees wanted Webster to appeal their cause to the US Supreme Court. Neither Smith nor Mason wished to travel to the capital city. Webster now faced the problem of getting the case on the US Supreme Court docket. As matters stood, the only way was a writ of error, saying that the state courts had misunderstood federal law and misapplied it in the present instance. The federal law in question was the Contract Clause. While this line of argument offered prospects of success, Webster was still provoked by Richardson's opinion. Webster did not want to rest the case on the Contract Clause alone and leave unanswered Richardson's dismissal of the law and politics, and public versus private questions. Instead, Webster saw the case resting precisely on those issues. Thus he would have preferred to bring the case to the High Court in a different way— by having it heard in a federal circuit court and having the district judge and the justice riding circuit (in this case his friend Story) agree to disagree. Then the issue on which he would appeal to the High Court would be one of vested rights of the trustees. He thought that the Court was sympathetic to all three of the arguments, however.[25]

The state's case was ultimately argued by William Wirt of Virginia and Congressman Salma Hale—Sullivan declining to travel to DC, citing the expense—and John Holmes, a Republican congressman from Massachusetts and later a US senator from Maine. Wirt was attorney general of the United States when he represented New Hampshire, a Jeffersonian Republican of high repute and unquestioned ability (federal law did not bar the US attorney general from representing private clients until the next decade). Hale was a printer, editor, and briefly a Jeffersonian Republican congressman, after which he returned to New Hampshire to practice law. The *Dartmouth College* case was clearly a question of national importance to the Republican political establishment and consequently to the remnant of the Federalist Party.

By now, the question of whether Dartmouth College, under its charter, was a private and not a public corporation, established for purposes of charity, or for education generally and thus a public corporation liable to the control of the legislature, had come to represent a lot more. As Webster wrote to Jeremiah Smith on the eve of his departure to argue the appeal in DC, "It is our misfortune that our cause goes to Washington on a single point . . . the repugnancy of these [New Hampshire] acts to the constitution of the United States." He wrote the same to Francis Brown, on a more positive note, "You are aware, that in the college case, the only question which can be argued at Washington, is, whether the recent Acts of the Legislature of N. Hampshire do not violate the Constitution of U.S." Webster wanted to argue the larger questions of vested rights and political partisanships but was, at least under the writ of error, constrained.[26]

Webster had no intention of confining his argument to the Contracts Clause, however. His aim was all three of the issues that Richardson had dismissed. Overcoming Richardson's bright-line distinction between public interest and private property was a tall order, and the chief justice's invocation of states' rights, coming after Webster had made a similar argument in favor of the Hartford Convention report, was almost a provocation. The slyness of the chief justice's assurance that politics had nothing to do with his decision would hardly be missed by the justices in Washington, DC, but how to confute Richardson's claim without crossing the line into politics himself was not easy. That he would refute all three of Richardson's points proved Webster's skill and determination.

At first, however, Webster was not sure that he could overturn Richardson's arguments. As much an act of deference as one of real necessity, Webster wrote to Mason, asking for his and Smith's notes on the case. "I will need help," he modestly admitted. A review of the notes, now preserved in the Dartmouth

College archives, shows them to be a list of bulleted points, interspersed with outlines. They emphasized the charitable nature of the charter and the English precedents. "What other English cases," the two men asked themselves, and followed with pages of more and more obscure precedent. These would have been useless to Webster without the English reports in front of him. So he wrote to opposing counsel William Wirt for the relevant volumes, even though he had already indicated that the case did not turn on English precedents. Still, counsel had to be ready to anticipate the arguments of opponents.[27]

Webster then enlisted the aid of Joseph Hopkinson, a Pennsylvania attorney, Federalist former member of Congress, trustee of the University of Pennsylvania, and later federal district judge in the state. Hopkinson did not argue often before the Supreme Court, but his presence at the counsel table added luster to Webster's cause. He also listened to Justice Story's hint to go beyond the question of whether New Hampshire's legislature had the authority under the state constitution to alter the terms of the charter. In this, Story was acting outside of his formal role as a member of the court. He might have waited to do this when Webster made his oral argument before the Court, through a helpful question. Justices do this all the time today, but it was not so common in the Court's early days. In any case, Story's conduct was simply unethical, and both men knew it, or should have. Judges then as now are supposed to be impartial arbiters.[28]

The *Dartmouth College* case was an opportunity to demonstrate how politics and law fit together, or rather had, but should not. According to R. Kent Newmyer, it "illuminates nicely the symbiotic nature of law and politics and the unity and strength of the conservative portion of the bench and bar." For the essence of Webster's legal practice was also the core of his political philosophy: private property must be protected against the excesses of democracy. In this sense, Webster was the last of the Federalists, long after the generation of the party founders had disappeared. He knew it, too.[29]

There is another facet to the case that Webster's preparation illuminated. He knew that he must argue for the supremacy of federal law over state law. He was on his way to becoming the spokesman for legal nationalism. In this, he had to demonstrate that legislative lawmaking must bow to judicial interpretation—this from a member of the US House of Representatives. The way ahead was full of booby traps.

Today, the value of oral argument before courts of appeals is much contested. Many judges and scholars agree that there is little use in it, and, in some state courts of appeal, preliminary decisions foreclose the need for oral argument. The US Supreme Court is, however, an exception to this development. Justices have gone on record attributing a change in their opinions due to oral argument. The importance of oral argument was even greater in the early nineteenth century. Not only was there no limit on the length of oral presentations (that came in 1849), only in 1834 did Congress require the justices to write all their opinions for the official reporter of the court. Beginning in 1795, attorneys had to present the Court with major points of their case in writing, but full briefs were not required until 1821. Orality was an essential part of the business of judging.[30]

Webster thought that the preliminary question before the High Court, according to his March 10, 1818, notes for oral argument, was whether the acts of the New Hampshire legislature were "valid and binding on the rights of the trustees, without their acceptance or assent." Answered in the negative, this would have disposed of the case as a simple contracts exercise. If they were not, could the Court declare the acts null and void? If it could, on what constitutional basis would that judgment rest? The Court had already asserted its authority to overturn acts of state legislatures when they violated the federal Constitution in *Chisholm v. Georgia* (1793) and *Fletcher v. Peck* (1810). Here Webster asked the Court to exercise this authority again. The case was thus one in a series that defined the relationship between the federal government and the states.[31]

Webster found ample evidence in the charter that Wheelock's college was a charitable institution, that the trustees were the owners of all its property, and that the charter was perpetual—that is, did not have a fixed end date. It was a corporation created by the grant that the state assumed when it became sovereign. Thus far, he was following Mason's and Smith's notes. He continued, "There are to be twelve trustees forever, and no more; and they are to have the right of filling vacancies occurring in their own body." Though created by a public grant, the college was private. "After the institution, thus created and constituted, had existed, uninterruptedly and usefully, nearly fifty years, the legislature of New-Hampshire passed the acts in question." These legislative acts, signed by the governor and council (a five-man advisory board elected by the voters to advise the governor), allowed him to appoint nine additional trustees, to rename the college a university, and transfer everything to a new state corporation to be run by a board of overseers, to be appointed by, not surprisingly, the governor and council. A second act was an enabling act, transferring all of the property to the care of Woodward, to hold until the new arrangements were in place—as if the trustees were going to remove the college in the middle of the night to a new location.[32]

If the legislation were valid, as held the state courts (like the governor and legislature Republican in personnel), the old grant would disappear. The assent of the trustees was not solicited and had no effect. "It was neither expected nor intended, that they should be members of the new corporation." The legislation had implied, in a kind of snide nod, that the old trustees still had a say in the new corporation, but anyone could see that was a façade. "These acts alter the whole constitution of the corporation. They affect the rights of the whole body, as a corporation, and the rights of the individuals who compose it. They revoke corporate powers and franchises. They alienate and transfer the property of the College to others." Webster went over the new provisions line by line, verse by verse, hammering away at the totality of the takeover and it brassiness. The trustees faced "heavy penalties, if they exercise their offices, or any of those powers and privileges granted them by charter, and which they had exercised for fifty years." Why bother? What the state could grant, could it not rescind?

Because this was a charitable trust, it fell under the general rules of equity. Although once these were the discretionary powers of the English chancellor, the king's secretary, to do justice when regular courts of law could not, by 1818 the rules of equity were well established. If a trust were properly managed for the benefit of its beneficiaries, here the students of the college, then the trust instrument was inviolable. If the grantor of the trust, here the state, wanted a court to dissolve it, the grantor had to come into court with "clean hands." Those who sought equitable relief had to do equity. Article VIII of the state constitution hinted that the trust idea lay at the very foundation of all republican government. But as Webster insisted, the state behaved badly, for it had not done equity. "All power residing originally in and being derived from the people, all the magistrates and officers of government are their substitutes and agents, and at all times accountable to them." Accountability was the essence of trusteeship. The trustees of the college had been accountable; the state was not.[33]

Webster professed astonishment at the arrogance of the legislature and the governor. "This, it must be confessed, is rather a summary mode of settling a question of constitutional right." His emotion was a little misplaced; after all, the superior and the supreme courts of the state had heard these same arguments and found that the coequal branches of state government had not exceeded their powers under the state constitution. Still, were they not to consider the established rights and privileges of the old grantees?

> The president, one of the old trustees, had a right to his office, salary, and emoluments, subject to the twelve trustees alone. His title to these is now changed, and he is made accountable to new masters. So also all the professors and tutors. If the legislature can at pleasure make these alterations and changes, in the rights and privileges of the plaintiffs, it may, with equal propriety, abolish these rights and privileges altogether.

What would prevent the popularly elected organs of government from destroying all property rights? Was nothing safe from the power of simple, temporary majorities? This was the slippery slope argument, a familiar one in court. Webster did not pursue this larger question, but he implied it, and by raising it, turned the Dartmouth grant into every man's claim to private property rights. He knew that Marshall and Story would be able to follow the logic of his argument, as they were now listening intently. What protection did the holders of private rights have against this monstrous doctrine that the state can take away what time, usage, and right had conveyed? For if "this is such a corporation as the legislature may abolish at pleasure; and that its members have no rights, liberties, franchises, property or privileges, which the legislature may not revoke, annul, alienate or transfer to others whenever it sees fit." Who was next?[34]

Webster had by now studied Mason's argument and Smith's notes. Their focus was on the question of English precedent—in particular, could Parliament dissolve a trust? If so, was the legislature of New Hampshire akin in this respect to Parliament? The analogy made little sense, however, for in England Parliament was supreme, but in New Hampshire, checks and balances prevented any of the three branches of government from having absolute dominion. Then again, the governor (Plumer), the legislature, and the courts all agreed that the act expanding the college into a university and taking its governance from the trustees was constitutional. The appeal from that agreement lay in a body that did not exist in England—the constitution of England was simply that body of law created by Parliament, the Crown, and the courts, and it could never restrict parliamentary law making (or unmaking), no matter what the American revolutionaries had argued.[35]

To this point, Webster's own contribution to the case had been minimal, glorious oratory but, according to Woodward, just wind. After all, the only issue properly before the High Court was whether the Contracts Clause applied in this case. Webster knew that the trustees had lost in the state courts, even though Mason and Smith were highly able and much-respected advocates. If he believed that they lost because the deck was stacked against them by political affiliation—they were Federalists and the justices on the bench were Republican—he might have hoped that rehearsing their arguments before a friendly tribunal would reverse the result. The US Supreme Court bench had a majority of Republicans, but all were conservative and rarely dissented from the chief justice's opinions. After all, they all boarded together, ate together, walked to and from the basement courthouse in the Capitol together, and thus far had almost always voted as a bloc—with the chief justice writing the opinion. Counting votes on the Court was an old and honored activity even in Webster's time. Webster must have realized that the Republicans on the bench outnumbered the Federalists. Thus he aimed most of his ammunition at Richardson's opinion.[36]

Webster was never a grand theorist, and what could by 1850 stand as a coherent constitutional jurisprudence was here appearing in bits and pieces. In part, that disarray was the result of the forum itself. Webster had to deal with arguments of opposing counsel, with the fact situation of the case, and with Smith and Mason's notes. Webster thus felt obligated to include a discussion of the English precedent, hardly necessary except as homage to Smith and Mason. Were he inclined (as he was not) to write an essay in the form of Hamilton's *Federalist* numbers on the judiciary, John C. Calhoun's "Exposition" of 1828, or Story's 1833 *Commentaries on the Constitution*, the bits and pieces would perhaps have reformed themselves into a coherent whole.

Nevertheless, even in fragmented fashion throughout his oral argument in *Dartmouth College*, Webster had invoked the need to draw strict separations between the political and the legal, as well as between the public and the private. The state's claims rested on politics in the legislature and the concomitant notion that the college was a public institution. By contrast, the trustees put their faith in the legal process and insisted that the college was a private one. The trustees' stance, he argued, rested on "common right," "the constitution of New-Hampshire," and "the constitution of the United States." Webster averred that he would not offer an argument on common right—that is, natural law—or on the state constitution. Instead, he went to "the single question, whether these acts are repugnant to the constitution of the United States," then, in true Ciceronian fashion, did exactly what he promised he would not do: circle back to common rights. "Yet it may assist in forming an opinion of their true nature and character, to compare them with those fundamental principles, introduced into the State governments for the purpose of limiting the exercise of the legislative power, and which the constitution of New-Hampshire expresses with great fullness and accuracy."[37]

A key portion of this endeavor was to make the case for common rights national by linking the cause of the trustees to the revolutionary foundations of republican government. Not democracy, but republicanism. It was this breath and daring of vision that made Webster such an effective advocate. Put in other terms, it was his training as an orator, free from the constraints of precise legal accuracy and precedent that confined Mason and Smith, that enabled him to go beyond their notes to confront Richardson's Republicanism directly.[38]

Webster conceded that the revolutionary constitutional settlement gave to the legislatures the foremost place in republican self-government. He did not challenge that, but just as the revolutionary constitutional theorists argued that Parliament was limited by fundamental rights, so Webster believed that the New Hampshire legislature was limited by common rights. In effect, he was returning to the question that had so concerned the framers of the state and federal constitutions: how could the rights of private individuals be protected in a system of government by electoral majorities? His answer was that these rights need not be included in the text of the state constitution, just as the Ninth Amendment to the federal Constitution recognized that the Bill of Rights did not specify all rights to which the people were entitled. Webster had to find the rights of the trustees in the interstices and penumbras of the New Hampshire Constitution of 1792. Its Article II stated, "All men have certain natural, essential, and inherent rights, among which are the enjoying and defending life and liberty, acquiring, possessing, and protecting property; and, in a word, of seeking an obtaining happiness." After all, Webster continued, the entire purpose of government was to insure liberty by limiting what governments could do to citizens. This was Webster's answer to Richardson: it was not government by the few that the trustees defended, but the rights of the few against the demands of the many.[39]

Webster next argued the state constitutional question that he had pressed before the New Hampshire Supreme Court bench. Why it belonged in his argument in Washington, DC, is unclear. Again, the only issue properly before the Court was whether the charter was a private contract. Webster's correspondence indicated that he wanted to challenge the conduct of the legislature. Perhaps his purpose was to reassert his Federalist credentials. He had not yet deserted the party, although its future in national politics was dim. Still, one of Webster's traits was loyalty, if not to causes, then to people. The trustees, Mason, Smith, Marshall, and Story had all been Federalists. Of the Republican-dominated legislature he warned, "Their object and effect is to take away from one, rights, property, and franchises, and to grant them to another. This is not the exercise of a legislative power." One should not trust Republicans in power. They had no respect for "vested rights" or for due process. "To justify the taking away of vested rights, there must be a forfeiture; to adjudge upon and declare which, is the proper province of the judiciary."[40]

Comparison is a feature of both legal argument and commonplace oratory. Webster stretched it by comparing state legislatures to Parliament. Parliament was both a legislature and a court. The legislature of New Hampshire was not a court. "Attainder and confiscation are acts of sovereign power, not acts of legislation. The British parliament, among other unlimited powers, claims that of altering and vacating charters; not as an act of ordinary legislation, but of uncontrolled authority. It is theoretically omnipotent." His audience knew where that went. Yet even Parliament used this power sparingly. "In modern times, it has attempted the exercise of this power very rarely. In a celebrated instance, those who asserted this power in parliament, vindicated its exercise only in a case, in which it could be shown, 1st. That the charter in question was a charter of political power. 2d. That there was a great and overruling state necessity, justifying the violation of the charter. 3d. That the charter had been abused, and justly forfeited." None of these were true in the *Dartmouth College* case. The comparison was thus irrelevant, but Webster insisted on making it because it applied to the revolutionary quarrel with Parliament. The revocation in question was that of the charter of Massachusetts, in 1684. "Its history is well known. . . . It cannot be pretended that the legislature, as successor to the king in this part of his prerogative, has any power to revoke, vacate, or alter this charter."[41]

Where was Webster going? Perhaps he thought that he had to neuter the winning argument that Sullivan had made at the state supreme court session. Sullivan had proposed that the charter was never private, that is, the corporation was a public one from the time it was granted. The assumption was that the state legislature inherited all of parliament's powers, including the power to make and unmake charters. Under this assumption, the legislature could call the college a public corporation and revise it in the public interest if the grantor could should that its purpose was better served in some other form. The problem with this was if the legislature was an interested party (say it wanted to use the new charter's trusteeship slots as patronage for its clients), it would be the judge in its own case. Webster objected: "But there are prohibitions in the constitution and bill of rights of New-Hampshire, introduced for the purpose of limiting the legislative power, and of protecting the rights and property of the citizens." But the New Hampshire courts had denied that the trustees, under the charter, had any property, immunity, liberty or privilege, in this corporation, within the meaning of the prohibition on taking in the state bill of rights.[42]

Again, ask why Webster was rehearsing a state constitution-based argument when the only relevant question this time was a federal one. The answer was that Webster distinguished between political acts and legal acts, that is, between the legislature's powers and the authority of courts. Legislatures could and did have purview of public matters, but the members of a private corporation had individual property rights which all republican government must respect. "It is necessary, therefore, to inquire into the true nature and character of the corporation, which was created by the charter of 1769." The legislature had power over civil corporations—of that there was no doubt. As Richardson had opined, these included "cities, counties, and the towns in New England. These may be changed and modified as public convenience may require, due regard being always had to the rights of property."[43]

There followed, probably from Smith's notes, a list of English cases and statutes to show the distinction between the two kinds of grants. While this show of erudition was impressive, it was also irrelevant. True, if the question were based on English law, the citations might have had weight. They were all present in Mason's argument before the New Hampshire Supreme Court. The sovereign state of New Hampshire was, however, the judge of which portions and distinctions in English common law were received in the state, and the ones offered by Mason made no headway. They might be brought in federal circuit court, which by the Judiciary Act used state law to settle diversity suits, but this was not a diversity suit (although the trustees had filed one already, about which more anon).

The nature of the corporation was one key to Webster's case, because from it he drew a clear line between public interests and private rights. "The case before the Court is clearly that of an eleemosynary corporation. It is, in the strictest legal sense, a private charity." So, the state could not abridge or alter its terms, unless it found fraud in the grant or misuse of funds in the conduct of the trustees (and a beneficiary of the trust brought a civil suit against it). Wheelock assumed all this, and "Little, probably, did he think, at that time, that the legislature would ever take away this property and these privileges, and give them to others. Little did he suppose, that this charter secured to him and his successors no legal rights. Little did the other donors think so." This was true of all the colleges that began with grants from the crown. It was true of those that began with corporate charters from the colonial governments. It was true of private schools that had corporate beginnings. "They hold their property by the same tenure, and no other." Now Webster, who was not always a nice or even a polite debater, took a whack at Richardson, a Harvard grad: "Nor has Harvard College any surer title than Dartmouth College. It may, to-day, have more friends; but to-morrow it may have more enemies. Its legal rights are the same." Later grants of land did not change the nature of the original charter, and "When donations are made, by the legislature, or others, to a charity already existing, without any condition, or the specification of any new use, the donation follows the nature of the charity."[44]

Finally, he connected the general argument about severing public from private and legislative from juridical to the particular fact pattern: "The very object sought in obtaining such charter, and in giving property to such a corporation, is to make and keep it private property, and to clothe it with all the security and inviolability of private property. The intent is, that there shall be a legal private ownership, and that the legal owners shall maintain and protect the property, for the benefit of those for whose use it was designed. Who ever endowed the public? Who ever appointed a legislature to administer his charity? Or who ever heard, before, that a gift to a College, or Hospital, or an Asylum, was, in reality, nothing but a gift to the State?" This should have ended the discussion of the nature of the grant. Once again, Webster was drawn into a tangential discourse on the New Hampshire constitution, a needless repetition of Mason's points. Or perhaps not, for one word followed or preceded rights—property. It was the trustees' property that was at stake, and property was Webster's lodestar.[45]

Until he had hammered home the primacy of the right to property, ensured and guarded it against the unjustified exactions of the state, he was not ready to rest the case on the Contracts Clause of the federal Constitution. Until he got there, he was free to talk endlessly about the sacredness of private property, but once he got there, what more would there be to say to the justices? So he delayed until there was nothing more to say about English precedent, the nature of corporations, the New Hampshire Constitution and goodness knows what else to prove that all law had the purpose of protecting private property. Mason's argument and Smith's notes did not have this aim; Webster turned what Mason had said and Smith had written to his own purpose—a treatise on the meaning and importance of the law of property.

Finally, he got to the relevant grounds for appeal, and the last of the three conundrums left by the framers—the relationship between the federal power and state sovereignty. "The plaintiffs contend, in the second place, that the acts in question are repugnant to the 10th section of the 1st article of the constitution of the United States." Webster's purpose was to win for his client, of course, but not just to win for his client. For even in the well of the courtroom, his politics and his political ideology infused his legalism. It was not merely legal instrumentalism, the oral argument having little relation to the Dartmouth College cause, but a thorough admixture of the case and a small land holder's conservatism. If the winning argument—at least the dispositive argument—could no longer be deferred, it was by now indissolubly linked to the Federalist ideal of private property.[46]

Webster now arrayed all the parts of his oral argument: "The object of these most important provisions in the national constitution has often been discussed, both here and elsewhere." The object of the provision was to protect private property rights against the invasion of legislatures. "Very properly, therefore, have the [constitutional] Convention added this constitutional bulwark in favour of personal security and private rights; and I am much deceived if they have not, in so doing, as faithfully consulted the genuine sentiments as the undoubted interests of their constituents." Personal security: "The sober people of America are weary of the fluctuating policy which has directed the public councils. They have seen with regret, and with indignation, that sudden changes, and legislative interferences, in cases affecting personal rights, become jobs in the hands of enterprising and influential speculators; and snares to the more industrious and less informed part of the community." Sober people were Webster's lookalikes and think-alikes. They had been the bulk of the Federalist Party, now rapidly receding in the rear mirror of American politics. But they were the ones who had secured personal property through the federal Constitution.[47]

Thus, once Webster got to the key constitutional issue, he needed to say relatively little about it. Precedent and plain text foreclosed any doubts about the applicability of the Contracts Clause to the *Dartmouth College* case. "This Court, then, does not admit the doctrine, that a legislature can repeal statutes creating private corporations. If it cannot repeal them altogether, of course it cannot repeal any part of them, or impair them, or essentially alter them, without the consent of the corporators." Scholars have wondered why Webster gave the issue comparatively short shrift if it was so vital to the case. The answer, again, is that it was simply the coda to his own cause—the defense of private property from state expropriation.[48]

The close of the oral argument was, like its opening and middle passages, concerned with the security of property against rapacious (presumably Republican) legislatures. "The case before the Court is not of ordinary importance, nor of every day occurrence. It affects not this college only, but every college, and all the literary institutions of the country. . . . They have all a common principle of existence, the inviolability of their charters. It will be a dangerous, a most dangerous experiment, to hold these institutions subject to the rise and fall of popular parties, and the fluctuations of political opinions. . . . Party and faction will be cherished in the places consecrated to piety and learning." The danger was not just or even primarily the indoctrination of the next generation of students in Republican doctrine. It was the threat to private property that the Republicans had already demonstrated. "If the franchise may be at any time taken away, or impaired, the property also may be taken away, or its use perverted."[49]

Webster's primary purpose at this point in his career, in this setting, was not to finish the incomplete Constitution. His aim was to win the appeal for his clients. But embedded in that appeal was the outline of answers to the three great questions the framers left for the next generation of jurists. Though the defense of private property, what later generations would decry as vested rights, stood in the forefront of the oral argument, that defense rested securely on the notions of strict divisions between public-interest lawmaking and private rights; between partisan politics (in legislatures) and neutral law (in courts); and between the claims of states and the authority given federal government by the Constitution. Cut away the facts of the particular case, and the framework of constitutional jurisprudence appears even more starkly.

Webster's oral argument went on for hours. The justices sat at their desks behind the railing (there was no bench) and listened. Story, pen at hand, never wrote a word. Marshall, characteristically, gave careful attention but did not take notes. A brief pause, followed by a peroration that Webster had not written and did not, in the end, provide to the Court reporter Henry Wheaton, supposedly brought tears to some in the courtroom. Webster's words were, however, remembered, and were quoted in his eulogy on the floor of the Senate. He had spoken of his love for Dartmouth and how the small college should be retained as it was. "You may destroy this little institution; it is weak; it is in your hands. But there are those of us who love it." That was not the most important part of the peroration, however. Instead, it was that "in some sense, [it is] the case of every man among us who has property of which he may be stripped."[50]

For secretary Woodward and the state, John Holmes spoke relatively briefly and, by all accounts, ineffectively. His co-counsel, Salma Hale, reported to a private correspondent, Holmes was "below our modest expectations." Webster was equally unimpressed by Holmes's contribution. Wirt spoke next, returning to the strongest part of Richardson's opinion—the trust was not a private contract. Webster remained unimpressed. Wirt was, he wrote to Mason, "completely unsuccessful." Hopkinson closed oral argument relying on the Contracts Clause. Of all of the participants, his was the most strictly relevant brief. He did not assay any of the other distinctions Webster made, again suggesting that they were Webster's own, rather than essential parts of the case.[51]

The case was heard and reserved (submitted) for judgment. Unsure of the outcome, Webster printed his arguments and sent them far and wide, including copies to the Dartmouth student body, to New York's chancellor James Kent, the doyen of state jurists, to Story of course, and to all "the commanding men in New England" and New York, according to a friend. He gave a copy to Wheaton, who saw to the publication of the decisions of the Court and the opinions of the justices. Wheaton also included the arguments of counsel, relying on what they gave him and editing the texts for publication. A practicing attorney and federal official, he did not give up private practice or his other offices when he acted as reporter of the court's opinions, from 1816 to 1827. In this he was aided by Story. Wheaton was a man of letters and a diplomat, composing a leading treatise on international law; and a biographer, ironically publishing in 1826 a biography of William Pinkney, Webster's great Court adversary.[52]

Webster also prepared a collateral attack on the state supreme court decision in the circuit federal court. The purpose of this was to bring before the
High Court the issue of the misconduct of the New Hampshire legislature.
The procedural devise would be a disagreement between the justice Story, riding circuit, and district court judge John S. Sherburne, formerly a Republican
congressman from New Hampshire and from 1804 to 1830 the federal district
court judge for the state. The grounds for the suit would be another common
law writ, the action of ejectment. In ejectment, the plaintiff argues that the
court should order the current possessor of property to return it to its lawful
owner. Some of the property of the college lay in Vermont. Because there was
diversity in the parties—that is, some of the trustees were not New Hampshire
residents—and Woodward was, the Judiciary Act of 1789 gave either party the
right to bring the suit in the federal circuit court. The plan was that Sherburne
would almost certainly find that the failure of the earlier trover suit decided
the ejectment suit. Story would disagree. That would certify the case to the US
Supreme Court, this time to be heard on state law grounds. When a suit was
heard in federal court on the diversity of residence of its parties, the court was
to use the state law to render a decision. This would allow Webster to bring
in the New Hampshire constitutional materials that had been irrelevant when
the only issue was the Contracts Clause of the federal Constitution. In any
event, the circuit court suit was filed in May 1818, was continued in the October meeting, and was heard after the Supreme Court decided the trover suit.[53]

When the High Court reserved judgment for the next session to convene in
January 1819, the state of New Hampshire asked Pinkney to represent its interests. Pinkney was the acknowledged leader of the Supreme Court bar. He had
studied in England and practiced in Maryland before a diplomatic mission
took him back to England. Informed that the Court might rehear argument
at the 1819 session, he prepared meticulously, as was his custom. According to
Hopkinson and others who spoke to Pinkney, he intended to make a states'
rights argument. Unlike Holmes and Wirt, who did not have access to Sullivan's notes until the last minute, Pinkney had before him the entire history
of the cause along with copies of all the relevant documents. He was present
in February 1819 when, to everyone's surprise, Marshall announced that the
Court had reached a decision and read it.[54]

Marshall's decision tracked Webster's brief on the Contracts Clause issue.
The chief justice was aware that the Court, if it found for the trustees, would

be voiding a state statute and overturning the opinion of its highest court. "This Court can be insensible neither to the magnitude nor delicacy of this question. The validity of a legislative act is to be examined; and the opinion of the highest law tribunal of a State is to be revised." Unstated but lurking in the shadows was the fact that the Court and Marshall were still Federalists and the state legislature and its supreme court were Republicans. Marshall's invocation of "cautious circumspection," a redundancy in itself, hardly banished the political question from anyone's thinking. But it was the "solemn duty" of the Court to apply the federal Constitution's language, and the Contracts Clause explicitly barred the states from impairing a contract. He then turned to the intentions of the framers, who plainly did not mean to prevent states from altering the regulation of their own inferior agencies. He next concluded that the charter grant was a contract with private individuals for a charitable institution, not a public one. Corporations were not public institutions unless they were framed as public institutions. "The particular interests of New-Hampshire never entered into the mind of the donors, never constituted a motive for their donation." Could New Hampshire simply declare that the college was a public institution? Here Marshall indulged in original intent. "There is no expression in the constitution, no sentiment delivered by its contemporaneous expounders, which would justify us in making" such an assumption. The Contracts Clause applied. "It results from this opinion, that the acts of the legislature of New-Hampshire, which are stated in the special verdict found in this cause, are repugnant to the constitution of the United States; and that the judgment on this special verdict ought to have been for the plaintiffs. The judgment of the State Court must, therefore, be reversed."[55]

Note here that Marshall's opinion did not accept Webster's invitation to demand a strict line be drawn between public interests and private rights, or between legislative and judicial powers. He simply assumed it. Marshall would insist throughout his career on the High Court bench that politics had nothing to do with the Court's decisions. The law and nothing but the law dictated the outcome, certainly no external sources; only principle, text, and precedent guided his hand.[56]

Justices Brockholst Livingston and William Johnson concurred, although both were Republicans, and Justices Bushrod Washington and Story wrote a concurring opinion to emphasize that the college was from its inception a charitable private institution. Gabriel Duvall dissented, without an opinion, which was something of a surprise, as he often voted with Marshall and was certainly not an avid Republican (though he was appointed by Republican president James Madison). Perhaps the fact that he, like Richardson, had been a chief justice of a state supreme court (of Maryland) may have influenced his views. Wirt and Pinkney were stunned. They must have thought that they had Livingston's and Johnson's votes, and perhaps Story's. Webster and Hopkinson were delighted. Webster moved for an order securing to the trustees their property. It was given. Pinkney objected that the state court and federal circuit courts had not given any orders to that effect, and that new facts had been produced in both forums. On May 1, 1819, Justice Story for the circuit court offered to hear any new facts in the diversity case. On May 27, he judged that they were not sufficient to require further judicial notice, repeating the substance of his longish disquisition on the nature of grants, contracts, and state powers. One year later, the superior court that had three years earlier heard the suit reversed itself and rendered its judgment that the college and its appurtenances did indeed belong to the original twelve trustees and their successors.[57]

The post-trial maneuvering, including a review, an appeal, and then a new round of trial in the circuit court, mirrored the relatively chaotic state of post-trial law. In New Hampshire, a new trial could be had on a motion of review. Judges routinely granted these when some point of law had not been thoroughly argued. Modern courts prefer the rule that an issue not raised in the initial trial cannot be the basis of an appeal, but courts in Webster's time did not foreclose new trials so preemptively. Even if the original trial court did not allow a new trial, an appeal to the state supreme court could gain an order for a new trial. Thus the paperwork of the original trial, the new writs, and the records of payments and bonds crisscrossed the mail to attorneys' offices. In sum, no one was pulling a fast one by trying to reopen the case.[58]

Webster's contribution to the unfinished Constitution in the *Dartmouth College* case was far more than the simple notion that the Contracts Clause protected private property, and thus it was a centerpiece of the Constitution. He understood that private property was not an absolute right—that the public had an interest in certain chartered corporations, and that legislatures legitimately protected these interests. Webster was not what modern theorists might call a strict libertarian. Perhaps Richardson had seen farther into the future, when government would create and protect public uses of property, but for the present, Webster's assessment was more accurate: the great age of private corporations had begun.[59]

In the meantime, Webster and Pinkney had turned to another cause in which they joined forces. It was an odd match—the convivial and often wordy Webster and the dour, arrogant and rigorously prepared Pinkney accepting fees to defend the Second Bank of the United States against Pinkney's home state of Maryland.[60]

3. "Necessary and Proper": *McCulloch v. Maryland* (1819)

Webster was no sooner done with his oral argument before the Court in *Dartmouth College*—indeed the case was still bouncing back and forth between the circuit court, the Supreme Court, and the state courts—when Webster argued for the Second Bank of the United States in *McCulloch v. Maryland*. *Dartmouth College* was a case of first importance, but *McCulloch* was a case of national significance. Like *Dartmouth College*, the bank case was both political and legal, for the bank was run by National Republicans, the heirs to the Federalists, and the opposition to the bank was led by Jeffersonian Republicans. What was more, unlike *Dartmouth College*, essentially an intrastate matter, *McCulloch* directly implicated federalism: could the state of Maryland tax a branch of a bank chartered by Congress? Finally, the bank issue crisscrossed the public/private divide, as the bank itself was a chartered corporation that had both public and private characteristics. All three of the conundrums of the incomplete Constitution came into play in *McCulloch*. Indeed, in a jurisprudential sense, so far as Webster was concerned, the case was the natural successor to *Dartmouth College*. And again, it demanded Webster draw boundaries left uncertain by the framers.

The recharter of the Bank of the United States (BUS II) in 1816 was not a popular move in many quarters. The first version of the bank, the brainchild of Secretary of the Treasury Alexander Hamilton and financier of the revolution Robert Morris, had a twenty-year lifespan and was not rechartered in 1812. While a national bank was defended as much-needed during the travail of the War of 1812, state banks that had appeared after the demise of the first Bank of the United States were not pleased that a successor was in the works. The problem was the power the BUS II would have to call in the reserves of state banks, when the latter were almost always overextended (having loaned out more than they could cover). In Congress, Daniel Webster proposed a compromise, arguing that some circulating medium acceptable throughout the nation was necessary for interstate and overseas trade. It was in a way the same problem the colonies had faced under the restrictive English currency acts. In 1815 a version of the revised second bank plan created a fund of $30 million, one-sixth of which would be in hard currency and the rest in treasury notes. President James Madison vetoed the plan, however, with a message that suggested the bank did not do enough to revive the credit of the federal government. A year later, in 1816, with peace reestablished, a new bill went through Congress creating a bank with $50 million in capital, chartered for twenty years, with twenty-five directors, five of whom were to be presidential nominees. John C. Calhoun had pushed through the compromise and written the new charter. Constitutional questions of the authority of Congress to create such a bank, a talking point for the opposition during the war, were not pressed, but opposition based on states' rights doctrine did raise its head. Nevertheless, the bill was passed and signed. The head branch was to be in Philadelphia, and state branches quickly appeared in ten states.[1]

Under the first president of the bank, William Jones, its policies were highly inflationary, giving out loans right and left when its primary function was to control the extravagances of state banks. By 1818, with the BUS II itself tottering on bankruptcy, the directors began to call in outstanding loans and press state banks to do the same. In response, some states—notably, Maryland and Tennessee, followed by Georgia, North Carolina, Ohio, and Kentucky—passed laws disfavoring the BUS II in favor of state banks. The Maryland legislature's act imposed a tax (via the use of prestamped paper Maryland sold) on all banks, or their branches within the state of Maryland, not chartered by the legislature. The only bank fitting this description was the BUS II. The penalty was levied for each violation, although it could be averted by paying a considerable lump sum. Other states' impositions on the BUS II branches were even more severe.[2]

The defendant, one James William M'Culloch, a cashier at the Bank of the United States, had issued notes that violated the Maryland law. M'Culloch was a Philadelphian of good family who found a home in Baltimore, served with honor in the militia in the War of 1812, and was a member of the city's mercantile community when he was chosen as the clerk of the BUS II branch. It was an important position and he was an ambitious man. He refused to use the stamped paper Maryland supplied. (Shades of the resistance to the Stamp Act of 1765!) The plaintiff, the state of Maryland, brought suit to recover penalties under the act. The county court found for the state, and the state court of appeals affirmed.[3]

The attack on the BUS II was a major political event that fell into a deeper constitutional crevasse. For in the Senate chamber just above the Supreme Court's room, members were debating Missouri's application for statehood.

Largely settled by slaveholders, its territorial legislature had proposed a constitution that would have permitted slavery, the internal slave trade, and the acquisition of slaves from outside the state. In the end, a compromise would be reached for Missouri, the rest of the Louisiana Territory purchase north of 36° 30', and the admission of Maine as a free state (keeping the balance in the Senate). In the meantime, pro- and antislavery voices were raised to fever pitch. The law and politics overlapped. Public policy and private rights of slaveholders were intertwined. States' rights was a centerpiece in the argument over slavery. The bank case was going to become part of the national referendum on states' rights.

The bank hired Webster and Pinkney to make its case. Webster would so often defend the bank that he sought and received a retainer from it. But the two lawyers in effect also represented the United States, because the cause of the bank was the cause of the congressional act that created the bank. They were joined by William Wirt, the attorney general of the United States, and Walter Jones, an attorney from the District of Columbia who had been its federal attorney from 1804 to 1821. A Jeffersonian Republican and a bookish man, Jones was thought by many to be the smartest man at the bar. The state of Maryland was represented by Joseph Hopkinson, Webster's ally in *Dartmouth College*, and by the attorney general of Maryland, Luther Martin. Martin was in his second term as the state's spokesman, the first coming nearly twenty years earlier. The circle of attorneys practicing before the High Court was small and elite; and many, like Hopkinson, Pinkney, and Webster, had worked with one another as often as they opposed one another.[4]

Webster now had to contend with Martin, a figure so important in the history of his state and the Union, and Hopkinson, Webster's rival at the federal bar. Besting Martin and Hopkinson was a project that spurred Webster's efforts, and it would lead to one of Webster's most far-reaching and persuasive intellectual achievements. What scholars sometimes miss in their eagerness to praise Marshall's opinion is that much of Marshall's opinion came directly from Webster.[5]

Webster began by confronting Martin's claim that the Congress had no power to incorporate a bank. "It is a question of the utmost magnitude, deeply interesting to the government itself, as well as to individuals." It was especially interesting to Webster because "the mere discussion of such a question may most essentially affect the value of a vast amount of private property." Once again, Webster thought that the Constitution's purpose, admittedly implied, was to draw a line between government and people; that is, he saw an opportunity to draw the correct line between public interest and private rights. The bank was a public institution, he argued, but its purpose was to create and enhance private enterprise. After all, the original aim of the bank was to ensure some security in the monetary supply. What could better facilitate both public and private interests than that?[6]

Martin was well aware that the BUS II held private capital as well as federal government monies. According to Webster, Martin should have known (after all, Luther Martin was a member of the Maryland delegation to the Philadelphia convention) that "this question arose early after the adoption of the constitution, and was discussed, and settled, as far as legislative decision could settle it, in the first Congress." Martin was Maryland's attorney general when Alexander Hamilton first proposed the Bank of the United States. Then, "The arguments drawn from the constitution in favour of this power, were stated, and exhausted, in that discussion. They were exhibited, with characteristic perspicuity and force, by the first Secretary of the Treasury, in his report to the President of the United States." Martin should have recalled that "the first Congress created and incorporated a bank. Nearly each succeeding Congress, if not every one, has acted and legislated on the presumption of the legal existence of such a power in the government." Again, the purpose of such a sweeping grant of discretion to Congress was to promote both public needs and private rights. In creating the bank, Congress was trying to accomplish what the framers had left open for Congress to do—merge public interest and private property.[7]

Martin had refused to sign the Constitution and had led Maryland Antifederalists during the ratification debates. Webster, it would seem, was directing his comments to Martin as well as to the bench. "Individuals, it is true, have doubted, or thought otherwise; but it cannot be shown that either branch of the legislature has, at any time, expressed an opinion against the existence of the power." Webster's defense of the bank charter and recharter was his (and Congress's) attempt to fill in the gap in the Constitution. "The executive government has acted upon it; and the courts of law have acted upon it." The bank's existence was thus proof that the line between politics (the executive and the legislative branches) and law (the courts) was not a barrier but a causeway. Finally, the relationship between the federal government and the states was not challenged by the two bank charters, because members of Congress were also leaders in their states. "Many of those who doubted or denied the existence of the power, when first attempted to be exercised, have yielded to the first decision, and acquiesced in it, as a settled question."[8]

Having made the general argument, Webster provided detailed evidence of his reading of the three issues. Here, as in *Dartmouth College*, there was something of a pedant in Webster, as though the country boy from New Hampshire was as literate and learned as any of the other members of the Supreme Court bar. So, too, combat against Martin and Hopkinson spurred Webster. He conceded that the creation of a Bank was not mentioned in the first article of the Constitution, but the Necessary and Proper Clause was there to enable the government to meet its needs. Such compromises between politics and law and between enumerated powers and reserved powers were required for the federal government to meet its responsibilities. "Congress, by the constitution, is invested with certain powers; and, as to the objects, and within the scope of these powers, it is sovereign." The power was implied. These need not be mentioned specifically. A government confined strictly within the letter of its enumerated powers could never respond to emergencies, long-term changes in social and economic needs, and operational necessities. The alternative, amending the Constitution, did not answer exigency. In effect, Webster was arguing that the strict construction of the powers of Congress under the Constitution would be a suicide pact.[9]

The Necessary and Proper Clause was the answer—not the only answer but a legitimate one—to felt needs and immediate problems. Unfortunately, the clause did not have any clear boundaries. These would have to be drawn around every act of Congress fitting the category. Were those boundaries merely political, or were they grounded in law? The legislative branch itself could not answer that question; it belonged to the courts. How far could the clause, and congressional legislation under it, advance into legislative territory claimed by the states? Was the clause an invitation for the federal government to destroy the sovereignty of the states?[10]

Webster, knowing that *Gibbons v. Ogden* was on the way to the Court and he was already approached by one of the parties to the case, assayed the following example: "Steam frigates, for example, were not in the minds of those who framed the constitution, as among the means of naval warfare; but no one doubts the power of Congress to use them, as means to an authorized end." Indeed, that was why the clause was put in Article I. Why else have it there if not to be used? "It is not enough to say, that it does not appear that a bank was in the contemplation of the framers of the constitution. It was not their intention, in these cases, to enumerate particulars." He then offered a rule for implied powers that is remarkable still: "The true view of the subject is, that if it be a fit instrument to an authorized purpose, it may be used, not being specially prohibited." Then he elaborated, just in case the elegance of his initial formulation was too hard to follow: "Congress is authorized to pass all laws 'necessary and proper' to carry into execution the powers conferred on it. These words, 'necessary and proper,' in such an instrument, are probably to be considered as synonymous."[11]

Necessary and *proper* were hardly synonyms, as Webster undoubtedly knew. *Necessary* meant "no choice." *Proper* meant "fitting." In fact, *proper* was added to *necessary* late in the Constitutional Convention. Together they make sense, however. Webster was trying to convince the Court to read the clause as a whole; that is, to find that a necessary act of Congress was also a proper one. A government "would hardly exist; at least, it would be wholly inadequate to the purposes of its formation" were some provision not made for the unforeseen or the suddenly necessitous. The framers were fully aware of the sudden turns that national emergencies could take. Financial crises were among these. "A bank is a proper and suitable instrument to assist the operations of the government, in the collection and disbursement of the revenue; in the occasional anticipations of taxes and imposts; and in the regulation of the actual currency, as being a part of the trade and exchange between the States." The decision of how such a bank was to operate, who was to run it, and the like were not matters for courts. They were objects of policy best left for the elected branches of government, and that is why the framers added the clause to Article I. If Congress elected to make the bank quasi-private, by a grant of incorporation, that too was the business of Congress, not the courts. Again, even though nothing explicit in the Constitution empowered Congress to grant corporate charters, that type of government activity was well established. Webster did not say "consider *Dartmouth College*," but then, he did not have to say it.[12]

Then on to his second intervention, "whether, if the bank be constitutionally created, the State governments have power to tax it?" The structure of federalism was accepted with ratification of the Constitution, and the powers conferred on the national government were established in that Constitution. The Constitution was the supreme law of the land "and shall control all State legislation and State constitutions, which may be incompatible therewith; and it confides to this Court the ultimate power of deciding all questions arising under the constitution and laws of the United States."[13]

If the Court found the bank constitutional, as Webster assumed it would, then the laws of the states that harmed the bank and its operations must fall. All that followed from the constitutionality of the bank. "The only inquiry, therefore, in this case is, whether the law of the state of Maryland imposing this tax be consistent with the free operation of the law establishing the bank, and the full enjoyment of the privileges conferred by it?" That question had an easy answer. "An unlimited power to tax involves, necessarily, a power to destroy; because there is a limit beyond which no institution and no property can bear taxation."[14]

States could impose taxes coincident with federal taxes, in which the discretion of the state government determined the extent of the tax. If the state could tax the BUS II, the amount of tax lay in the hands of the state. It could, if it wished, tax the bank out of existence. It could use taxes to harry the bank or to interfere with its operation. Webster did not go behind Maryland's thinking (which he knew) to argue that the state wanted to destroy the bank. He merely followed his own logic. "A question of constitutional power can hardly be made to depend on a question of more or less" taxes. "The object in laying this tax, may have been revenue to the State. In the next case, the object may be to expel the bank from the State."[15]

The purpose of the state did not matter—taxing a creature of the federal government, in effect federal property, violated the Constitution. Could the state next tax the federal customs houses? Federal courthouses in the state? Other federal property? Of course not. Could it tax federal treasury notes? Could it impose a stamp tax on federal official documents? The power to tax was the power to destroy. Could the state of Maryland, using an unrestrained taxing power, destroy the federal government operations in Maryland? Of course not.

Hopkinson disagreed. The bank was not a legitimate exercise of federal congressional authority. Maybe the first Bank of the US was necessary and proper in 1791, but it was no longer so in 1816. Conditions had changed. State banks had appeared and were doing a fine job (ignoring the collapse of the state banking industry in the Panic of 1819). What was more, even if Congress

determined what was necessary and proper in 1816, Congress had not authorized the BUS II to establish branch banks in the states. This was the act of
the directors of the bank, and it exceeded their authority under the charter.
The directors of the bank were not immediately responsible to Congress or
to the people. In creating the branch banks, they had acted as private bank-
ers rather than fiduciaries for the public. Finally, nothing in the enabling act
creating the bank said that it or its branches would be exempt from ordinary
and equal taxation of property in the state by the state. "This overwhelm-
ing invasion of State sovereignty is not warranted by any express clause or
grant in the constitution, and never was imagined by any State that adopted
and ratified that constitution." In short, a states' rights argument was the
strongest Hopkinson could muster to defend the Maryland tax and its penal
impositions on agents of the BUS II.[16]

Hopkinson's peroration was perhaps the high point of the rhetorical exercise: "What have we opposed to these doctrines, so just and reasonable?
Distressing inconveniences ingeniously contrived; supposed dangers; fearful
distrusts; anticipated violence and injustice from the States, and consequent
ruin to the bank." Next up, Martin railed against the comparative mildness
of Webster's rhetoric. Webster had not warned against the end of days, but
Martin saw that peril in sight. He dismissed the core of Webster's argument,
sneering, "A right to tax is a right to destroy, is the whole amount of the argument, however varied by ingenuity, or embellished by eloquence." But this
he thought a chimera, for if the states had the power, then nothing in the appellants' arguments could resist it. Not to worry, however, for state taxes were
no threat. They were using it "modestly and discreetly." Trust the state, he
offered, for only "a reasonable confidence in each other" could enable federal
and state governments to operate in the same space.[17]

Martin, Pinkney, and Jones covered already plowed ground, the first two ill
and on their last legs, and Jones with little to say that was news. Marshall's
opinion for the Court seemed to open a new seam of controversy, however. It
was long—longer than any of the lawyers' briefs, and it recognized the issues
of the case as monumentally important, not just for the Constitution but for
the politics of the nation's future. It thus had the character of a political as
well as a legal statement that Marshall had so pointedly avoided in *Dartmouth
College*. "In the case now to be determined, the defendant, a sovereign State,

denies the obligation of a law enacted by the legislature of the Union." Maryland had intentionally and blatantly claimed it could confute federal law. This was, in a way, a more threatening posture than interposition or nullification in the Virginia and Kentucky resolves, which applied only to the state and its people. Maryland's stance, were it duplicated around the country, would destroy the power of Congress to pass any legislation. Marshall would not allow this to happen. "The constitution of our country, in its most interesting and vital parts, is to be considered; the conflicting powers of the government of the Union and of its members, as marked in that constitution, are to be discussed; and an opinion given, which may essentially influence the great operations of the government." He recognized that the issue was the opening salvo of what might become "a source of hostile legislation, perhaps of hostility of a still more serious nature."[18]

The authority of Congress to create the bank could not be questioned. It had happened once before, in 1791. (In fact, the constitutionality of that bank had never been tested in court.) Then, as in 1816, it was the work of the people's assembly. In that assembly, the BUS II had been hotly debated. Still, opponents like Maryland proposed a compact theory of the federal system, "to consider that instrument not as emanating from the people, but as the act of sovereign and independent States. The powers of the general government, it has been said, are delegated by the States, who alone are truly sovereign; and must be exercised in subordination to the States, who alone possess supreme dominion." As history and as law, that argument, he thought, was settled. The ratification of the Constitution by elected conventions settled it. A more perfect union was the product of we the people, not the states. For this, Marshall relied on the text of the preamble as well as the ratification process.[19]

Reason and experience coincided in Marshall's thinking. The federal government was supreme in its sphere, and "though any one State may be willing to control its operations, no State is willing to allow others to control them." Nothing in the enumerated powers mentioned creating a bank by corporate charter, but the Necessary and Proper Clause was there precisely for this reason. Here, clearly, was Webster's argument. Though phrased in Marshall's somewhat clunkier language, Webster's logic reappeared. "A constitution, to contain an accurate detail of all the subdivisions of which its great powers will admit, and of all the means by which they may be carried into execution, would partake of the prolixity of a legal code, and could scarcely be embraced by the human mind." The Constitution was not such a code, but the "great outline" whose minor ingredients (a mixed metaphor) could be deduced from the experience of the framers and the needs of a growing nation. "In considering this question, then, we must never forget, that it is a constitution we are expounding," not a code.[20]

While in context the meaning of the last phrase in the paragraph is simple—a constitution was not a minutely detailed code—over time the phrase has gained a much larger place in constitutional jurisprudence. Repeatedly cited in later cases, it endows the judge with a power to see in the Constitution all manner of necessities and properties not visible to the naked eye. Marshall did not intend it to be an "open sesame" to an all-powerful central government. Consider that the very next passage demonstrated just how far Marshall intended to go. The bank was not mentioned, but

> although, among the enumerated powers of government, we do not find the word "bank" or "incorporation," we find the great powers to lay and collect taxes; to borrow money; to regulate commerce; to declare and conduct a war; and to raise and support armies and navies. The sword and the purse, all the external relations, and no inconsiderable portion of the industry of the nation, are entrusted to its government.

The bank was like these latter enumerated powers. Indeed, the bank was a much inferior power to those explicitly granted.[21]

Surely no one could doubt that the federal government had the power to grant a charter of incorporation. Every government had such power. What was the bank but such a grant—more of Webster's thinking. Even if this power was not expressly conferred on Congress, if Congress could not do what every other government could, how could Congress function? The BUS II was merely the means that Congress had selected to perform what Congress had to perform. The means surely was left to the Congress, for Congress was the agency of a sovereign government, to wit, the United States. "The subject is the execution of those great powers on which the welfare of a nation essentially depends. It must have been the intention of those who gave these powers, to insure, as far as human prudence could insure, their beneficial execution. This could not be done by confiding the choice of means to such narrow limits as not to leave it in the power of Congress to adopt any which might be appropriate, and which were conducive to the end."[22]

It was unnecessary to have specific provisions for all of these exigencies.

At best, the country would be left with a code rather than a constitution. At worst, even the most comprehensive code would leave out powers that, in future, would become necessary. "To have prescribed the means by which government should, in all future time, execute its powers, would have been to change, entirely, the character of the instrument." Not a code, Marshall repeated, as if there were another, unseen, auditor in the courtroom. European jurisprudence, in particular the Code Napoleon, were exactly what Marshall disparaged. He knew about the Code Napoleon and had been in Paris when Napoleon returned from war to accolades and took up the project. One can, with a little imagination, read the repetitions in the passage as a slap at Napoleon's legal efforts. In any case, Marshall concluded that his view was not an open-ended grant of absolute power to Congress. Instead, it was simply the rational extension of the necessary and proper powers.[23]

Marshall's thinking was functional, practical, and logical. "The baneful influence of this narrow construction on all the operations of the government, and the absolute impracticability of maintaining it without rendering the government incompetent to its great objects, might be illustrated by numerous examples drawn from the constitution, and from our laws." The examples then supported the proposition. This is the style of reasoning, and writing, of a diplomat (he had been secretary of state under John Adams) and a member of Congress, rather than someone who spent his entire government career on the bench. Webster too would later serve as secretary of state. In this sense, as in others, the thinking of the two men would align, not just by conservative ideology or nationalism, but by experience.[24]

Marshall, unlike Webster, engaged in simple parsing of text. This was in modern parlance textualism—finding the commonsense meaning of words. For Marshall, so close to the framing, textualism made sense, for it rested upon contemporary usages. "If the word 'necessary' means 'needful,' 'requisite,' 'essential,' 'conducive to' . . . is it not equally comprehensive when required to authorize the use of means which facilitate the execution of the powers of government." Marshall assumed that he could divine the meaning of words the framers used. "In ascertaining the sense in which the word 'necessary' is used in this clause of the constitution, we may derive some aid from that with which it is associated." Look for *necessary* and *proper* throughout the debates, and you will find that they were not employed to constrain but to free government to act. After all, the clause was placed among the powers of Congress, not among its limitations.[25]

With the *Dartmouth College* case just decided, Marshall assumed that the creation of a public corporation was a perfectly legitimate means to effectuate the ends Congress had in mind. "If a corporation may be employed indiscriminately with other means to carry into execution the powers of the government, no particular reason can be assigned for excluding the use of a bank, if required for its fiscal operations." The chief justice then borrowed from Hamilton's original justification for the bank: "All those who have been concerned in the administration of our finances, have concurred in representing its importance and necessity."[26]

Next Marshall turned to the question of whether Maryland violated the Constitution by taxing the branch bank. Maryland had the power to tax individuals and institutions that did business within its borders. Taxation was a concurrent power. States could not tax imports or exports, however, and the operations of a federal bank fell into that category. The federal government's power to create and preserve must not be curbed by the operation of a state, for the federal government "must not yield to that over which it is supreme." That the power to tax was the power to destroy for Marshall was "too obvious to be denied." Maryland asked that the federal government trust it not to overstep state powers. In this case, it had. States could tax their own property and property held by their citizens, but not property held by agencies of the federal government.[27]

Near to closing, Marshall considered the implications of the Maryland tax. "If the States may tax one instrument, employed by the government in the execution of its powers, they may tax any and every other instrument." He then offered examples, a list of horribles. Again, the list came from Webster. "They may tax all the means employed by the government, to an excess which would defeat all the ends of government." In short, "the power to tax is the power to destroy."[28]

A little more history to close the wound: according to Marshall, the Publius newspaper essays (i.e., *The Federalist Papers*) rightly read, and remember that at this time no one knew who had written which of the essays—that was only nailed down in 1944 by historian Douglas Adair—was still not compelling jurisprudence. It was political opinion. The argument that a reciprocity between the federal government and the states conferred on the states the power to tax the federal government was inane. Anything that the state did to impede the lawful operation of the federal government was null and void. The conclusion was inescapable:

> The Court has bestowed on this subject its most deliberate consideration. The result is a conviction that the States have no power, by taxation or otherwise, to retard, impede, burden, or in any manner control, the operations of the constitutional laws enacted by Congress to carry into execution the powers vested in the general government. This is, we think, the unavoidable consequence of that supremacy which the constitution has declared.

Marshall had laid the groundwork for a strong federal government, but he closed with a remark that seemed to offer peace to those in favor of moderate states' rights: "This opinion does not deprive the States of any resources which they originally possessed." The peace offering would shortly be rejected by opponents of his reasoning.[29]

Marshall's opinion shielded Webster from the full force of strident states' rights advocacy. The response to the decision and even more to Marshall's opinion was fierce, if predictable, and surprisingly swift. Coming on top of the Missouri statehood crisis in Congress, it appeared that states' rights doctrine had taken a body blow. Thomas Richie's *Richmond Enquirer* newspaper published a series of thinly disguised (assumed at the time to be Spencer Roane but actually William Brockenbrough) attacks on the opinion. Marshall had allegedly destroyed federalism. Both Roane and Brockenbrough came from leading Virginia families, in much the same circle as Marshall, although both remained in state rather than federal judicial service. The anonymous essayist, Amphictyon, was respectful, but only because one had to be respectful to the chief justice and another Virginia gentleman: "That this opinion is very able, every one must admit. This was to have been expected, proceeding as it does from a man of the most profound legal attainments, and upon a subject which has employed his thoughts, his tongue, and his pen, as a politician, and an historian, for more than thirty years." The author of the newspaper piece made no secret of the political party divide he believed lay between himself (and Jefferson) and Marshall. "The subject too, is one which has, perhaps more than any other, heretofore drawn a broad line of distinction between the two great parties in this country, in which line no one has taken a more distinguished and decided rank than the judge who has thus expounded the supreme law of the land." A concession to the length and depth of the opinion followed, but this part of the compliment was almost satirical:

> It is not in my power to carry on a contest upon such a subject with a man of his gigantic powers, but I trust that it will not be thought rash or presumptuous to endeavor to point out the consequences of some of the doctrines maintained by the supreme court, and to oppose to their adjudication some of the principles which have heretofore been advocated by the republican party in this country.[30]

The speed with which the Richmond paper's essay followed the opinion showed that the issues were long discussed by Brockenbrough, Roane, Richie, and others in their circle. They were Jeffersonians of a decidedly nonradical type. They were as much worried about the rise of democracy as Federalists like Webster and Marshall. The essence of their quarrel with Marshall, and by proxy with Webster, was simple:

> There are two principles advocated and decided on by the supreme court, which appear to me to endanger the very existence of state rights. The first is the denial that the powers of the federal government were delegated by the states; and the second is, that the grant of powers to that government, and particularly the grant of powers "necessary and proper" to carry the other powers into effect, ought to be construed in a liberal, rather than a restricted sense.

In some sense, the author had gotten it wrong—it was Webster rather than Marshall who argued the strong version of the old Federalist position. But *McCulloch* could certainly have been read as a warning shot across the bow of states' rights.

> Both of these principles tend directly to consolidation of the states, and to strip them of some of the most important attributes of their sovereignty. If the Congress of the United States should think proper to legislate to the full extent, upon the principles now adjudicated by the supreme court, it is difficult to say how small would be the remnant of power left in the hands of the state authorities.[31]

Marshall, following Webster, had expounded on the necessary separation of powers, and on the supremacy of the federal power when the object was necessary and proper. Marshall had not addressed Webster's other contributions—that political partisanship must be curbed by law, and that legislative acts were subject to judicial scrutiny. Marshall assumed these boundaries but, as was his wont, did not go into political thickets.

With the resolution of the Missouri statehood question by compromise in 1821, the decision in a series of cases following *McCulloch* that fully established the power of Congress to create the bank, and finally the return of prosperity, the immediate threat to states' rights seemed to wane. States continued to dispute and in some cases reject Supreme Court decisions curtailing state discretion. For a time the line between law and politics seemed clear. But another decision of the court, following another brilliant performance by Webster, would relight those fires.[32]

4. "Commerce among the Several States": *Gibbons v. Ogden* (1824)

After his victories in the Dartmouth College case and *McCulloch*, Webster was very much in demand among petitioners to the High Court. His fee of $1,000 was no object to some of the potential clients. Their expected payoff from a successful suit was far greater than Webster's fee, and their prospective return would repay their investment many times over. Between *McCulloch* and *Gibbons v. Ogden* (1824), the third of the trilogy, he argued twenty cases before the Supreme Court. But none was as central to the chance of mapping the three great spaces in the unfinished Constitution as *Gibbons v. Ogden* (1824). The "Steamboat Case," as it was called at the time, once again implicated all three of the constitutional conundrums. It was a federalism case, pitting a state monopoly charter for commerce on the Hudson River against the Federal Coasting Act, hence the Interstate Commerce Clause. It raised questions along the political/legal boundary, as all the parties used political leverage to gain legal advantage. Finally, it asked whether riverine traffic was public, in the sense of belonging to all, or private, a form of property whose profits could be limited to a single enterpriser. Webster, preparing to run for the First Congressional District of Massachusetts, representing Boston in the House of Representatives, was in a unique position to comment on all three of these issues.[1]

The Hudson River had been a major commercial thoroughfare from the time that the Dutch West Indian Company contracted with Henry Hudson to navigate the river. With the construction of the Erie Canal, the Hudson became the gateway to the Great Lakes (via the Lake Ontario–Lake Erie connection) and thus to the Midwest. None of this was lost on entrepreneurs in New York City, the entrepôt of imports and exports. The use of the Hudson was made even more valuable by Robert Fulton's perfection of the steamboat, although the idea was older, with various experimental versions of the craft predating Fulton's boat by decades. Fulton died in 1815 before realizing the value of his efforts, but his patents were defended by Aaron Ogden, governor of New Jersey and himself a partner in the Fulton company. Replacing wind power, the steamboat was a more reliable form of transportation up and down the river. If potential shippers could gain control of the Hudson, in effect monopolizing the route, they could expect a windfall in profits with the new form of transportation. This is exactly what John R. Livingston, whose family was a major power in New York politics since the early eighteenth century, brought to the Fulton-Ogden enterprise. In 1808 the state legislature granted a thirty-year monopoly of steamboat navigation of the Hudson to their North River Company.[2]

At this point, two of the three players in the drama held political office. They surely realized that politics of a state-imposed monopoly over such valuable natural resources as river traffic would entail political questions. In this, the law followed politics. As well, any line between private and public interests was ignored. Under the Articles of Confederation, states were relatively free to restrict their own businessmen's rivals' river trade. The issue was the formal reason for the Annapolis Conference of 1786, whose leading voices (Hamilton and Madison) in turn called for a constitutional convention. At the Philadelphia meeting the next year, delegates addressed the problems of proprietary state control of riverways with the Interstate Commerce Clause. As finally framed in Article I, section 8, clause 3, it gave to Congress the authority "to regulate commerce with foreign nations, and among the several states, and with the Indian tribes." Did it also give to Congress an exclusive right to that regulation, or could states continue to regulate river trade wholly within the state? Did Congress have to act for the clause to rise from sleep?

The question of regulation of the river trade had thus occupied political leaders for nearly forty years when the steamboat controversy erupted. None of this stopped New York from granting exclusive use of the Hudson to the Fulton-Livingston partnership. This gave the North River Company command of the steamboat route up and down the Hudson. Aaron Ogden, formerly governor of New Jersey and an entrepreneur himself, though not yet allied with the two New Yorkers, had secretly entered into an arrangement with their great New Jersey rival, Thomas Gibbons. Gibbons, an adventurous investor, had been one of the disappointed grantees of Yazoo lands—and found steamboat trade appetizing. He was highly litigious, fiercely competitive, and well-schooled in law. Together, the two men persuaded the New Jersey legislature to pass a law fining foreign businesses (for which read the Fulton-Livingston steamboat company) plying New Jersey waters. Failure to pay the fines meant forfeiture of the vessels. After a personal squabble, Gibbons, dissatisfied with his deal with Ogden, formed his own steamboat company in 1816 and sought legal aid to undo the New York state monopoly. Ogden, similarly, tried to convince New Jersey to drop its retaliatory legislation.[3]

In the meantime, the Fulton-Livingston company was fighting rivals within the state, and in 1812 it had sought an injunction, a court order against all rivals navigating the Hudson, from the court of chancery (an injunction being one equitable remedy the court offered). Chancellor John Lansing declined to issue it. The waters, like the air, he thought belonged to everyone. Petitioners appealed to the Court of Impeachments and Errors, which issued the injunction. The three judges of that court agreed that the New York law was constitutional, and that an injunction rather than a trial at law was the proper way to protect property rights from diminution. One of the judges, James Kent, who could rightly be classed with Story and Marshall as a jurist, added that Congress had not yet passed any law regulating the use of waterways, and until it did, the Commerce Clause of Article I did not apply.[4]

The case, *Livingston v. Van Lingen*, produced a typical Kent opinion. Wide ranging and thoughtful, in it Kent recognized the dominance of the federal rule, but only when it came in the form of a positive law. That is, until Congress exercised its control over interstate commerce, the states' residual sovereignty was intact. Kent relied on a strong version of states' rights. "If they are void, it must be because the people of this State have alienated to the government of the United States their whole original power over the subject matter of the grant." He was unwilling to make this kind of open-ended gift of power to the federal government. After all, there was a sovereign state of New York prior to the federal Constitution. "No one can entertain a doubt of a competent power existing in the Legislature, prior to the adoption of the federal Constitution."

The state's power was not just historical—it was inherent in every sovereign governmental body. "The capacity to grant separate and exclusive privileges appertains to every sovereign authority. It is a necessary attribute of every independent government." New York had long operated on that assumption without interference from Washington, DC. "These grants may possibly be inexpedient or unwise, but that has nothing to do with the question of constitutional right." The result was a "concurrent" authority that both state and federal government might exercise. In effect, this limited federal power over the states, a states' rights position similar to that New Hampshire claimed in Richardson's opinion in *Dartmouth College*. "The question here is, not what powers are granted to that [federal] government, but what powers are retained by this, and, particularly, whether the States have absolutely parted with their original power of granting such an exclusive privilege as the one now before us."

The powers reserved to the states were only limited by the powers explicitly enumerated in the federal Constitution, and then only when those powers were expressed in positive law. "We ought to bear in mind certain great rules or principles of construction peculiar to the case of a confederated government, and by attending to them in the examination of the subject, all our seeming difficulties will vanish." It was a neatly framed combination of states' rights and legislative supremacy in a decision by a court. Kent simply erased the line between the political and the legal, his court having rubberstamped the legislature's action. It proved Kent still the master where Richardson was a journeyman.[5]

The continuing fight by Gibbons to undo the injunction made no headway against such a combination of political muscle and juridical logic. His appeal in 1820 to the New York high court only succeeded giving subsequent federal litigation the name by which it was known: in the court's terse opinion, basically repeating what Kent had opined, the case became *Gibbons v. Ogden*. The important point is that in the 1810s, before slavery became the fulcrum of states' rights thinking, chief justices and courts in the North were recurring to states' rights to protect the commercial regulations of their jurisdictions.[6]

The Fulton-Livingston partnership was also eyeing prospects for steamboat traffic beyond the Hudson River. Indeed, it was because the Hudson was the gateway to the upper Midwest via the Erie Canal and the Great Lakes that it was such a potentially valuable monopoly for the North River Company. The partners sought and for a short time gained a monopoly of the route between New Orleans and Natchez, Mississippi, a cotton and slaves trade bonanza. That monopoly did not last, in part because Henry Shreve had pioneered a shallow draft steamboat better suited to the Mississippi waters. Meanwhile, the monopoly in New York was finding opposition. Passenger travel on steamboats was becoming more attractive, and competition, particularly from Gibbons and his investors, was gaining ground. Fulton was gone. Livingston was gone. Ogden inherited all these problems when he bought up controlling interest in the North River line, and this pitted him against Gibbons in court.

———

With Gibbons unable to break the injunction in New York courts, he turned to federal court and Webster. Gibbons was struggling with complications from diabetes, and time was of the essence. Gibbons had hired William Pinkney as well as Webster, the winning team from *McCulloch*, but Pinkney died and the case was held over. In the interim, justice Brockholst Livingston had died, he a cousin of the Livingston family member whose interest in the litigation would have created some questions of partisanship. No matter—that potential bias was renewed with the appointment of Smith Thompson as Livingston's replacement. Thompson was a close associate of Kent and came to the Court by way of the New York Supreme Court. His participation in the case was, however, delayed by the severe illness of his daughter, and he did not take his seat until late February, when the case had already been submitted. By this time, the case had already killed half of the original parties and was now slaying counsel and judges. When it was finally heard, at the winter 1824 session, Webster was joined by William Wirt, and New York's case, as well as Ogden's, was presented by Thomas Oakley, formerly New York's attorney general, and Thomas A. Emmet, whose brother Robert had been attorney general of New York ten years earlier. But the real opponent in Webster's mind was Kent himself, perhaps, along with Story and Marshall, the foremost living authority on constitutional law.[7]

Why the state was involved is a matter of some interest. The party who benefited from the monopoly was Ogden, not, presumably, the state. True, the state's interests were indirectly at stake, but Gibbons was not challenging the state directly. He had suffered enough at its hands already—arrested for violating Kent's injunction, out of pocket for losing in the Court of Errors, seriously ill with tuberculosis on top of diabetes; he simply wanted the federal court to overturn the state decisions favoring Ogden. It was the state itself that decided to intervene by offering to defend Ogden. This lifted the financial burden from Ogden, as well as removing from him the power to hire and direct his own counsel. In effect, the state of New York regarded this case as a threat to its sovereignty and the untouchability of state law. In the meantime, Gibbons was pursing Ogden with injunctions in New Jersey courts, and even threatened to duel with one of Ogden's allies (though Gibbons admitted that his sight was all but gone—the duel would have been something like that between King Arthur and the black knight in *Monty Python and the Holy Grail*). The duel was averted at the last minute.[8]

The formal grounds for the appeal lay in the federal jurisdiction section of the Judiciary Act, giving to federal courts supervision of cases involving federal acts. The act in question was the Federal Coasting Act of 1793, affording the federal government regulation of all coasting trade on the Atlantic, under which Gibbons had a license to run his steamboats along the coast of New Jersey. The New York injunction interfered with this license, he claimed.

Webster, arguing by his own preference the Commerce Clause part of the case (Wirt would argue the patent rights portion), recognized the part that New York had played in the affair, and thus the reason for Ogden choosing counsel with experience in New York in the federal hearing. His competitive juices released by a virtual combat with Kent, Webster gave the state its due. "There was a very respectable weight of authority in favour of the decision [to grant the injunction], which was sought to be reversed." At every level, from the state assembly, to the governor, to the various courts of the state, the monopoly had been upheld. An echo of the *Dartmouth College* case? Again the public interest was confused with a private monopoly. Was this ordinary (partisan) politics, or law? He noted also that the case could not come to the federal courts until it had been heard at every level of the state courts. From these, Gibbons appealed, properly, to the Supreme Court. Such a process alone gave the Court jurisdiction; and therefore, "while they are to be respected as the judgments of learned Judges, they are yet in the condition of all decisions from which the law allows an appeal."[9]

Webster even conceded a possible basis for the rulings Ogden had won from the state court: Ogden had the goods. "It would not be a waste of time to advert to the existing state of the facts connected with the subject of this litigation. The use of steam boats, on the coasts, and in the bays and rivers of the country, had become very general. The intercourse of its different parts essentially depended upon this mode of conveyance and transportation." But the conflict between New York and New Jersey, featuring dueling injunctions, was the very gravamen that had led to federal intervention. "Rivers and bays, in many cases, form the divisions between States; and thence it was obvious, that if the States should make regulations for the navigation of these waters, and such regulations should be repugnant and hostile [to other states], embarrassment would necessarily happen to the general intercourse of the community." That is exactly what happened in *Gibbons v. Ogden*.[10]

A kind of economic war of each against all had in fact ensued. New York refused to let anyone navigate any of the waters within the state without a license from the state. The violator would lose his vessel. Connecticut had the same law regarding steamships. New Jersey imposed a reciprocal law—if anyone lost a ship under the New York law, he could bring an action for triple damages, in New Jersey, against "the party who thus restrains or impedes him under the law of New-York." Presumably that meant New York magistrates hailed into New Jersey courts because they enforced a New York law in New York. What a calamity, and with no resolution in sight so long as state sovereignty commanded the issue. But they did not. "It would hardly be contended, that all these acts were consistent with the laws and constitution of the United States. If there were no power in the general government, to control this extreme belligerent legislation of the States," the calamity would fall on everyone.[11]

Webster's recitation of the facts of the case was substantially accurate, going back to the first of the New York monopolies for river steamboat travel in 1787; the act of 1798 repealing that grant and conferring the privilege on Robert R. Livingston; then the 1803 act including Robert Fulton in the monopoly; then another act in 1808, allowing for more Livingston-Fulton boats and extending the monopoly for thirty years; and finally, an act in 1811 providing for forfeiture of offending (rival) steamboats. Webster did not add anything of the way that the monopolists managed their enterprise. The lobbying power of the Livingston family in the state could hardly be more evident, though Webster did not raise the issue of corruption in the granting of the monopoly. Livingston himself did not ask for the seizure of his rivals' boats, preferring to work out arrangements in the shadow of the courthouse steps. Everyone in court knew that the rigor of the law was mitigated by commercial and political concerns.[12]

Still, Gibbons thought he could navigate his way through these waters, making secret deals with Ogden, successor to Fulton and Livingston, and when these fell through, seeking the aid of the courts. He failed, of course, and a bill in equity against him "was filed against him by Ogden, in October, 1818, and an injunction granted, restraining him from such use of his boat. This injunction was made perpetual, on the final hearing of the cause, in the Court of Chancery; and the decree of the Chancellor has been duly affirmed in the Court of Errors." Gibbons had only the slender thread of the license for coastal navigation under the Federal Coasting Act of 1793 on which to hang his hopes. One wonders why he persisted, as Webster and Wirt commanded substantial legal fees that Gibbons would owe whether he won or not. Sometimes, more is at stake than simple economic opportunity. By this time, Gibbons no doubt felt that he had been cheated, that his honor as a businessman and a gentleman had been traversed, and he hoped that winning in court would restore that honor.[13]

Webster did not rely on the federal issue jurisdiction to bring the suit to the High Court. He offered a diversity grounds for the appeal. Gibbons was a citizen of New Jersey, and his opponent a citizen of New York. That should have brought the case into the federal circuit court in New York, which would then have applied New York law to settle it. The only way to win there was to argue the federal issue (the coasting license). So the diversity question was raised and dropped. Instead, Webster turned to the federal license. The laws of New York "were void, still, as against any right enjoyed under the laws of the United States, with which they came in collision; and that, in this case, they were found interfering with such rights." The Coasting Act rested on the Interstate Commerce Clause. "The power of Congress to regulate commerce, was complete and entire, and, to a certain extent, necessarily exclusive." *Exclusive* sounded absolute, but the "to a certain extent" was a hedge that would reappear in Marshall's opinion for the Court. Webster asserted the primacy of the federal government "guardedly." "He did not mean to say that all regulations which might, in their operation, affect commerce, were exclusively in the power of Congress; but that such power as had been exercised in this case, did not remain with the States." Navigation of waterways that ran between states was within the commerce power.[14]

What then was commerce? The term is not defined in the Constitution, no more than *obligations* or *necessary and proper*. Did it mean any gainful activity, or was it limited to trade? If limited, surely shipping was included in trade. Webster tackled its ambiguity. Was it a public activity, or ancillary to private property acquisition? Was it primarily a subject of legislation, or a subject for courts? "Nothing was more complex than commerce; and in such an age as this, no words embraced a wider field than commercial regulation. Almost all the business and intercourse of life may be connected, incidentally, more or less, with commercial regulations." Commerce was thus public—involving more than one person—and private, apportioning property among buyers and sellers. It was a matter of law, that is, subject to decisions in the courts, and a matter of everyday politics, regulated by legislatures. Of course, when the Commerce Clause was involved, it entailed analysis of federalism. The framers had not defined it; Webster did.

Plainly, Webster adopted the broad definition. How limited was the power of Congress to regulate commerce? Here Webster had to work harder, for the issue was not settled by earlier case law. Still, "it was only necessary to apply to this part of the constitution the well settled rules of construction. Some powers are holden to be exclusive in Congress, from the use of exclusive words in the grant; others, from the prohibitions on the States to exercise similar powers; and others, again, from the nature of the powers themselves." What was granted to Congress explicitly could be assumed to be granted exclusively; else, if a state exercised the power, the state regulation could interfere with the federal regulation. That would deny to the federal government regulation any effect.[15]

Webster had not quite finished. His reading of the Constitution might persuade him, but it was the Court's reading that decided the question. The problem for him was to tell the justices how to read the document. One would be hard pressed to find a passage in Webster's brief so tangled as the one that followed:

> As some powers have been holden exclusive, and others not so, under the same form of expression, from the nature of the different powers respectively; so, where the power, on any one subject, is given in general words, like the power to regulate commerce, the true method of construction would be, to consider of what parts the grant is composed, and which of those, from the nature of the thing, ought to be considered exclusive.

The only explanation one can give of this convoluted phrasing is that Henry Wheaton was taking down Webster's words but did not have Webster's own corrected brief. There are other evidences in the text of Wheaton's report of the case where Wheaton wrote "Webster said," or "he thought it reasonable to say"—evidence that Wheaton was composing rather than reprinting. Wheaton did correct errors in materials given him before he gave them to the printer. In any case, Webster seemed to be telling the Court that the justices had to look closely at what New York was doing with its legislation to see if it were commercial.

Webster explained that the key to finding the boundary between state and federal powers—that is, the key to federalism—was the substance of the state enactments. Match that with the Constitution and you have your answer. "The right set up in this case, under the laws of New-York, is a monopoly." What kind of monopoly? A monopoly over steamboat traffic on the river. Surely this was commerce, but "the constitution never intended to leave with the States the power of granting monopolies, either of trade or of navigation; and, therefore, that as to this, the commercial power was exclusive in Congress." Could Congress have created such a monopoly, for example by limiting coasting trade to a single shipper, rather than giving licenses and charging fees? Restraint of trade, that is, a privately created monopoly, was long outlawed by the common law, but the first federal act to embody this doctrine was the Sherman Antitrust Act of 1890. Webster was ahead of his time in suggesting the evils of monopoly, but he had long been an advocate of free trade when he represented the merchants of Portsmouth. His shift to defense of high tariffs and the manufacturing interests of Massachusetts would come in 1828.[16]

Did Congress exceed its implied powers in claiming an exclusive purview of interstate navigation? "It was in vain to look for a precise and exact definition of the powers of Congress, on several subjects. The constitution did not undertake the task of making such exact definitions." How could it, lest the document be of infinite length. "In conferring powers, it proceeded in the way of enumeration, stating the powers conferred, one after another, in few words; and, where the power was general, or complex in its nature, the extent of the grant must necessarily be judged of, and limited, by its object, and by the nature of the power."

This formula, almost as obscure as that above, might be open to a different kind of elaboration: historical context. Different from original intent (peering into the minds of the framers), historical context looked at the objective, external needs of national commerce at the time of the framing. From these manifest historical conditions, the extent of powers conferred on Congress by the framers could be inferred. "Few things were better known than the immediate causes which led to the adoption of the present constitution; and he thought nothing clearer, than that the prevailing motive was to regulate commerce; to rescue it from the embarrassing and destructive consequences, resulting from the legislation of so many different States, and to place it under the protection of a uniform law."

What followed was a history lesson based on Webster's own knowledge of the confederation period. He had heard line and verse when he was young. The conclusion was part of every story he heard from his merchant clients in

Portsmouth. He found the same theme in the confederation-era resolutions of Virginia and New Jersey calling for a uniform, exclusive regulation of commerce—when "the States could still, each for itself, regulate commerce, and the consequence [there] was, a perpetual jarring and hostility of commercial regulation." The driving force behind the federalist movement according to Webster was the need to provide a sound basis for interstate and overseas trade. That basis was a uniform federal law wielded by a strong federal government. "In the history of the times, it was accordingly found, that the great topic, urged on all occasions, as showing the necessity of a new and different government, was the state of trade and commerce.[17]

One strand of that argument paralleled Webster's brief for *Dartmouth* that the basis of the federal Constitution was the protection of private property. For what was commerce but the production of private property? "To benefit and improve these, was a great object in itself: and it became greater when it was regarded as the only means of enabling the country to pay the public debt, and to do justice to those who had most effectually laboured for its independence." Men of substance and understanding had ventured their lives and fortunes in the revolution to protect private property in commerce:

> The leading state papers of the time are full of this topic. . . . Over whatever other interests of the country this government may diffuse its benefits, and its blessings, it will always be true, as matter of historical fact, that it had its immediate origin in the necessities of commerce; and, for its immediate object, the relief of those necessities, by removing their causes, and by establishing a uniform and steady system.[18]

Webster also rejected New York's claim of a concurrent power. "We do not find, in the history of the formation and adoption of the constitution, that any man speaks of a general concurrent power, in the regulation of foreign and domestic trade, as still residing in the States." A concurrent power would diminish the federal authority. It could not be admitted and was not by anyone at the Philadelphia convention. "Henceforth, the commerce of the States was to be a unit; and the system by which it was to exist and be governed, must necessarily be complete, entire, and uniform." Any exception would be an invitation to "manifest encroachment and confusion."[19]

Webster did not try to make a distinction between commerce and manufacturing, the arbitrary distinction later made by the majority in *United States v.*

E. C. Knight (1894) (a sugar-refining monopoly was not a restraint of trade under the Sherman Antitrust Act because it was not commerce), or between interstate and intrastate commerce that was part of a larger system of interstate commerce (e.g., the Hudson River led out to New Jersey ports). He did allow states to impose their own inspection laws for products grown or sold within the state. Whether this was a concession to the slave states, whose laws included regulation of slave sales, he did not say. In the short term, that question would become a central concern of interstate slave traders.[20]

There was of course the great obstacle to Webster's purpose: the foremost authority on the common law in his time, Chancellor Kent. How to honor and yet confute Kent was Webster's greatest challenge. His tactic was, for want of a better word, masterful:

> If the present state of things—these laws of New-York, the laws of Connecticut, and the laws of New-Jersey, had been all presented, in the convention of New-York, to the eminent person whose name is on this record, and who acted, on that occasion, so important a part; if he had been told, that, after all he had said in favour of the new government, and of its salutary effects on commercial regulations, the time should yet come, when the North River would be shut up by a monopoly from New-York; the [Long Island] Sound interdicted by a penal law of Connecticut; reprisals authorized by New-Jersey, against citizens of New-York; and when one could not cross a ferry, without transshipment; does any one suppose he would have admitted all this, as compatible with the government which he was recommending?

Of course not, Webster himself concluded. For had Kent raised his eyes from New York's interests to consider the property interests of citizens of other states, he would see that "this doctrine of a general concurrent power in the States, is insidious and dangerous. If it be admitted, no one can say where it will stop."

The war of each against all that seventeenth-century English political philosopher Thomas Hobbes had seen in the wilds of the New World, and the framers of the Constitution had seen in the confederation period, would return. States would again impose burdens on one another, and national trade would suffer. Counsel for Ogden might argue that "the States may legislate, it is said, wherever Congress has not made a plenary exercise of its power, But who is to judge whether Congress has made this plenary exercise of power?" For Congress's regulatory power to work, it must be exclusive. "All useful regulation does not consist in restraint; and that which Congress sees fit to leave free, is a part of its regulation, as much as the rest." Noncommercial state regulations, for example health and welfare, were—as before—left to the states unless Congress intervened. Even then, for example in the construction of roads, there could be concurrent activity.[21]

Webster insisted that the proper comparison was not the regulation of slaves or the construction of ferries, but federal admiralty jurisdiction. "It might further be argued, that the power of Congress over these high branches of commerce was exclusive, from the consideration that Congress possessed an exclusive admiralty jurisdiction. That it did possess such exclusive jurisdiction, would hardly be contested. No State pretended to exercise any jurisdiction of that kind." The New York monopoly reached out into waters that federal admiralty law already occupied. "Over these waters, therefore, or, at least, some of them, which are the subject of this monopoly, New-York has no jurisdiction whatever. They are a part of the high sea." Federal criminal law, for example the Federal Crimes Act of 1790, provided punishment for piracy and other crimes on the high seas. New York law did not extend to these crimes. "This restraining of the States from all jurisdiction, out of the bodies of their own counties, shows plainly enough, that navigation on the high seas, was understood to be a matter to be regulated only by Congress." The exclusive regulation of navigable waters within states was a not unreasonable extension of this doctrine. "It is a common principle, that arms of the sea, including navigable rivers, belong to the sovereign, so far as navigation is concerned."[22]

That in itself should have ended the question of the New York monopoly. Surely the Hudson was navigable? Why then the long excursus into the Commerce Clause? The answer lay outside of the case at hand, to the larger issue of private property in interstate commerce. Courts in the nineteenth century were to find law, not make it. They were to confine themselves to past wrongs, not project themselves into possible future wrongs. They were not to make policy—that was the task of the legislative branch. None of these self-imposed jurisprudential restrictions restricted Webster. In this he was a modern thinker, seeing the case as one of many likely to arise in the future, and regarding the Court as a miniature legislature. "It might now be well to take a nearer view of these laws, to see more exactly what their provisions were, what consequences have followed from them, and what would and might follow from other similar laws."[23]

As in the Dartmouth College case, for Webster the underlying issue was the constitutional protection of private property from undue state interference. "The first grant to John Fitch, gave him the sole and exclusive right of making, employing, and navigating, all boats impelled by fire or steam, 'in all creeks, rivers, bays, and waters, within the territory and jurisdiction of the State.'" This was a property right. "The subsequent acts repeal this, and grant similar privileges to Livingston and Fulton: and the act of 1811 provides the extraordinary and summary remedy." The State of New York had taken from individuals the right to enjoy their property. The monopoly extended that denial to all but the single grantee. "The river, the bay, and the marine league along the shore, are all within the scope of this grant. Any vessel, therefore, of this description, coming into any of those waters, without a license, whether from another State, or from abroad, whether it be a public or private vessel, is instantly forfeited to the grantees of the monopoly."[24]

Everyone's property rights were then at risk if the state exercised its sovereign power to take from one person and give to another. "If the State could grant this monopoly for that purpose, it could also grant it for any other purpose. . . . If it can grant these exclusive privileges to a few, it may grant them to many; that is, it may grant them to all its own citizens, to the exclusion of every body else." The monopoly restrained trade. Did it do so unfairly? Clearly, as Ogden had an "in" with the state judiciary. But who could say that Chancellor Kent was nothing but a pol? Not Webster, with the result that he had to back and fill around the question of the partisan politics of the monopoly.[25]

The way to avoid pointing fingers at the New York judges was to expand the argument to include more than New York. "The waters of New-York are no more the subject of exclusive grants by that State, than the waters of other States are subjects of such grants by those other States. Virginia may well exercise, over the entrance of the Chesapeake, all the power that New-York can exercise over the bay of New-York, and the waters on the shore. The Chesapeake, therefore, upon the principle of these laws, may be the subject of State monopoly; and so may the bay of Massachusetts." Nice step away from the abyss, this, a demonstration of Webster at his rhetorical best. A final touch, showing that Webster was not anti–New York: "The people of New-York have a right to be protected against this monopoly."[26]

Then, Webster returned to the right to enjoy one's property. "The appellant had a right to go from New-Jersey to New-York, in a vessel, owned by himself, of the proper legal description, and enrolled and licensed according to law. This right belonged to him as a citizen of the United States. It was derived under the laws of the United States, and no act of the Legislature of New-York can deprive him of it, any more than such act could deprive him of the right of holding lands in that State, or of suing in its Courts." The Constitution protected the property rights of the citizens of the United States, and, by implication, that was the highest duty of a constitutional lawyer. "Now, this right was expressly conferred by the laws of the United States." The Coasting Act of 1793 conferred this right explicitly. "Words could not make this authority more express," despite what the New York courts had determined. The license under the act conferred a property right: "It is the authority which the master carries with him, to prove his right to navigate freely the waters of the United States, and to carry on the coasting trade." The right was not limited to ownership of the vessel. It extended to the occupation, that is, property gained through labor. Webster here hinted, as he had already stated in various celebratory addresses, that free labor created property rights. It was the basis of his condemnation of slave labor, for the slave's labor created profits for the master alone. The slave gained no property through his labor and had no way to benefit from that labor.[27]

Marshall's opinion for the appellants agreed that the Interstate Commerce Clause was more important than the patents issue. First came the boiler-plate acknowledgment of how well the case was argued and its importance:

> No tribunal can approach the decision of this question without feeling a just and real respect for that opinion which is sustained by such authority [i.e., a bow to Chancellor Kent's opinion and his reputation], but it is the province of this Court, while it respects, not to bow to it implicitly, and the Judges must exercise, in the examination of the subject, that understanding which Providence has bestowed upon them, with that independence which the people of the United States expect from this department of the government.[28]

Next came recognition and recapitulation of Webster's history lesson, Marshall agreeing with every point. "This instrument contains an enumeration of powers expressly granted by the people to their government. It has been said that these powers ought to be construed strictly. But why ought they to be so construed? Is there one sentence in the Constitution which gives countenance to this rule?" So much for the Republicans' canon of strict construction of the Constitution, a stance that Marshall had dismissed in many prior opinions, but this time, instead of simply discarding strict construction, Marshall jumped up and down on the corpse.

> We do not, therefore, think ourselves justified in adopting it. What do gentlemen mean by a "strict construction?" If they contend only against that enlarged construction, which would extend words beyond their natural and obvious import, we might question the application of the term, but should not controvert the principle. If they contend for that narrow construction which, in support or some theory not to be found in the Constitution, would deny to the government those powers which the words of the grant, as usually understood, import, and which are consistent with the general views and objects of the instrument; for that narrow construction which would cripple the government and render it unequal to the object for which it is declared to be instituted, and to which the powers given, as fairly understood, render it competent; then we cannot perceive the propriety of this strict construction, nor adopt it as the rule by which the Constitution is to be expounded.

That finished that.[29]

Again following Webster, Marshall offered a disquisition on the meaning of the word *commerce.* "The subject to be regulated is commerce, and our Constitution being, as was aptly said at the bar [i.e., by Webster], one of enumeration, and not of definition, to ascertain the extent of the power, it becomes necessary to settle the meaning of the word." New York had contended that commerce meant buying and selling, and nothing more. It did not mean the transportation of goods. "This would restrict a general term, applicable to many objects, to one of its significations." That made no sense to Marshall. Commerce was intercourse of all mercantile kinds, "in all its branches." After all, the provision in the Constitution included commerce with other nations. How could this be performed without shipping? Overseas trade, so vital to the American economy, could hardly be excluded from commerce even if the Constitution had not included trade with other nations. "The convention must have used the word in that sense, because all have understood it in that sense, and the attempt to restrict it comes too late." "All understood it" is a form of originalism called original intent. That is, one understands the meaning of terms in the Constitution by reference to the intent of the framers. Marshall was not at the Constitutional Convention, but he was practicing law in Virginia at the time and he knew all of the Virginia signers and all of the ratification convention members because he was one of the Henrico County delegation to it. (He voted aye.)[30]

Marshall found other parts of the Constitution whose plain sense supported his reading of the Commerce Clause. The form of interpretation is today called *textualism*. Take, for example, the embargo of 1808, so hated by the merchants of New England. They objected to it on many practical grounds, "Yet they never suspected that navigation was no branch of trade, and was therefore not comprehended in the power to regulate commerce." In other words, they read the plain meaning of the term. "They did, indeed, contest the constitutionality of the act. . . . They denied that the particular law in question was made in pursuance of the Constitution not because the power could not act directly on vessels, but because a perpetual embargo was the annihilation, and not the regulation, of commerce." In other words, the New England Federalists "admitted the applicability of the words used in the Constitution to vessels. . . . No example could more strongly illustrate the universal understanding of the American people on this subject. It was always understood to comprehend navigation within its meaning."[31]

Marshall then reintroduced Webster's analogy to overseas trade, which had to include shipping, then added that if navigation of the high seas was an essential part of the first item in the sentence, it must be included in the interstate commerce portion. "Among the several states" meant any commerce between states, a "plain, intelligible reading" of the text. Note that unlike some modern textualists, Marshall was willing to use more than the text itself to explain himself. As he had with the framers and with the Federalist opponents of the embargo, he brought navigable waters into the discussion. "The deep streams which penetrate our country in every direction pass through the interior of almost every State in the Union, and furnish the means of exercising this right. If Congress has the power to regulate it, that power must be exercised whenever the subject exists. If it exists within the States, if a foreign voyage may commence or terminate at a port within a State, then the power of Congress may be exercised within a State."

By following the waters, as much as the logic of his own argument, commerce among the several states had become commerce that reached into a single state—including New York's Hudson River. After all, "Can a trading expedition between two adjoining States, commence and terminate outside of each? And if the trading intercourse be between two States remote from each other, must it not commence in one, terminate in the other, and probably pass through a third? Commerce among the States must, of necessity, be commerce with the States." This is not textualism. It is, and was, plain common sense. Marshall's genius was here in full view: the ability to see the law in its everyday context. It is not legal positivism, the law as the command of the state—but legal realism, reading the law so that actual life was reflected in law.[32]

Congress had passed laws regarding navigation. Did these preclude the New York monopoly the appellees claimed was permitted by the absence of explicit federal law on steamboat traffic? "The power to regulate, that is, to prescribe the rule by which commerce is to be governed . . . like all others vested in Congress, is complete in itself, may be exercised to its utmost extent." Because Congress had not yet done so, however, did this allow for a concurrent exercise of state and federal riverine regulation? Marshall had already established that the congressional regulatory power extended to commerce within the states. Nothing in the sovereignty of the states, which Marshall conceded, diminished Congress's power to regulate river traffic, for concurrent power would automatically diminish the authority of Congress. Webster had argued, and Marshall repeated, "Full power to regulate a particular subject implies the whole power, and leaves no residuum; that a grant of the whole is incompatible with the existence of a right in another to any part of it." What about the concurrent power states had to tax? Was this not analogous to regulation of commerce? How about the right to inspect goods coming into the state? Marshall again turned to recent history to reject these analogies:

> The idea that the same measure might, according to circumstances, be arranged with different classes of power was no novelty to the framers of our Constitution. Those illustrious statesmen and patriots had been, many of them, deeply engaged in the discussions which preceded the war of our revolution, and all of them were well read in those discussions. The right to regulate commerce, even by the imposition of duties, was not controverted.[33]

Historians have noted that the issue of federal intervention in states' regulations was raised during the Missouri Compromise debate. Advocates of slavery feared that Congress would adopt laws for Missouri effectively barring slavery. Marshall weighed in on this question on the side of a robust nationalism. "In making these provisions [for regulation of importation of goods, and prohibition of the importation of slaves] . . . the opinion is unequivocally manifested that Congress may control the State laws so far as it may be necessary to control them for the regulation of commerce." Indeed, the slavery issue lurked in the shadows at every junction of Marshall's opinion, for the slave states treated the internal, interstate slave trade as commerce in persons, rather than things, and hotly resented any federal interference. If the federal government, whether Congress or the High Court, could define an exclusive regulatory power of commerce in the federal government, might not Congress or the Court, in some future time, outlaw the internal slave trade?

> If this inference were correct, if this power was exercised not under any particular clause in the Constitution, but in virtue of a general right over the subject of commerce, to exist as long as the Constitution itself, it might now be exercised. Any State might now import African slaves into its own territory. But it is obvious that the power of the States over this subject, previous to the year 1808, constitutes an exception to the power of Congress to regulate commerce, and the exception is expressed in such words, as to manifest clearly the intention to continue the preexisting right of the States to admit or exclude, for a limited period."[34]

States exercised some concurrent powers with the federal government, for example, the licensing of pilots, the building of lighthouses, and of course taxation, but none of these could be extended to the regulation of commerce generally. "These acts were cited at the bar for the purpose of showing an opinion in Congress that the States possess, concurrently with the Legislature of the Union, the power to regulate commerce with foreign nations and among the States." Marshall and his brethren rejected the analogy of these state powers to the present case. "Upon reviewing them, we think they do not establish the proposition they were intended to prove. They show the opinion that the States retain powers enabling them to pass the laws to which allusion has been made, not that those laws proceed from the particular power which has been delegated to Congress."[35]

Marshall, as was his wont, was moving in parallel with counsels' briefs. In effect, instead of simply standing above the case and calling it, like a referee or umpire, he was acting as a third counsel, commenting on the work of fellow counsels. This explains why Marshall felt the need to deal with every point raised by counsel, particularly when he intended to rule against that side. One must remember that Marshall went from practicing law to Congress, then to secretary of state, then to the center seat on the Supreme Court. He had never been a judge until he was placed on the Court; thus his natural affinity for regarding cases, and counsels' briefs, as a lawyer rather than a judge. This made him amenable to Webster's arguments—that is, to reading closely and adopting language and ideas that fit his own view of the matter. In this way, Webster's advocacy became constitutional law.

Oakley's and Emmet's attempt to make concurrent powers doctrine part of constitutional law, arguments that actually outran Webster's and Wirt's in length and detail, were heavily supplemented with citations to cases and history. Neither Oakley's long and carefully prepared defense of the New York monopoly nor Emmet's passionate defense of the state's role in promoting commerce and invention, however, swayed the Court. Emmet did make one point based on original intent that was striking—Judge Lansing, whose opinion in favor of the monopoly, was himself a member of the Constitutional Convention in 1787. Emmet neglected to add that Lansing refused to sign the Constitution, in fact leaving before the convention ended, and led the fight against the Constitution in New York. The two counsellors' emphasis on the importance of protecting the Fulton patent fell on deaf ears. Parenthetically, both men seemed to have missed the point that a case based on examples from the pre-federal constitutional period and on state precedent was not going to win in federal court. Instead, Oakley and Emmet should have relied on prior federal cases. That they could not or did not try to do so suggests that the Marshall Court's prior jurisprudence on federalism leaned against them.[36]

Leaned, but did not fall. If Marshall was not convinced, he was still conciliatory. For him, the federal Constitution was not a compact among sovereign states but rather the creation of a new sovereignty, the United States, whose sovereign powers overlapped with state powers and sometimes overmatched them. States should trust the federal government not to abuse its powers, as federal officials were as beholden to the will of the American people as states' officials were to the citizens of those states. In *Gibbons*, Marshall struck down every argument for concurrent power that Oakley and Emmet made, but he did not insist on the absolute power of the federal government. The delicate balance of federalism proposed in Philadelphia in 1787 and defended at the Virginia ratification convention the next year, rather than an all-powerful central government, was Marshall's preferred view. In accord with that, he allowed that if a state regulated commerce entirely within its boundaries, that regulation could stand untouched—unless it contravened an existing federal law. This equivocation was what set off a loud and continuing debate over the federal government's intrusion into states' slavery laws and led, albeit indirectly, to Webster's next great constitutional passage of arms in a Senate debate with Robert V. Hayne of South Carolina.[37]

5. "True Principles of the Constitution": Webster-Hayne Debate, January 19–27, 1830

Four decades after the federal government began operation under the new Constitution, the unmapped portions of text left by the framers had grown smaller, but debate over controversial guideposts still roiled national politics. In courtrooms, courtesy and cases constrained lawyers' exchanges over what was public policy and what private rights, what belonged to the legislative branches and what was the province of the courts, and the line between federal authority and state sovereignty. Webster, aided and abetted by Chief Justice John Marshall, had partially addressed the three questions in *Dartmouth College*, *McCulloch*, and *Gibbons*. After his victory in the steamboat cases, Webster became even busier in the courtroom.

Between his successful advocacy of Gibbons' rights and his appearance on the Senate floor to debate Robert Y. Hayne, early in 1830, Webster was counsel in fifty-two cases that came to the US Supreme Court. None of these were as momentous as *Gibbons*, but all involved substantial preparation and correspondence. With William Pinkney gone from the scene, Webster was the most sought-after appellate lawyer in the nation. He worked with rivals, allies, and many of the most famous politician/lawyers of his time. In *Kirk v. Smith* (1824), for example, Webster teamed with Henry Clay to defend the land titles of Pennsylvanians resting on grants from the colonial proprietor. In arguments eerily similar to his in *Dartmouth College*, Webster successfully defended the rights of the occupiers of the land. In addition, Webster was involved in a project to relieve the justices of much of the burden of circuit riding, although he did not subscribe to Jeremiah Mason's plan to create a new set of purely circuit court judges (a plan that would bear fruit in the 1869 Judiciary Act and in the Evarts Act of 1891).[1]

In 1824 Webster was returned by the Massachusetts legislature to a seat in the US Senate. There, the ideal Constitution that he promoted in the Supreme Court was hotly contested by Jacksonian Democrats and states' rights advocates. In the so-called Webster-Hayne Debate of January 19–27, 1830, he took his now fifteen-year project of supplying answers to the incomplete Constitution into the nation's deliberative chamber. There, Webster fitted his courtroom jurisprudence into a vision of the good republic. In the process, Webster was becoming, bit by bit, a more complete constitutional thinker. He rejected partisan alliances of East and West or South and West in favor of the rule of settled law, insisted that public space uses must sometimes bow to private rights, and demanded that individual states' interests were subordinate to the national good. In short, what looked and sounded to contemporaries like a political oration was in fact the continuation of his arguments in *Dartmouth College, McCulloch,* and *Gibbons.*[2]

On its face, the exchange between Webster and Hayne concerned federal land policy, a sectionally divisive issue in itself, but one that cannot be understood without seeing it in light of tariff policy. In 1828 Webster appeared to have changed his colors on the defense of free trade. Having fought against a protective tariff for years, he now, somewhat belatedly and reluctantly, became a supporter of it. The key issue was a rise in rates for imported textiles. To the manufacturers of textiles in Massachusetts, Webster's new clients and friends, this was a boon. To purchasers of cheap textiles, in particular the slave owners of the South who provided clothing for their bond laborers, the new tariff was a burden. They also feared that it was likely to spur dismay among their English cotton buyers (who also manufactured and shipped textile goods to the United States) and that it would hurt southern export trade. Because it fell on the owners who bought clothing, it seemed like the opening wedge of a federal assault on slavery itself.[3]

In 1828 South Carolina's response was an exposition of the reasons why the tariff was unconstitutional. In it, the author blurred the partisan political and the legal. Constitutional law was to be a defense of South Carolina's particular politics, a legalistic exposition of the grounds for its resistance, but that exposition was politically motivated and infused with partisanship. No attempt was made to concede or conciliate under older precedents. The defense of the law was also the strongest defense of states' rights, in direct conflict with a congressional power to set tariffs explicitly and exclusively enumerated in Article I. Finally, the exposition of the law saw no division between the state and the individual; the state's needs trumped all individual rights. It was this answer to the third of the constitutional lacuna that has convinced some scholars that South Carolina was more interested in defending slavery than in protesting the tariff rates.[4]

The exposition (explanation) of this ordinance was secretly drafted by the vice president of the United States, John C. Calhoun. South Carolina political leaders had turned to him to frame the grounds for their objection to the tariff. All of them knew that setting tariffs was one of the enumerated powers of Congress in Article I, so the task of exposition was a difficult one. What was more, when he was secretary of war from 1817 to 1825, Calhoun was an outspoken nationalist, in favor of protective tariffs, internal improvements, and a strong federal government. He concealed his authorship of the exposition, though just about everyone knew it was his work.[5]

Calhoun's case against the imposition of the "tariff of abominations" was a constitutional one. It was Calhoun's own attempt to address the same questions that Webster had assayed. The answers Calhoun offered, however, were the very opposite of Webster's. Beginning with Thomas Jefferson's secretly authored 1798 Kentucky Resolves, then going beyond them, Calhoun argued that the federal government was the creature of the states, and the Constitution a mere compact among sovereign political entities. These entities had lost none of their puissance when they ratified the document and could, if they chose, withdraw from the compact when its agent, the federal government, violated any of the terms of the contract. The political aims of the majority in the state, embodied its legislation, erased any line between the political and the legal. The public policy of the state outweighed any private rights its citizens might claim. Rights belonged to the corporate identity of the state, not to individuals.

Nullification ignored the fact that the tariff was an enumerated power of Congress in Article I, and that states were barred from imposing tariffs on their own. Instead, Calhoun wrote that the tariff of 1828 violated the rights of South Carolina. A constitutional tariff was meant for a revenue only, according to Calhoun, but the tariff of 1828 was a bounty to certain manufacturing regions paid for by agricultural producers. The remedy, going beyond the Jeffersonian Republicans' response to the Alien and Sedition Act of 1798, was nullification. In this, again based on his compact theory of the Constitution, a state could nullify the effect of an act of Congress within its borders.[6]

Webster had no doubt that Calhoun was the author of the exposition. In his second reply to Hayne, while staring directly at the raised bench on which the president of the Senate, Calhoun, sat (speakers in the Senate were to address the chair or presiding officer), Webster called nullification the "Carolina Doctrine." One can easily imagine Webster's voice and manner at that moment; a pause, almost a sneer, certainly an increase in volume. (These performance effects were one reason that his speeches were so well attended.) For it was the not-so-shadowy presence of Calhoun that drew from Webster two of the finest Senate orations in history. Calhoun was Webster's real opponent in this virtual courtroom.[7]

On the basis of earlier events, Webster was an unlikely defender of a protective tariff, or indeed a critic of nullification. He had been the spokesman of New England obstructionism during the embargo period and then in the War of 1812. Infuriated by then secretary of war James Monroe's conscription plan, Webster even used language reminiscent of the Kentucky resolves and this on the floor of the House of Representatives. But times had changed, and Webster had moved away from a strict states' rights stance to the more nationalist pose he took in *McCulloch* and *Gibbons*. To be sure, in these cases, his clients relied on federal action against state interposition. In April 1824 Senator Webster gave a speech defending low tariffs. Still, as New England became a manufacturing center, Webster's clients came to include its major textile firms as well as the Second Bank. Webster reluctantly supported the tariff of 1828. By contrast, South Carolina's senatorial delegation, which had in past favored protective tariffs, had changed course 180 degrees, to oppose them. It was the tariff dispute, not the land sales issue, that set the stage for the Hayne-Webster debate over the fate of the Union.[8]

On January 19, 1830, the senators were discussing Samuel Foot's motion. He asked the Senate to limit further sales of western lands in the national domain to those already surveyed and on the market and not open new lands until those still untaken were sold. He also wanted the office of federal land survey abolished. Speculation in western lands had led to one grievous economic crisis already, the Panic of 1819; and the Land Act of 1820, designed to curb runaway speculation, had failed to satisfy western leaders' lust for rapid development of federal lands. An 1824 bill for a survey of western lands and land sale effects had little traction. Plans for "graduation," lowering the price on federal parcels and allowing smaller parcel sales, and cession, giving the federal lands within existing states to the state governments, were alternatives to Foot's proposal. By 1828, aided by the election of Tennessee's Andrew Jackson, a land speculator himself, western senators were pressing for even more rapid land sales, as these fueled the growing influence of the region in the

Senate (by laying the groundwork for additional states). More plans for western lands appeared on the Senate floor, including using the receipts from the sales to pay the national debt, to fund education, and to return the sales to the states. Farm interests argued for a preemption policy, in effect giving the lands to those who occupied them and improved them. The most vociferous of the western spokesmen, Senator Thomas Hart Benton of Missouri, repeatedly insisted that Foot's resolution was a body blow to western expansion.[9]

Like the tariff, the land sales policy of the United States was firmly rooted in Article I, but also like the tariff, too much was at stake for South Carolina to let others, though they might be more immediately concerned, frame the policy. South Carolina rice, one of the richest staple crops in the world, and South Carolina upland cotton were both planted and harvested by slaves. The surplus of these slaves could be sold to cotton growers of the Delta region of Mississippi, Arkansas, and Louisiana. But South Carolina agriculture, and influence in the nation, faced a crisis. As a result of the Panic of 1819, thousands of free whites had left the state and taken over 80,000 slaves with them. The state had thus tried to protect its interests by nullifying the tariff of 1828, but alone, or even with southern state allies, South Carolina did not have the ability to enforce its own policies.[10]

Rising to oppose Foot's resolution was Robert Y. Hayne of South Carolina, self-appointed spokesman for his state. A wealthy planter and lawyer, well spoken, and self-confident, Hayne was an associate of Calhoun, his fellow South Carolinian and currently the vice president. The two men had conferenced over the issue, and everyone in the upper house knew that Hayne spoke for Calhoun as well as for himself. When Calhoun resigned the vice presidency, in 1832, he would take Hayne's place in the Senate. Hayne would become governor of South Carolina.[11]

Arriving at the Senate chamber from the Court in the basement below, Webster heard Hayne deliver his address at the close of the session on the January 19, 1830. After conferring with other New England senators, all of whom were concerned that the interests of their region were imperiled by the nascent western-southern alliance in the Senate, Webster went to his residence and prepared a reply. We know that Webster had been following the debate on western lands before and during Foot's intervention. The conventional explanation for his interest was that Foot, a fellow New Englander, was concerned about declining New England influence in American political and economic life. This is surely true, but Webster had other, legal concerns. Webster knew that Hayne would take positions on the three issues directly opposed to what Webster had argued in Court. That is one reason why he dropped everything in a very busy Supreme Court session (over a dozen cases at hand and as many more docketed) to hear Hayne's address—though he said later that he happened to listen by chance—and the very next morning to respond.[12]

Hayne believed that public interest and private right converged on the protection of slavery. Slavery was a public good and had to be protected by law. Slavery was also a private good, for many southerners, including Hayne, had fortunes invested in slaves. The private good required a friendly public land policy, for slavery relentlessly sought new lands to be fully profitable. The internal slave trade, carrying millions of slaves from the East Coast to the west, had replaced the overseas slave trade as a supplier of labor for southern staple crop agriculture. Almost every southerner in the course of their lives—slave and free—was somehow involved in the trade. The rapid expansion to the west, with southern speculators opening up new lands to southern planters, and planters moving slaves onto that land, was not only a fact of life, it was slavery's lifeblood. So when Hayne, speaking not only for Calhoun or for South Carolina, but for the slave South, entered the lists, he was representing a different idea of the public/private divide from that Webster promoted.[13]

Nor did Hayne see a necessary separation of politics and law. Southern politics was devoted to the law of slavery. Advocacy of slavery was the litmus test of political advancement in the slave South. That became clear in the debates over Missouri's application for statehood in 1819. When New York's James Tallmadge moved to amend the Missouri application to bar slave owners from bringing their slaves to Missouri and to free all persons at age twenty-five born to slaves already in the state, Southern representatives seethed with animosity. Southern speaker after speaker rose not only to defend Missouri's desire to enter the Union as a slave state, but threatened dire consequences if antislavery congressmen prevented Missouri from joining the slave states in Congress. For southerners, politics and law were the same on the Missouri issue, and the Foot resolution, though not directly antislavery, raised the same concerns.[14]

Finally, though not least, Hayne argued for the strongest possible states' rights stance short of secession. Again, the fear of an obtrusive and intrusive federal government lay precisely in such policies as Foot's—a limitation on the expansion of slavery. Were the slave interest not in play, there is no reason that the South would have stressed such a view of federalism. For when federal policy favored southern interests, for example in the Fugitive Slave Acts, southern spokesmen put aside their qualms about states' rights.

Although filled with oratorical flourishes, the Webster-Hayne exchange had the character of oral argument—two counsel, representing opposing sides of a legal issue. Bear in mind that the Congress was a law-making body, and legislation, although it was prospective and policy-focused rather than focused on the past and a case or controversy, was otherwise similar to the opinion of an appeals court. The latitude given counsel's oral argument in the early modern federal courts looked and sounded like the latitude taken by members of the two legislative houses, with the exception that sometimes speakers in Congress engaged in personal affront. That tone, not permissible in court between two counsel for opposing sides, was allowed in congressional oratory. Indeed, mention of slavery seemed to bring out that kind of personal vituperation.

Slavery had created a kind of intersectionality of the three constitutional issues, so overlapping one another that they had become almost indistinguishable. In the Missouri statehood admission debates, and in the debates over the gag-rule in Congress between 1835 and 1850, in the quarrel over the Compromise of 1850 and later "Bleeding Kansas," members of both houses, particularly the lower house, spat defiance and threats of disunion and threatened rivers of blood would flow—language not heard in courts. Thus Foot's resolution itself soon faded from view in the Hayne-Webster exchange. As historian Christopher Childers has written, "the mere mention of the slavery issue changed the character of the debate."[15]

Hayne began in an almost conciliatory manner—a South Carolina gentleman addressing other gentlemen: "What ought to be the future policy of the Government in relation to the Public Lands? We find the most opposite and irreconcilable opinions between the two parties." That was politics. "On the one side it is contended that the public land ought to be reserved as a permanent fund for revenue, and future distribution among the States, while, on the other, it is insisted that the whole of these lands of right belong to, and ought to be relinquished to, the States in which they lie." In other words, graduation versus cession. Rather than regard the issue as old West versus new West, however, Hayne saw it as a state-versus-nation question. "Would it be safe to confide such a treasure to the keeping of our national rulers? To expose them to the temptations inseparable from the direction and control of a fund which might be enlarged or diminished almost at pleasure, without imposing burthens upon the people?"

Hayne was using a code that everyone understood. He denied that he spoke as a sectionalist for the South. Instead, he spoke against an overweening central government with a major permanent source of income from land sales. Taxation required the consent of the governed, by which he meant people of property, and that was an acceptable form of government self-finance, but the land sales violated "one of the greatest safeguards of liberty." The highest duty of the statesman was "a jealous watchfulness on the part of the people, over the collection and expenditure of the public money." Speaking as a statesman, Hayne reckoned that an independent source of income "has done much to weaken the responsibility of our federal rulers to the people, and has made them, in some measure, careless of their rights, and regardless of the high trust committed to their care." This applied to the tariff as well as to the land sales. That is, the interests of South Carolina citizens were ignored when a majority in the Congress could impose land sale policies or tariff policies that disfavored South Carolina.[16]

One would thus suppose that Hayne would favor Foot's resolution. But he opposed both graduation and cession (fearing that the lands would become Free Soil, though he did not say so). Moreover, Hayne was not really interested in land sales policy. He had, to be sure, engaged in a conciliatory exchange with Thomas Hart Benton and other western advocates of cheap land, but the alliance of the South and the West, built in part on the election of Jackson and in part on enmity to the tariff of 1828, was a frail one.

Instead, Hayne's adoption of western views was mainly based on a perceived states' rights platform—and (again because he opposed ceding the land to the states) on the right of states to impose slavery on some of their people. "I distrust, therefore, sir, the policy of creating a great permanent national treasury, whether to be derived from public lands or from any other source." The "any other source" tied the debate directly to the ongoing contest over the tariff. A source of income independent of the citizens of the states "would enable Congress and the Executive to exercise a control over States, as well as over great interests in the country, nay, even over corporations and individuals—utterly destructive of the purity, and fatal to the duration of our institutions." The reference to "our institutions" could hardly be misunderstood, though vague on its face. Everyone knew that South Carolina was defending slavery, its "peculiar institution." So, too, such an uncontrolled federal government "would be equally fatal to the sovereignty and independence of the States."[17]

Hayne was now in full gallop toward his actual destination—a defense of states' rights that collapsed into the defense of slavery. Note that the individual right to hold slaves was tied to the states' rights to protect slavery. The two were inseparable. The public and the private were one and the same. "Sir, I am one of those who believe that the very life of our system is the independence of the States, and that there is no evil more to be deprecated than the consolidation of this Government." Allowing the federal government to set sales prices, limit or expand the minimum size of parcels, and survey new lands was a violation of "strict adherence to the limitations imposed by the constitution on the Federal Government." Webster had seen this dragon when it emerged from the cave in *McCulloch* and *Gibbons*. Here, the dragon not only had teeth, it breathed fire. Hayne vowed, "I am opposed, therefore, in any shape, to all unnecessary extension of the powers, or the influence of the Legislature or Executive of the Union over the States, or the people of the States." Once again, without mentioning it, Hayne made the slave South's position in the Union the real complaint. For all centralizing measures "create an abject spirit of dependence [and] to sow the seeds of dissolution." For *dependence*, read the growing sense in the South that its finances and exports were dependent on the North but did not benefit commensurably. In the end, "The people of the South might be considered as strangers in the land of their fathers." For *dissolution*, read the threat of disunion.[18]

The next day, Webster's reply began on a quiet note. "Every actual settler should be able to buy good land, at a cheap rate; but, on the other hand, speculation by individuals, on a large scale, should not be encouraged; nor should the value of all lands, sold or unsold, be reduced to nothing, by throwing new and vast quantities into the market at prices merely nominal." So far, an uncontroversial salute to the yeoman farmer, a warning against unconstrained land speculators, and more, the argument that individual ownership rights should not be dependent on the state. But he was not done. For Webster, land was for settlement and individual family use. He did not favor the speculator. "The lands cannot be settled but by settlers; nor faster than settlers can be found." Land policy should "encourage settlement and cultivation as rapidly as the increasing population of the country is competent to extend settlement and cultivation." In short, law should facilitate individual rights.[19]

Webster next revealed that his quarry had been Hayne, and Hayne's veiled defenses of the southern idea of property. He would bait Hayne to say so, turning a conversation about land policy into a national debate about the Constitution, the Union, and slavery. "I now proceed, sir, to some of the opinions expressed by the gentleman from South Carolina. Two or three topics were touched by him, in regard to which he expressed sentiments in which I do not at all concur." After a brief rehearsal of New England's solicitude for the West—or to be precise, for the western settler—Webster offered a history lesson. "The original North American colonists either fled from Europe, like our New England ancestors, to avoid persecution, or came hither at their own charges, and often at the ruin of their fortunes, as private adventurers." They did not need the state to protect them, as they had only the works of their own hands and their families' labor. "Generally speaking, they derived neither succor nor protection from their governments at home." Look closely at the history lesson: no slaves. Free men came to seek freedom. Hayne from his seat, Calhoun presiding from the raised rostrum just above Webster, the Senate galleries, and the nation take notice—this discourse was about freedom and, lurking in the shadows, slavery.[20]

The settlers were protected "through necessary sacrifices, made for proper ends." The Indians had to go. Slavery was barred. "A parental government at home was still ever mindful of their condition, and their wants; and nothing was spared, which a just sense of their necessities required." War against the native possessors was justified. It was inevitable, but the expansion of the southern system was not, and it was not allowed. The land, in the infancy of the nation a wilderness, "Over all that is now Ohio, there then stretched one vast wilderness, unbroken, except by . . . the arm of the frontiersman [that] had leveled the forest, and let in the sun." But the flood of free men, farmers, "a million of inhabitants! an amount of population greater than that of all the cantons of Switzerland; equal to one-third of all the people of the United States, when they undertook to accomplish their independence."

The state might be necessary to protect property in slaves; nothing was necessary to protect the property that free labor created except freedom itself. "If, sir, we may judge of measures by their results, what lessons do these facts read us, upon the policy of the government?" What policy was that? Webster did not say; he had no need to say it; everyone knew it—barring slavery had drawn the republican farmer into Ohio, and the result was a veritable Eden, without any snakes. "Sir, does it not require some portion of self-respect in us, to imagine, that if our light had shone on the path of government, if our wisdom could have been consulted in its measures, a more rapid advance of strength and prosperity would have been experienced?" Never once, not yet, did Webster mention slavery.[21]

The western lands were a national trust, held for the people by the confederation and then by the national government. If government intervention was necessary to add to the expanse of free land, it should be the federal government, not the state governments. The lands of the West were held "as deed of trust" for the people of the nation. The federal government spoke for the people, the freeholders. Congress had acted, "putting it into the power of every man in the country, however poor, but who has health and strength to become a freeholder if he desires, not of barren acres, but of rich and fertile soil. The government has performed all the conditions of the grant." The barb in this offering was sharp: "Every man in the country"—were not some of these men held in bondage?[22]

In debate, it is clever to rephrase one's opponent's accusation. Hayne accused defenders of the current land policy of wishing to create an independent source of funds for the federal government untouchable by the voters. Webster recast the accusation. "Consolidation!—that perpetual cry both of terror and delusion—consolidation!" What was this but "any thing more than that the union of the states will be strengthened, by whatever continues or furnishes inducements to the people of the states to hold together?" Such consolidation was a good thing, "and lo this species of consolidation every true American ought to be attached; it is neither more nor less than strengthening the union itself." A strong union was a strong nation. Surely every patriot aspired to that end, "the greatest interest of every true American, the consolidation of our union, in which is involved our prosperity, felicity, safety, perhaps our national existence." Who better to make the avatar of that goal than the father of the country? "This, sir, is general Washington's consolidation. This is the true constitutional consolidation. . . . I rejoice in whatever tends to strengthen the bond that unites us; and encourages the hope that our union may be perpetual."[23]

With that, Webster swung into his attack on states' rights. He did not mention slavery, as part of the National Republican (later the Whig) Party to which he belonged and for whose nomination to the presidency he longed had support in the South, but he could fire salvos at states' rights. "And, therefore, I cannot but feel regret at the expression of such opinions as the gentleman has avowed; because I think their obvious tendency is to weaken the bond of our connexion." Disunionism was a southern phenomenon, he implied. "I know that there are some persons in the part of the country from which the hon[orable]. member comes, who habitually speak of the union in terms of indifference, or even of disparagement." Of course Hayne was not tainted with that disease Webster proposed (a Ciceronian touch), but the end of such "ideas and sentiments is obviously to bring the union into discussion, as a mere question of present and temporary expediency—nothing more than a mere matter of profit and loss." Such men did not love the Union, but regarded it as a temporary expedient that could be "sundered whenever it shall be found to thwart" their purposes. The real enemy—secession, secession to protect against the threat to slavery that the sale of land to free men posed—poked its nose around the corner of Webster's rhetoric.[24]

This was a serious accusation, for it touched treason itself. Webster proclaimed himself free of this taint. "I am a unionist, and in this sense, a national republican. I would strengthen the ties that hold us together." Never mind the Hartford Convention. The hook for Hayne was baited. He could hardly have ignored the accusation, or at least the implication that he and those whom he represented were not patriotic. The galleries filled and overflowed with men and women into the Senate chamber aisles as Webster concluded. The penny newspaper editors were there, along with stenographers for Gales and Seaton's and Niles' weekly newspapers.

Webster's speech was not quite done, however. "I come now, Mr. President, to that part of the gentleman's speech, which has been the main occasion of my addressing the senate. The East! the obnoxious, the rebuked the always reproached East!!" Webster raised the tariff issue—and with it summoned the specter of nullification. "And the cause of all this narrow and selfish policy the gentleman finds in the tariff I think he called it the accursed policy of the tariff. This policy the gentleman tells us, requires multitudes of dependent laborers, a population of paupers, and that it is to secure these at home that the east opposes whatever may induce to western emigration."

The rapier—no mention of nullification, but who could miss the implication of nullification: "But the tariff! the tariff!! Sir, I beg to say, in regard to the east that the original policy of the tariff is not hers whether it be wise or unwise. New England is not its author." The tariff of 1816, the first protection-ist tariff, "was not carried by New England votes. It was truly more a southern than an eastern measure." And what votes carried the tariff of 1824? "Certainly, not those of New England." New England (and Webster) opposed the tariff of 1824. Who had supported that tariff? Not Hayne, but sitting behind Hayne, Calhoun had supported the tariff of 1824. Hayne knew it. Calhoun knew it. Everyone in the Senate knew it. Presumably everyone who had followed na-tional politics for the past decade knew it. In fact, Webster had opposed that tariff, and by this twisting of the rapier he excused his own volte face and that of New England. "It was literally forced upon New England and this shows how groundless bow void of all probability any charge must be, which imputes to her hostility to the growth of the western states as naturally flowing from a cherished policy of her own."[25]

Webster did not close with his remarks on states' rights or a discourse on the tariff. There is an old debater's tactic, certainly as old as Cicero's speeches against Mark Anthony, and, ironically, enshrined in Mark Anthony's speech at the burial of Julius Caesar in the Shakespeare play: deny that you mean to disagree with something your opponent has said, and in the process, pillory it. That is what Webster did at the close of his first speech. Webster had skirted the slavery issue, clothing it in a favorable comparison of free territory versus slave territory. He had never directly attacked it, although Hayne felt and the rest of the auditory surely knew that was Webster's intent. "The plan of the gentleman [Hayne] went to reverse the order of nature, vainly expecting to re-tain men within a small and comparatively unproductive territory 'who have all the world before them whose to choose.'"

For his own part, he was in favor of letting population take its own course. Slaves could not take their own course; they were taken away from family to new lands. Webster "should experience no feeling of mortification if any of his con-stituents liked better to settle on the Kansas or the Arkansas, or the lord knows where, within our territory; let them go, and be happier if they could." Happier because they could choose to go, not because they would willingly settle among slaves and slave masters. "The settlement of a new and fertile country? Such a country present[ed] the most alluring of all prospects to a young and laboring man; it gives him a freehold—it offers to him weight and respectability in so-ciety; and above all, it presents to him a prospect of a permanent provision for his children." None of this applied to slaves, of course, for there were no slaves among the New England men who ventured out into new lands.[26]

Woven into his reply, Webster had outlined a powerful ideal of American constitutionalism. It was a Constitution that favored the free enterpriser over the slave driver, the family farmer over the large planter, and the industrious over the indolent. It was a Constitution that spread the New England way, its farms and its factories, westward. Its heroes were the framers of the Northwest Ordinance. One might almost call it a Constitution of rugged individualism were it not for the danger of anachronism. Above all it was a Constitution that favored property created by one's own labor, rather than forced labor of others. To this end, all three of the framers' missing pieces contributed. The Constitution was for the individual's rights, not for the state; law and politics should not be conflated; and states must bow to the supremacy of the Union.

Perhaps Hayne should have allowed Benton to respond to Webster, and Benton, no shrinking violet when it came to floor debate, immediately rose to defend the interests of the West. But Webster had turned the debate away from the sale of lands to the occupation and improvement of lands, and by implication, the supremacy of free settlers over those who brought slaves to new lands. He had posed, in direct opposition to Hayne, answers to the three constitutional conundrums. And so for the next two days, Hayne held the floor to spit defiance at Webster. No longer about Foot's resolution, nor Benton's plans for western expansion, the debate had become a national referendum on states' rights. That, at least, was Hayne's purpose, and ultimately the weakness of his cause. For the extremity of states' rights was nullification, a project associated with South Carolina's response to the tariff, and South Carolina alone. How Calhoun must have squirmed in his seat at the front of the chamber as his ally defended a post that no other state adopted, in the name of states' rights. Hayne nevertheless decided that the threat to the expansion of slavery could not be ignored. The duel was now between Webster's rapier and Hayne's claymore. Hayne also turned the policy debate into a frank confrontation between the two sections, and public opinion agreed that Hayne attacked New England and Webster personally.[27]

Hayne began, once again, in the measured tones of a gentleman. "Sir, I questioned no man's opinions; I impeached no man's motives; I charged no party, or state, or section of country with hostility to any other, but ventured, as I thought, in a becoming spirit, to put forth my own sentiments in relation to a great national question of public policy." Again, he could have stopped there, but he did not. This was not a courtroom exchange, not any longer; it was a duel with words as weapons. Hayne would never back down from such a challenge; he had already fought one duel with real ammunition. "The honorable gentleman from Massachusetts . . . chooses to consider me as the author of those charges; and, losing sight entirely of that gentleman, selects me as his adversary, and pours out all the vials of his mighty wrath upon my devoted head." Even that a gentleman might bear, but Hayne saw himself as the representative of the South and he had to defend its honor. Webster "goes on to assail the institutions and policy of the South, and calls in question the principles and conduct of the State which I have the honor to represent."

In fact, Webster had skirted, danced, and merely implied such as Hayne believed, but so acutely did a southern gentleman sense any affront to his or his region's honor that even the most subtly couched insult as Webster offered had to be challenged. "When I find a gentleman of mature age and experience, of acknowledged talents and profound sagacity, pursuing a course like this, declining the contest offered from the West, and making war upon the unoffending South, I must believe, I am bound to believe, he has some object in view that he has not ventured to disclose." Well, that was true.[28]

Webster had raised the issue of the tariff, not exactly on point, but slyly impugning South Carolina nullification. Hayne rejected all subtlety when he reprised New England's participation in the Hartford Convention at the end of the War of 1812. That meeting had also called for something very close to nullification. How lambasting the Hartford Convention for its nullification stance defended South Carolina's similar position was not obvious, but Hayne was determined to defend South Carolina by attacking New England. It was not a winning tactic, but he kept at it. "Did that gentleman, sir, when he formed the determination to cross the southern border, in order to invade the State of South Carolina, deem it prudent, or necessary, to enlist under his banners the prejudices of the world." What could those be—of course, those against slavery. "Or was it supposed, sir, that, in a premeditated and unprovoked attack upon the South, it was advisable to begin by a gentle admonition of our supposed weakness [again, slavery], in order to prevent us from making that firm and manly resistance, due to our own character, and our dearest interest?" The dearest interest and the weakness were one and the same: "Was the significant hint of the weakness of slave-holding States, when contrasted with the superior strength of free States—like the glare of the weapon half drawn from its scabbard—intended to enforce the lessons of prudence and of patriotism?" Hayne had gone far beyond where Webster had stopped, into a full-blown defense of slavery.[29]

Hayne offered that the South had found slavery rather than created it. Slaves were brought to southern shores by New England slave traders, Hayne announced. His history was not entirely accurate—there were slaves in Virginia before there was a New England, brought there by Dutch raiders of Portuguese slavers—but no one was fact-checking Hayne's speech.

> We met it as a practical question of obligation and duty. We resolved to make the best of the situation in which Providence had placed us, and to fulfil the high trust which had developed upon us as the owners of slaves, in the only way in which such a trust could be fulfilled, without spreading misery and ruin throughout the land. We found that we had to deal with a people whose physical, moral, and intellectual habits and character, totally disqualified them from the enjoyment of the blessings of freedom.

Slavery was good for the slave, apparently. It was also good for the South, as Haynes reported the profits of slave labor. Slavery was better than the condition of urban workers in the North. "Sir, there does not exist, on the face of the whole earth, a population so poor, so wretched, so vile, so loathsome, so utterly destitute of all the comforts, conveniences, and decencies of life, as the unfortunate blacks of Philadelphia, and New York, and Boston. Liberty has been to them the greatest of calamities, the heaviest of curses." How did Hayne know this? Firsthand observation and on the spot interviews? Hayne had never traveled in the North. No matter: "Sir, I have had some opportunities of making comparisons between the condition of the free negroes of the North and the slaves of the South, and the comparison has left not only an indelible impression of the superior advantages of the latter." Hayne's refrain was to become the mantra of the slave South: "On this subject, as in all others, we ask nothing of our Northern brethren but to 'let us alone'; leave us to the undisturbed management of our domestic concerns, and the direction of our own industry, and we will ask no more."[30]

Had Hayne stopped here, proclaiming slavery as a strength rather than a weakness, he would not have opened himself or the South to greater blame than Webster had already cast upon it. But Hayne had another goal entirely, and that connected the dots of the land sales, the tariff, slavery, and states' rights: the defense of nullification. It was the mirror opposite of Webster's constitutionalism. Politics and law, public and private, federal and state all converged on the protection of slavery. Unfortunately, the means to protect slavery, nullification, isolated South Carolina from its allies. Hayne thus promoted his own view of the Constitution: "The object of the framers of the constitution, as disclosed in that address, was not the consolidation of the government, but 'the consolidation of the Union.' It was not to draw power from the states, in order to transfer it to a great national government." Webster had misunderstood the meaning of consolidation. Here Hayne was clearly getting help from an outside source, in all likelihood Calhoun himself. For this was Calhoun's exposition, a positive interpretation, rather than the negativity of Hayne's own views. *Make it positive*, one can hear Calhoun urging his friend and fellow nullifier. Contemporaries reported that Hayne and Calhoun, who shared the same lodging, went over the next steps together.[31]

Hayne could not resist throwing Webster's earlier free trade views back at him. This was hardly the conduct allowed a lawyer in a courtroom, but the exchange had long since passed into a personal one. "But, sir, that gentleman has thought proper, for purposes best known to himself, to strike the South through me, the most unworthy of her servants. He has crossed the border, he has invaded the State of South Carolina, is making war upon her citizens, and endeavoring to overthrow her principles and her institutions." Words had become deeds in Hayne's mind.[32]

The Constitution according to South Carolina "would confine the federal government strictly within the limits prescribed by the constitution—who would preserve to the States and the people all powers not expressly delegated—who would make this a federal and not a national Union." Others wanted a consolidated national government "constantly stealing power from the States and adding strength to the federal government." South Carolina had found the answer to consolidationists: "the idea that a State has any constitutional remedy by the exercise of its sovereign authority against 'a gross, palpable, and deliberate violation of the Constitution.'" Despite what Webster sneered, Hayne proposed that this was no idle or ridiculous notion, nor would it make the Union a rope of sand. The opposite idea, that "the Federal Government is the exclusive judge of the extent as well as the limitations of its powers, it seems to be utterly subversive of the sovereignty and independence of the States." What was the end of Webster's centrist doctrine—nothing but the reduction of sovereign states to mere departments of an all-powerful and autocratic central government.

To be fair, this was not what Webster wanted. He did not want to destroy the sovereignty of New Hampshire or Massachusetts any more than of South Carolina. He simply wanted the federal government to have absolute control of the powers explicitly granted to it—including land sales and tariff levels. Hayne feared (quite without grounds as far as Webster was concerned, but not without grounds as far as the abolitionists were starting to argue) that the federal government could harm South Carolina's dearest interest. Hayne warned, "This is practically 'a Government without limitation of powers'; the States are at once reduced to mere petty corporations, and the people are entirely at your mercy." Were the issue simply South Carolina's nullification, that soon would be solved by President Jackson sending gunboats to Charleston Harbor to aid in the collection of the tariff. But Hayne gave away the game in his final passage: "The measures of the Federal Government have, it is true, prostrated [South Carolina's] interests, and will soon involve the whole South in irretrievable ruin." The "whole South" had not embraced nullification. It had embraced slavery. Like Webster's, Hayne's constitution protected property, but that property was largely in slave laborers.[33]

Webster could not reply immediately. He was, he said, summoned elsewhere, and in any case, the hour was late. Benton then spoke. Webster returned to the foot of the speaker's desk on January 26 and continued for hours—until the next day—in what has been regarded as one of the finest examples of American oratory. He opened by comparing Hayne's conduct to a duelist's: "He had a shot, he said, to return, and he wished to discharge it. That shot, Sir, which he thus kindly informed us was coming, that we might stand out of the way, or prepare ourselves to fall by it and die with decency, has now been received." Webster brushed it aside.

He then spent hours going back over every point Hayne made, having now had the time to prepare rebuttal. He did not agree with any of it and did not attempt to reply to the citations of his earlier opinions. Instead, he spoke in glowing terms of the once-cordial relations between the two states, "in refreshing rememberance of the past; let me remind you that, in early times, no States cherished greater harmony, both of principle and feeling, than Massachusetts and South Carolina." It demonstrated that he was the true gentleman, wishing nothing but harmony. He then called to mind Massachusetts's glories: "There is Boston, and Concord, and Lexington, and Bunker Hill; and there they will remain for ever. The bones of her sons, falling in the great struggle for Independence, now lie mingled with the soil of every State from New England to Georgia." Why had so many been sacrificed? For American "liberty," of course—but not from British tyranny; no mention of that. What tyranny then? He let the point lie. He decried discord and disunion, party strife and "blind ambition." Who could object?[34]

As for slavery, well, "I spoke, Sir, of the Ordinance of 1787, which prohibits slavery, in all future times, northwest of the Ohio, as a measure of great wisdom and foresight, and one which had been attended with highly beneficial and permanent consequences." Webster professed surprise that "on this point, no two gentlemen in the Senate could entertain different opinions." This was rank nonsense, as Hayne had already expressed a different opinion. "But the simple expression of this sentiment has led the gentleman, not only into a labored defence of slavery, in the abstract, and on principle, but also into a warm accusation against me, as having attacked the system of domestic slavery now existing in the Southern States."

No—he had not attacked slavery where it existed, but merely proposed that it was wise and judicious not to introduce it where it did not exist—the very policy of Free Soil that Hayne feared. "There is not, and never has been, a disposition in the North to interfere with these interests of the South. Such interference has never been supposed to be within the power of government; nor has it been in any way attempted." But, he wanted to be clear: "I regard domestic slavery as one of the greatest evils, both moral and political." And then a parting shot at the Three-Fifths Clause of the Constitution: "Nor do I complain of the peculiar effect which the magnitude of that population has had in the distribution of power under this Federal government. We know, Sir, that the representation of the States in the other house is not equal. We know that great advantage in that respect is enjoyed by the slave-holding States." The so-called three-fifths compromise of including three-fifths of the slave population in the calculation of representatives in the House was one way in which the partisan politics of slavery had mangled a law of equal representation that should have been neutral in its effect.[35]

Webster then turned away from South Carolina and Hayne and to the Constitution and "we the people." "Sir, we narrow-minded people of New England do not reason thus. Our *notion* of things is entirely different. We look upon the States, not as separated, but as united. . . . In whatever is within the proper sphere of the constitutional power of this government, we look upon the States as one." With this single phrase, repeated in various ways throughout the rest of the speech, Webster transformed the united states into the United States, one nation rather than a federation of states.[36]

The "Carolina doctrine" would have it otherwise. "I [i.e., Webster] understand him [Hayne] to maintain an authority, on the part of the States, thus to interfere, for the purpose of correcting the exercise of power by the general government, of checking it, and of compelling it to conform to their opinion of the extend of its powers." That was a fair exposition of nullification, along with "I understand him to insist, that, if the exigency of the case, in the opinion of any State government, require it, such State government may, by its own sovereign authority, annul an act of the general government which it deems plainly and palpably unconstitutional." But it was wrong. The federal government was not the creature of the states. It was the agent of the people of the whole country. "Sir, the people's Constitution, the people's government, made for the people, made by the people, and answerable to the people. The people of the United States have declared that the Constitution shall be the supreme law. . . . We are all agents of the same supreme power, the people."[37]

Webster could not close without alluding to the forum in which he had made his greatest contributions to constitutional jurisprudence—the High Court. "To whom lies the last appeal? This, Sir, the Constitution itself decides also, by declaring, '*That the judicial power shall extend to all cases arising under the Constitution and laws of the United States.*' These two provisions cover the whole ground. They are, in truth, the keystone of the arch! With these it is a government; without them it is a confederation." Need he remind the members that the Court, in part at his prodding and certainly with his support, had adopted the very sentiments he now espoused? In *McCulloch* and *Gibbons*, his view of an expansive Necessary and Proper Clause and his approval of an exclusive Interstate Commerce Clause, respectively, had become the law of the land. From the Senate floor, they had taken wing: "Liberty and Union, now and fore ever, one and inseparable."[38]

The evening after Webster had finished, he and Hayne attended a reception at the White House. The two men, both lawyers, greeted one another jovially, as lawyers often do after a pitched battle in the courtroom. "How are you tonight?" Webster asked Hayne. "None the better for you, sir," Hayne smiled in reply. In fact, the evening brought respite in the Nullification Controversy.

That would require more weeks of perfervid Senate debate, a presidential election that brought Jackson a second term, Jackson's inaugural address warning South Carolina of continued disobedience to the law, a compromise tariff in 1833, and the passage of the Force Act giving Jackson the authority he needed to bring South Carolina to heel. It was ominous stuff, and Webster played his role in it, ironically as Jackson's ally.[39]

Between January 20 and January 26, 1830, something remarkable had happened in Webster's thinking about the Constitution. The separation of law and politics, of public interest and private rights, was no longer just the aegis for private property. These notions, combined with the supremacy of the Union, had become an icon in itself for him. The first reply to Hayne rested on the superiority of one kind of property over another, reflecting Webster's long-standing prioritization of private property in a free society. During that speech, he realized that slave property was also private property and could be defended, along with the South's way of life, based on the same principles he had previously espoused. That shook him. When Hayne defended the South in his reply, Webster probed the problem—what was different in the land the free settlers improved from the land that the slaves improved for their masters? Whether Webster's thinking had matured in that week, or he saw the fallacy in his first reply to Hayne, or he saw the dream of financial independence slipping away, he shifted his ground to a defense of the unitary union and "we the people." *The people*, he said, over and over. "I would not regard the Constitution with idolatrous admiration, but this side of idolatry, I hold it in profound respect." Later, reflecting on the exchange with Hayne, Webster opined, "I felt it to be a contest for the integrity of the Constitution." This too was a criticism of Hayne, for surely Hayne knew that slaves were people, and Webster's Constitution began with "we the people." Hayne had associated the South with nullification; Webster associated the East, or New England, with the proper interpretation of the Constitution: a national union.[40]

In the meantime, Webster still supported a protective tariff on imported textiles in the Senate debates, and he busied himself with cases on the High Court docket. His reputation as the nation's orator, if it had needed burnishing, now shown with high gloss. But his prospects for advancement to the highest office had dimmed with the growing strength of the Jacksonian Democracy. Perhaps worse, in 1835, Jackson's secretary of the treasury, Roger Taney, replaced John Marshall in the center seat of the Court, surrounded by a fleet of Democrats. Webster had labored to table the Taney nomination, including a sophisticated (but easily unveiled) attempt to replace an eastern federal judicial circuit with a western one, but in the end, Jackson's ally went on to the center seat. He was not as strong an advocate of states' rights as Hayne or Calhoun, but neither did he share Webster's view of the implied powers of the federal government. Webster ran for president on the new Whig Party ticket in 1836 but lost to Vice President Martin Van Buren.[41]

Perhaps another victory in the courts would give Webster the chance to shine once more? In 1827 the Charles River Bridge Company had secured his services to protect its monopoly against a rival newcomer, the Warren Bridge Company. The issues were familiar—a corporate charter under attack from a legislature. The case arrived at the High Court in 1831 and was not decided until 1837. Could Webster once again win in a familiar battleground?

6. "Secur[ing] Individual Property against Legislative Assumption": *Charles River Bridge v. Warren Bridge* (1837)

Between 1820 and 1840, the US economy and society were profoundly transformed by what historians have called "the transportation revolution." Before 1820, commercial traffic on roads, steamboats, and canals carried agricultural and manufactured goods, including consumer durables, along east-west and north-south routes. Unfortunately for sellers and buyers, roads were unreliable in spring (mud) and winter (snow), and river ports and canals did not reach every town and village. As demand for cheap foodstuffs in the cities and cheap clothing and tools in the countryside increased with population growth, a new technology appeared to service the demand: railroads. Investment in rail lines, railroad companies, and the manufacture of locomotives and rolling stock was a boon to transportation, lowering the cost and increasing the reliability of delivery. Supported by state and local bonds, right of way soon expanded exponentially, and private capital, often the investment of thousands of individuals, made railroads king.[1]

Along with the railroad boom came a new way of looking at the economy—an embrace of competition. In industries as varied as textile manufacturing and firearms, no technological advance was free from pilferage by one's competitors. Free, or at least freer, enterprise meant that the old idea of chartered monopolies must bow to the newer idea of best use. *Best use* meant that older private rights to water, air, and even freedom from nuisances must make way for more productive (and profitable) enterprises. The law of property followed the changing commercial landscape.[2]

Legal historian Morton Horwitz rightly believes that *Charles River Bridge v. Warren Bridge* (1837) tested the new ideology of competition in the courts. At the center of the case stood Daniel Webster. In its near-decade course from 1828 to 1837, it overturned Webster's view of the divisions between the political and the legal, and the public interest and private rights. It also nearly drove him to distraction, for his antagonist was untouchable: Chief Justice Roger Taney.[3]

The suit began in the Massachusetts courts, between the proprietors of a bridge chartered in 1795 by the state to cross the Charles River between Boston and Cambridge (the Charles River Bridge) and the sponsors of a new bridge built in 1828 under a state charter to cross the river closer to its mouth near Charlestown (the Warren Bridge). Webster was drawn into the battle in 1826, when on behalf of the company that operated the older bridge he sought an injunction to prevent construction of the newer rival. The grounds for his plea were similar to the *Dartmouth College* case—the state charter created a private property right in the Charles Bridge's owners. Allowing construction of a competing bridge denied those owners' toll revenue (as the new bridge would be toll-free after six years). In the Supreme Judicial Court of Massachusetts, on October 8, 1829, Webster argued "upon strict principle to private rights" to property against the Warren Bridge's counsels' invocation of "free competition" and "public improvements." Webster pleaded that the judiciary, in the form of an injunction against the new bridge (ironic in light of his arguments in *Gibbons* against such impositions on competition), should trump legislative determinations of legal questions (the new bridge being based on an act of the legislature, much like the revision of the Dartmouth charter by legislative action). The older bridge's charter rights conferred real estate rights that the legislature would abridge by sanctioning the new bridge. The Supreme Judicial Court divided, its two Federalists favoring Webster's argument while the two Jacksonian Democrats opposed him. At that point the Charles Bridge proprietors appealed to the US Supreme Court. Argument there in 1831 ended in a deadlocked court. The case was rescheduled.[4]

Charles River Bridge was more than just another case for Webster. Over the first years of its course, Andrew Jackson and his party had swept into the White House and Congress. Appointment of Jacksonians to the federal district courts and the US Supreme Court followed. All that Webster thought secure in politics was vanishing, along with his hope that he would sit in the White House. Perhaps even worse, his legacy in *Dartmouth College, McCulloch,* and *Gibbons* might disappear as populist majorities undermined the security of all private property. For Webster, the winning streak was less important than the precedents. *Charles River Bridge* became a test case of all this, pitting the courts' defense of property against Jacksonian unregulated majoritarianism. Lose this, and what next? Could Webster, by force of personality, legal skill, and precedent, win out?[5]

By 1831 Webster had invested five years of time and research on the case, and it was not nearly over. In the next six years, Webster extensively prepared once again for the US Supreme Court hearing, by which time an archenemy, Roger Taney, had become chief justice. He knew that winning would be difficult, even though he could count on Justice Story's vote (and indeed Story was working for a favorable decision throughout the years between the first and the second hearing, in 1837). It was the presence of Taney in the center chair of the Supreme Court bench that motivated Webster to prove himself the chief justice's intellectual master, but the task was an impossible one.

At oral argument, Webster's co-counsel, Warren Dutton, a lawyer who often worked with Webster, asked, over and over, what is our franchise worth without tolls? What would the profits be if a rival bridge in a more lucrative site competed with us? Surely the power of the legislature to make such policy was limited by natural law. "It may well be doubted whether the nature of society and of government does not prescribe some limits to the legislative power; and if any be prescribed, where are they to be found, if the property of an individual, fairly and honestly acquired, may be seized without compensation." Dutton's views were sincerely held. A former Federalist with a Boston practice, he had gone public with his approval of *McCulloch*, in that the Court had rightly protected the rights of citizens against the impositions of uncontrolled popular legislatures.[6]

Webster's oral argument followed the presentations of the defense counsel. He saw the present suit in light of precedent—in fact, precedent that he helped fashion. It was "was one of a private right, and was to be determined by the fair construction of a contract." Webster was aware that his views were not popular; the proprietors of the old bridge stood in the way of progress. They did it for the wrong reason—to impose tolls. The opposition to tolls was old. It had caused turnpike riots in England. Two years after Webster spoke, Welshmen dressed as women tore down tollbooths to protest taxation there. No one liked tolls. "Much had been said to bring the claims of the plaintiffs in error into reproach," but "this course of remark does not affect their right to their property."[7]

Apparently tired, somewhat grumpy, and already sliding into the increasingly antisocial demeanor that would mark his later days, Webster once again confronted the intractable problem: politically infused law made in the assembly that threatened private rights protected by the courts (he hoped). Once again, as in *Dartmouth College*, *McCulloch*, and *Gibbons*, both the state legislature and state courts favored the political majority. Now the public interest was framed as competitive choice: let the users decide which bridge to cross. Webster had fought for a charter in the *Dartmouth College* case and against a monopolistic charter in *Gibbons*, but the argument in both had been the same—private rights could not be violated and private property diminished because a state government was lobbied to undo the value of a prior contract. The *Charles River Bridge* cause was not merely one of profits, as Dutton implied, but a matter of the inviolability of contract, Webster argued. "It is a question of contract; and if it is so, where is the necessity to inquire whether the plaintiffs have laid out a million, or nothing. If there was a contract, the question is not what was the amount of profit to be derived from it, but what was its provisions." Opposing counsel had obscured that question by opening "new and enlarged grounds." They were "if it gave an exclusive right of making all communications between two places, to a corporation, or to an individual, would operate to prevent the introduction of improved modes of intercourse, as by rail roads; and thus be most extensively injurious to the interests, and stay, to a fatal extent, the prosperity of the community."[8]

Webster turned the tolls argument on its head. For him a vested right was not mere greed; it was a matter of basic principle. "That one [bridge] is sufficient, is shown by the fact, which is not denied, that since the Warren Bridge has become free, all travelers pass over it, and no tolls are received by the proprietors of the Charles River Bridge." Was this proof that only one bridge was necessary? Well, perhaps not. He nevertheless had to concede "that Boston has many of such bridges as that constructed by the plaintiffs. This must necessarily be so." Webster made a distinction. "In fact, in all the cases where rival bridges, or bridges affecting prior rights have been put up; it is understood that there have been agreements with those who were or might be affected by them." When the Harvard College ferry was supplanted by the Charles River Bridge, for example, the college agreed to the arrangement and was compensated with a yearly payment. In all other cases of a similar type, the operators of new bridges came to an accord with the Charles River Bridge corporation. In no case until the present one did a rival bridge company ask the legislature to use its power to authorize direct competition without compensation to the original charter holder. By contrast, the Warren Bridge project in the state legislature "began with a clamour about monopoly! It was asserted, that the public had a right to break up the monopoly which was held by the Charles River Bridge Company; that they had a right to have a free bridge."[9]

What had in the uncertain politics of the postrevolutionary period been a need to establish legal rules for vested rights in the Jacksonian era seemed to be supplanted by a fluidity of property rights. The older public-interest rationale for a monopoly was replaced by a new ethic of fierce and unrelenting competition. Webster offered that "Such a violation of a contract would be fatal to the confidence of the governed in those who govern; and would destroy the security of all property, and all rights derived under it." Thus the issue was framed as competing visions of public/private dichotomy: were the people's property rights better secured by a utilitarian greater good politically determined, or by a strict vested rights jurisprudence?[10]

For a time, the old (that is, Webster's own) version of the public/private divide held sway, at least according to Webster's brief. "Applications were frequently made to the legislature on those principles and for that purpose, during five years, without success; and the bill, authorizing the bridge, when it was first passed by the legislature of Massachusetts, was rejected by the veto of the governor." Then the weight of modernity, of populist property law and legislative law-making, changed the balance.

Webster revisited the federal/state boundary argument with speculation about the thinking of the state legislators. "Members of the legislature consented to the law, on the ground that if it interfered with chartered rights, this Court would set it aside. The argument was, that if the law was a violation of the charter, it would be of no avail. Thus it passed." In fact, the legislature had reversed itself on the petition of the Warren Bridge proprietors in the name of "public convenience and necessity" (after a massive lobbying campaign), not because the legislators wanted the federal courts to tell them what was permissible. It was politics, not law, that won that day for the Warren Bridge in 1828. Webster, not the Massachusetts General Assembly, nor the Massachusetts Supreme Judicial Court, hoped that the US Supreme Court would find for the Charles River Bridge proprietors.[11]

Webster knew perfectly well that the jurisprudential arguments he had made over the years mapping the terrain of the Constitution were losing ground in the federal courts. He could not say that politics had invaded that sanctuary of law, not while facing a political adversary in the center seat on the bench, but he implied it. "It is said, take care! You are treading on burning embers! You are asking to interfere with the rights of the state to make rail roads, and modern improvements, which supersede those of past times by their superiority! You prevent the progress of improvements, essential to the prosperity of the community!" He almost continued that the Constitution must bow to the politics of the day. "It is said that the public are on one side, and the plaintiffs [Charles River Bridge] are on the other." The democracy must have the right of way.

Webster's voice had risen, and he indulged a kind of hyperbolic excess that made little sense in the courtroom but made a lot of sense if he were defending his entire career. For he was once again offering his version of the three issues, this time knowing that he would lose, and with that loss, his bid to join the framers as an interpreter of the Constitution had failed. Realizing this, he allowed something of the rhetorical display of his second reply to Hayne to make its way into the chamber below the Senate.[12]

Of course, one can speculate that the two bridges had for Webster taken on a more intimate and symbolic meaning. The Charles River Bridge had its origin close to Webster's birth. The Warren Bridge was the enterprise of the next generation. To the very real extent that the new bridge would supplant the old in traffic and utility, perhaps, somewhere in the back of Webster's capacious mind, he saw himself being supplanted by the next generation. The replacement of Marshall by Taney reinforced this sense of replacement, and the difference between Marshall's Federalism and Taney's Jacksonianism replicated the ouster of Webster's take on the public/private and political/legal issues by a democratic ethos. One can find generational hints in his argument. For example: "The rights of the plaintiffs are no monopoly. They are the enjoyments of the property for which they had paid in advance; and which, by a contract made by the law, they were entitled to enjoy for twenty years yet to come."[13]

Then Webster returned to the grounds for seeking injunctive relief, the federal Constitution. Bear in mind that at the Constitutional Convention, William Samuel Johnson of Connecticut, who had a large equity practice, added equitable jurisdiction to the powers of the US Supreme Court in Article III. Webster: "The only issue here is the question whether the defendants have infringed the rights of the plaintiffs, and have violated the constitution of the United States"; that is, the Contracts Clause. Webster noted that the Warren Bridge belonged now not to its proprietors but to the State of Massachusetts. This made no difference to him, as the vested right of his client did not derive from a public-interest charter whatever the status of the defendant's bridge might be. In other words, for him it was a straight replay of the *Dartmouth College* case. Could the state be brought into the Court as a party? No, said the Warren Bridge counsel. Yes, said *Fletcher v. Peck*, and yes, said *Osborn v.*

Bank of the United States. Webster had the modesty not to mention *McCulloch*, although it was the precedent for *Osborn.* Everyone on the bench knew, of course, that he had pleaded for the BUS II in both cases.[14]

On and on Webster ran, so long that the reporter, Richard Peters, periodically summarized: "Mr. Webster cited several cases" and "Mr. Webster answered." Webster excused Massachusetts for getting the case wrong. "This particular case, formed an exception to the usual caution exercised by Massachusetts, in legislating upon matters of this kind." Kind of him. He was not so kind to the opposition:

> And there was one other subject, which, though it had no bearing upon the case
> at bar whatever, had been made a great deal of, in the argument of defendants'
> counsel. Some observations upon it had been advanced, by way of connecting
> it with the case, of so novel a kind, as to require, however, some notice. And this
> was, that in chartering the Warren Bridge, the legislature did but exercise its
> power over the eminent domain of the state.

Webster then spent over an hour refuting opposing counsel argument that was irrelevant, "that it cannot tie up its hands in any wise, in regard to its eminent domain." So upset was opposing counsel Simon Greenleaf, on leave as Royall Professor of Law at Harvard Law School, that he interrupted Webster to assert that Massachusetts "was pledged to indemnify the parties; by making full compensation for whatever property the state might take, and for all the injury which should be done to private rights."[15]

On and on Webster trudged, through the English precedents, the rules of equity, another recitation of the facts, a narrative of ferries in Boston from 1641 to the ferry that the Charles River Bridge replaced, a miniature lecture on eminent domain that had little relevance to the case, and an aside on New Jersey franchise law. On and on, as if by wearying the bench he could sway its majority. As long as he was talking, he had not lost. In the end, he conceded the crucial point: "The plaintiffs have placed their reliance upon the precedents and authority established by this honourable Court, in the course of the last thirty years, in support of that constitution which secured individual property against legislative assumption." Then he added a pregnant last note, a note that was neither necessary to make his case nor familiar to anyone who heard him argue cases: "If [the appellants] have not succeeded in sustaining their complaint upon legal and constitutional grounds

. . . they must, as good citizens of this republic, remain satisfied with the decision of the Court."[16]

Whatever did that coda mean? That Webster believed the Supreme Court was the final arbiter of both state and federal litigation was hardly news. That he and other counsel were the least likely to raise rebellion against the decisions of a court of law was common knowledge. He did not need to recite his fidelity to the Constitution. But his enmity toward Taney was so notorious that he may have thought this peace offering was appropriate. It was civil, even polite, and certainly politic. It was unlikely to affect the outcome—Taney was not going to change his mind because Webster avowed his obligation to accept the decision of the Court. No, the last part of the opinion was not about Taney or the Charles River Bridge. It was about Webster. In it, he affirmed his allegiance to the rule of law. That concept would not be formally elucidated until British jurist A. V. Dicey enshrined it in his *Introduction to the Study of the Constitution* (1885). Its central pillars were that law was above political factions and that law duly framed must be obeyed. Webster had already arrived at those conclusions, and his concluding remarks in *Charles River Bridge* affirmed the rule of law.[17]

The Court then held, in a 5 to 2 decision by Taney, that Massachusetts had not violated its contract with the Charles River Bridge Company, and what was more, the interest of the community in cheap and easy transportation outweighed any private chartered rights the Charles River Bridge Company might claim. Webster's oral argument, it might be noted, came second and was the shortest of any of the co-counsel for the two sides. He relied upon co-counsel Warren Dutton's briefs of cases and notes. There was, as well, a discernable note of weariness of mind and body in it. "He rambled" instead of roared, "as if he knew he would lose."[18]

In one narrow sense, the outcome of the case demonstrated that Webster's briefs in *Dartmouth College* and *Gibbons* were at odds, the former holding a private contract based on a state grant safe from state interference, the latter attacking a state grant creating a monopoly for a private entrepreneur. What had held the two briefs together was Webster's energetic certitude that the defense of private property was a public virtue and that courts, not legislatures, were the proper fora for deciding questions of private property. In this sense, private property bridged the gap between political and legal, it being the purpose of the former and the lodestar of the latter. In *Charles River Bridge* the Court found that private property rights bowed before public interest, and competition among private grantees superseded any exclusive right one of those grantees might claim. Before he died, Marshall had come to agree with this position, and Taney, advocating it, carried all but Story and Thompson. Story was on record favoring Webster's view of chartered grants, and Thompson was still indebted to Chancellor Kent and his view of the steamboat cases. The jewel in Webster's crown, *Dartmouth College,* had lost its luster.[19]

Webster's long winning streak had not exactly come to an end, and he was employed to argue cases before the High Court often enough over the next thirteen years, although he was no longer assured of victory. For example, in the so-called Alabama Bank Cases (1837) Webster, as counsel for the BUS II—chartered in Pennsylvania and effectually crippled from doing business in Alabama by a state law favoring its own chartered bank—convinced Taney and the Court to lift the obstacle to operations of out-of-state banks. Webster had based his argument on two grounds: the first that corporations were persons, and so protected by the Privileges and Immunities Clause of the Constitution (Article IV, sec 2, cl. 1), and second that states were obliged to give full faith and credit (the Comity Clause) to the acts of other states. Taney rested his decision on the latter argument. In the License Cases and the Passenger Cases, Webster was again employed by, respectively, opponents of the Massachusetts liquor licensing laws (*Thurlow v. Massachusetts* [1847]) and the Massachusetts tax on incoming ship passengers (*Norris v. City of Boston* [1849]). He lost the former and won the latter, but the Court was so fragmented and the justices' opinions so varied that Webster could hardly have been said to have swayed anyone. While his performance was, according to newspaper reports, up to his usual elegance, his views did not become part of the body of the law. In particular, his belief that federal law trumped state failed in the latter cases, a harbinger of the rising tide of states' rights jurisprudence on the Court.[20]

When he lost, Webster was so upset that he took to his rented rooms and refused to join in any of DC's storied festivities. He never would bring himself to praise Taney in public or in private. He knew as well, as the modern editor of Webster's legal papers relates, that arguments that "went too far in tying the hands of the states" could not prevail in the Taney Court. "If the Court chose to sweep away substantive barriers safeguarding property rights [against the state impositions], at least he could struggle to maintain the integrity of the constitutional process." Webster was still capable of adding bits to constitutional jurisprudence, however; for example, political question exceptions to judicial intervention in *Luther v. Borden* (1849). In representing a group of men who acted as agents of the existing government of Rhode Island against those who forcibly tried to impose a new (and more democratic) constitution, he told the Court: "What do the Constitution and laws of the United States say upon this point? The Constitution recognizes the existence of States, and guarantees to each a republican form of government, and to protect them against domestic violence. The thing which is to be protected is the existing State government." These arguments were acceptable to the Taney Court not least because they deferred to state sovereignty.[21]

The lines that Webster had so carefully drawn between ordinary politics and court-made law seemed to him erased. So too were the distinctions between the public interest and private rights. In the rage for democracy, no one's property was safe. The federal courts no longer stood as sentinels against state legislative encroachment on the private sphere. The lessons of the American Revolution—as Webster understood them, and the basis of republican virtue, as he understood it—had been forgotten. As he wrote in his notes for argument in *Boston and Lowell Railroad*, on January 20, 1845, "the duties of the Legislature [of Massachusetts] are grave; especially as they may alter charters. This is an outcry against 'Vested Rights.' It began with *Warren Bridge*."[22]

Webster would have other opportunities to defend his version of the Constitution. For example, as co-counsel (with his great rival Henry Clay) in *Groves v. Slaughter* (1841) he tried to reassert portions of his jurisprudence into a case that ill fit them. The issue was whether a purchaser of slaves could refuse to honor the promissory notes he had given the sellers, in part payment for the slaves. The buyer's case rested on a provision of the Mississippi constitution (where he lived) that no slaves could be brought into the state from out of state after 1833. The legislature of Mississippi had not, however, passed enabling legislation until 1837. Knowing this, or perhaps ignoring it, he had attempted to bring slaves into the state from the New Orleans slave market, the leading source of slaves in the Deep South in 1836. The buyer lost in the circuit court, and again in the US Supreme Court. But the case raised collateral issues familiar to Webster. Could the federal courts, in ruling for the sellers, confute both the Constitution and the legislation of Missouri? Could courts uphold a contract for sale of slaves in the face of a popular measure against the importation of slaves passed by a state legislature? Would property (and the law of property) be safe against local politics? Webster's argument was condensed. Richard Peters, the Supreme Court reporter, did not accord Webster's arguments the license that his predecessor, Henry Wheaton, allowed. But Webster's central point was clear, even in summary form.

> For what purpose, but for such as is exhibited in this case, was the judicial power given to the Courts of the United States, to be exercised in controversies between the citizens of different states? This was the very object. It was intended to give the citizens of one state a power to sue citizens of another state, in an independent tribunal. Now, it is contended, that when a citizen of Virginia sues in a Court of the United States, he is to be bound by the decisions of the state tribunals. This defeats the provision in the Constitution of the United States. It is a mockery, if this is to be the law.[23]

In 1840 Webster's yearning for the presidency was once more dashed when he agreed to step aside for Indiana's William Henry Harrison, an aging scion of one of the first families of Virginia then living in Indiana. The consolation prize was appointment to Harrison's cabinet as secretary of state. Harrison died shortly after his inauguration, weary with years. Vice President John Tyler, a Democrat, kept Webster on for a time, and from 1841 to 1843, Webster negotiated the end of unofficial hostilities with Great Britain over the Maine and Great Lakes borders. The secretary of state post gave Webster a chance to burnish his reputation as a statesman and, secretly, to find the means to pay off some of his debts. Moreover, his stint in the state department afforded Webster the chance to explore constitutional jurisprudence from an international perspective. It should have ended well.[24]

7. "The Rule of Law": Webster the Diplomat, 1841–1843

Chastened by the failure of the Whigs to nominate him for the presidency in the 1840 campaign and harried by his creditors, Webster looked for respite across the Atlantic to England. He was, according to his foremost biographer, "an ardent, almost rabid, Anglophile." He could not convince President Martin Van Buren, a Democrat and Jackson follower, to name him as a special envoy to Britain (the Canadian-US boundary dispute was again overheating), but Webster was able to pledge his western lands as collateral for the funds to travel and stay abroad. Among the "lions" he met were members of Britain's diplomatic corps. He and wife Caroline also had an audience with Queen Victoria. Feted and refreshed, Webster returned to the United States to find that he would officially negotiate the boundary dispute. For newly elected Whig president William Henry Harrison would name Webster his secretary of state.[1]

One of the foremost duties of the secretary of state was assisting the president in the conduct of diplomacy. As many of the leading American politicians had held this post, including Jefferson, Madison, James Monroe, John Quincy Adams, and Henry Clay, Webster could hardly refuse, though his personal finances were once more in considerable disarray. It was a time when the Texas Question (and with that, potential war with the Mexican Republic) and the hostilities along the Maine–New Brunswick border raised the prospect of war. Britain's aggressive naval suppression of the overseas slave trade, aggravated by the Jackson administration's refusal to pay alleged debts, made the job of negotiating with Britain anything but easy. On top of these ongoing diplomatic quarrels, the issues raised with the Spanish government by the *Amistad* case had finally to be resolved, and the impressment of seamen by the Royal Navy had once again arisen. Webster's signal triumph in office, however, was the Webster-Ashburton Treaty of 1842.[2]

The relationship between the treaty power, defined in the US Constitution, and domestic sources of law, including the decisions of the US Supreme Court and the acts of Congress, has always been a complicated one. Article II, section 2, clause 2, addresses the treaty power, "[The President] shall have Power, by and with the Advice and Consent of the Senate, to make Treaties, provided two-thirds of the Senators present concur." The Supremacy Clause of the US

Constitution classes treaties with federal laws as the supreme law of the land, but it does not say that either type of law is superior to the other. Some very early statute law suggests that concepts of international law (law of nations; law of war) apply in federal courts with or without a treaty. For example, the Alien Tort Statute of 1789 said that "the district courts shall have original jurisdiction of any civil action by an alien for a tort only, committed in violation of the law of nations or a treaty of the united states."[3]

However, the federal courts have regularly found that domestic legislation, in the words of constitutional scholar Akhil Amar, trumps treaties. As well, Congress has the practical power to void or repeal a treaty by legislation, which suggests that the treaty is subject to domestic federal law. If a treaty is executory, that is, requires legislation (for example, appropriations) to go into effect, Congress can simply refuse to pass the legislation. The president has the power to abrogate a treaty by not enforcing it. In reverse fashion, some constitutional scholars have argued that the US Constitution is international law. If that is so, then the federal government's relations with foreign nations should conform to general international law precepts. As Chief Justice Marshall opined in *The Schooner Peggy* (1801), "Where a treaty is the law of the land, and as such affects the rights of parties litigating in court, that treaty as much binds those rights and is as much to be regarded by the court as an act of congress." Nevertheless, modern cases have shown that international law does not bind domestic courts, either of the states or the United States. While many of these are later than the period covered in this volume, the classics of international law of treaties in the works of Emmerich de Vattel, Hugo Grotius, and Samuel von Pufendorf were well known to American diplomats like John Adams and Thomas Jefferson, and presumably they and their generation faced the same problems of adjudication that exist today.[4]

The American experience with actual treaties was complicated. The nation began with two treaties, one among the states, creating the Articles of Confederation and its Congress (fully ratified in 1781), and the other, the Treaty of Paris (1783), ending the War for Independence against Great Britain, and ratified by the warring powers in that year. The provisions of both treaties were soon the subject of considerable controversy. Questions about the efficacy of the Articles were finally settled with the federal Constitution, with the exception of the three issues discussed throughout this book. The peace treaty of 1783 also raised serious problems, in particular concerning British occupation of portions of the Great Lakes, Royal Navy impressing of American sailors and seizure of American ships and cargoes during the Wars of the French Revolution and the Napoleonic period, and the unwillingness of American debtors to repay pre-war debts to British creditors. Commissions set up to settle the matter failed to resolve anything, and the Jay Treaty of 1795 did little more. The War of 1812 and the Treaty of Ghent (1815) did not resolve these issues, save to demonstrate a growing British interest in exploiting the Canadian interior. A simmering war along the Maine frontier with the British colony of New Brunswick and a looming conflict over the border between the Oregon Territory and British Columbia in the West added to the potential for a new war between the two powers. To be sure, treaties with foreign lands had not always brought troubles in their train. Treaties added the Louisiana Territory and West Florida to the national domain, and treaties quieted relations between the US and Spanish possessions in the Southwest and later the Mexican Republic—at least until Texas declared and won its independence from Mexico in 1836 and began to agitate for annexation.[5]

Treatises with Indian nations did not settle anything. Although the Indians were classed in law as foreign nations, and relations with them took the form of diplomatic negotiations, as soon as the number and political clout of their US neighbors was sufficient, Indian treaties were abrogated by an act of Congress or not enforced at all. In Webster's time, the Indian Removal Act of 1830 trumped a slew of US-Indian treaties, insofar as it permitted President Jackson to renegotiate treaties guaranteeing Indian peoples' possession of the lands they occupied. The act would "exchange" lands west of the Mississippi owned by the federal government with lands primarily in the Southeast presently occupied by the Cherokee and other peoples, guaranteeing to those who voluntarily agreed to the exchange that the new residence would be theirs in perpetuity. The act was a fraud, as everyone on both sides of the issue knew that Jackson wanted the removal of the Indians, by force if necessary, with or without their consent. The state of Georgia intervened in this process by ordering the removal of resident Indians—a removal that shortly thereafter federal troops abetted. Jackson and Governor Wilson Lumpkin of Georgia ignored the decision of the Marshall Court in *Wooster v. Georgia* (1832) that the treaty obligations superseded state law and that the US government was required to fulfill its obligations to the Cherokee and other tribes under the treaties. Jackson, hardly a friend to native peoples, portrayed himself instead as their protector. Webster knew differently and voted against the Indian Removal Act and the forcible relocation of the Indians, but he did not speak on the matter.[6]

In sum, the treaty was a third type of law mentioned in the Constitution, alongside case law (precedent) and legislation, whose precise status relative to those more familiar domestic sources of law was unclear. Indeed, the expression itself, like the terms *obligation, necessary and proper,* and *commerce,* was not defined elsewhere in the Constitution. Could Webster apply his answers to the three conundrums to the treaty power? For example, were treaties supposed to be above politics? Were treaties that affected private rights subject to public policy concerns? Could states interfere in treaty commitments? Appointment as secretary of state would, Webster hoped, remove him from party politics, though he owed the appointment to his strong support for Harrison, and, as he told a correspondent during the campaign, he could never take a seat on the High Court bench because he was too "mixed up" in politics.[7]

When president-elect William Henry Harrison died and vice-president elect John Tyler made clear his intention to assume the full duties and honors of the position, Webster had to decide where his loyalties lay. He had been Harrison's right-hand man from the time that the Indiana politician arrived in Washington—despite their party and regional differences—but Webster soon developed a strong working relationship with Tyler. They had known one another from the Senate, and they both detested Henry Clay. This, and Webster's attachment to the emoluments of the Department of State, convinced him to remain as along as he was wanted. His diplomatic performance was greatly helped by his admiration of the English and his accord with Alexander Baring, Lord Ashburton when the latter finally arrived in Washington at the end of 1841. At the end of the grueling negotiations over the northern boundary, for example, Webster hosted a dinner for Ashburton and President Tyler. The toasts were genuine, even effusive, and none more so than Tyler's "blessed are the peacemakers." Blessed too were Webster's New England allies, whose lobbying got the treaty past Senate Whigs hostile to both Tyler and Webster.[8]

Webster's service was highly useful, but without a real antagonist against whom to match his abilities, Webster did not shine as he had in Court or in Congress. His more menial instincts instead leeched away any higher sense of duty, and he used the post to repay debts and settle petty spites. The secretary of state was supposed to be a statesman, representing his country to the world. Cast literally and figurative in this way, the secretary of state's role in the treaty power could be the epitome of constitutional lawmaking: above politics, an embodiment of federal supremacy, a clearly distinguishing mark of public interest. Unfortunately, during his tenure, from 1841 through mid-1843, Webster could not escape his personal woes. There was the house in Washington, DC, that he must have. And have it he did. And his estate in Marshfield must have a fish pond, which he added. To repay or put off debts, Webster needed cash, and for that he began to auction off diplomatic positions in his command. The venality of even the most revered statesmen will hardly surprise readers of history, but oh those debts. Webster was a desperate man.[9]

If there was any form of salvation, it would come in his work. He took his diplomatic tasks seriously by all accounts. To them he brought not only his well-honed skills as a negotiator but his conceptions of jurisprudence and his political acumen. The main event in Webster's tenure as Tyler's secretary of state was settling the long-standing and sometimes violent border dispute between the state of Maine and the British-Canadian colony of New Brunswick. The northern border was apparently the home of both settlers and ruffians, a border crossed with ill intent during the Revolutionary War, the War of 1812, and the so-called Aroostook War of 1838–1839. In fact, one might say that peace only occasionally broke out along the northern border. During the War of 1812, the British coveted eastern Maine, but the Treaty of Ghent did not result in any territorial transfers. So the undeclared, sporadic conflict between the Americans and the Canadians, with Indians on both sides, continued. The final phase—the war of words, threats, and occasional musket discharges (no one died; no formal military forces were involved, however) along the Aroostook River Valley, with its valuable store of white pines—plagued both the United States and Britain. Earlier attempts at settlements, including rival census taking and the solicited mediation of the king of the Netherlands (ironically a settlement that almost perfectly anticipated that of 1842), ended with no resolution. A treaty proposed in 1831 was rejected by the US Senate as well as by the state of Maine. In the meantime, Maine was engaging in both diplomatic and military activities that violated the federal Constitution. In an attempt to forestall Maine's actions, Congress authorized the raising of troops to defend Maine should the troops New Brunswick had armed crossed the border—wherever that might be.[10]

Webster thus had a task that none before him had achieved: an amicable settlement to which Maine, Massachusetts, Canadian, and British authorities agreed, none more seriously than the negotiation that led to the northern border. The negotiations actually began informally when Webster was in England.

When he returned, after he began his correspondence with Edward Everett, the US ambassador in Westminster, Webster laid out his approach. No sword rattling. Instead, "it is only by the exercise of calm reason, that truth can be arrived at in questions of a complicated nature." This was especially true in the northern boundary case, "between states, each of which understands and respect the intelligence of the power of the other." Thus the best diplomacy was like a law case, and negotiations in it "necessarily constitute a tribunal august in character and formidable in its decisions." Diplomacy, rightly performed, "upon the rules of natural justice, moral property, the usages of modern times, and the prescriptions of public law," could resolve all differences between nations. They must accept the outcome, as the parties to a lawsuit must accept the court's decision. Everett, himself a Whig, an educator, an orator, and a former Massachusetts governor and member of Congress, surely understood what Webster meant. In fact, the two were close friends from the time that young Everett attended Webster's brother Ezekiel's school, and later in life the two men visited one another often. There was thus no need for Webster to tutor, enlighten, prompt, or condescend to Everett. In effect, Webster was simply stating their shared ideals for diplomacy.[11]

Webster kept his eye out for maps of the disputed lands between the Canadian colony of New Brunswick and the state of Maine. Earlier attempts at drawing the line had failed to use maps in King George III's map room that favored the US position. Webster found one that seemed to grant most of the land to Canada, a later map that was used at the peace talks in 1781, which he concealed from Ashburton. According to the *Federal Rules of Civil Procedure*, the concealment of evidence is not today allowed in "discovery" during litigation. Then it was commonplace. Instead of producing the map, Webster placed newspaper pieces in Whig venues, lobbied the Maine legislature, and made payments to Maine political figures from a secret congressional fund. He managed to arrange a deal. Webster was careful to write as the representative of the president: "The president thinks it a highly desirable object to prevent the delays," he told Governor John Fairfield of Maine in April, as the negotiations progressed. New Brunswick got 50,000 square miles, Maine got 75,000 square miles, and both sides got a $125,000 sweetener from the from the British government.[12]

The fact that Webster knew and had developed a strong personal relationship with his British counterpart, Lord Ashburton, a financier and merchant rather than a career diplomat, and that the British government wanted the issue resolved swiftly, did not hurt either. Ashburton arrived in the United States in late February, and although the two men met frequently thereafter in Washington, formal diplomatic relations also required writing notes to one another. These were formulaic to some extent, but neither man was a veteran or career diplomat, and neither relied on an assistant or staff to write the notes. Indeed, among the powers of the West, the United States had invested the least in the pomp and circumstance of diplomacy, relying on talented amateurs like Everett, a minister by trade, and Webster. (Even the greats of early American diplomacy, like Benjamin Franklin, John Jay, John Quincy Adams, and Robert Livingston, were not career diplomats.) Some historians have even accused Webster of accepting bribes from various sources in the course of the negotiations. The solicitation of bribes, for example in the XYZ Affair of 1797–1798, was not unusual in diplomatic relations. Whatever the truth of such allegations, for Webster, the notes he prepared were something very much like his notes for oral argument, albeit in complete sentences rather than bullet points.[13]

Consider next the case of Alexander McLeod. McLeod had (or had not, depending on whom one believed) taken part on a British-run attack on an American ship, the *Caroline*, moored in American waters in 1837 during the Upper (eastern) Canadian Rebellion against Great Britain. Three years later, he was apprehended in New York after boasting of his role in the raid. A New York State grand jury had handed down a true bill against him for murder and arson. The British government appealed to Webster's predecessor, John Forsythe, to free McLeod, as he had acted under the orders of the British colonial government as a soldier in a military operation. When the State Department delayed, demanding evidence of the latter claim from the appropriate British authority, British prime minister Lord Palmerston threatened to begin military operations against the state of New York. When evidence in the form of a letter from British ambassador Henry Fox was delivered to Webster that McLeod had acted under orders, he promised that the matter would be laid before President Tyler.

In his reply to Fox, Webster could simply have stated that the federal government could not intervene in a state criminal prosecution (the Habeas Corpus Act of 1869 allowed for such removal). Recognizing the discomfort of the British, Webster reported that the president and the state of New York had agreed to move the trial from the vicinage, inflamed over the events, to the state supreme court in Albany. Webster then treated Fox to a long and detailed treatise on the respective jurisdictions of the federal and state governments, an essay similar to those he interspersed throughout his oral arguments in court.

Enclosed in the reply to Fox was a letter he had written three days after receiving Fox's appeal, to John J. Crittenden, attorney general of the United states, that the president wished Crittenden to attend the trial, and that should the trial court not accept the evidence that McLeod acted in the capacity of a soldier under orders, Crittenden should aid McLeod's American counsel in removing the case by a writ of error to the Supreme Court of the United States. There the law of war, part of the law of nations, could be applied to the case. New York governor William Henry Seward wanted the trial to go forward, not because he wanted to embarrass Tyler's administration but because he desired to protect the state's criminal justice system (he had long been in favor of reform in prisons and law enforcement). When McLeod's attorney turned out to be Tyler's new attorney for the district of New York, Joshua Spencer, Seward cried foul. Webster backed away, but he continued to watch the trial closely. The preparation that went into these diplomatic notes was equivalent to that Webster put into his arguments before the High Court. In fact, the New York jury did not convict McLeod, as an alibi conveniently provided at the trial proved decisive.[14]

In his letter to Fox, perhaps the reason that it took over a month for him to reply, Webster set out a test for McLeod's conduct that went far beyond Webster's role as a diplomat. Donning the robes of the judge (that he refused to wear throughout his career), he argued that the destruction of the *Caroline*, at anchor on an island in the Niagara River between the United States and Canada, could only be justified if it was done in self-defense against imminent attack by the ship or those on it against Canada. Then, McLeod, who was a sheriff on the Canadian side of the river, would be judged innocent under international law. The opinion was not official in any sense—Webster was not a judge on a court of international law. Neither was he asked for an opinion as an expert on the law of war. However, his criteria, that the preemptive attack must be the only alternative open to the attackers, has become known as the "*Caroline* test" and is still in use.[15]

A second, more relevant issue, at least insofar as Webster's prior thinking about federalism was involved, was this: How was the federal government to tell a sovereign state (here, New York) how to run its criminal justice system? In international law, the case was relatively simple. McLeod was a soldier acting under orders to suppress a domestic rebellion. The state of New York, actually Seward, did not see it that way. Its constitution had explicitly received (adopted) the common law, which many authorities believed included the law of war. Instead, it applied its own criminal law to the case, the case presented to the grand jury in New York simply as one of murder and arson. Civil War–era legislation would provide for removal of such trials from state courts to federal courts, but at this time only crimes defined by federal law (for example, piracy), crimes committed against the federal government (for example, treason), and crimes committed on federal territory were triable in federal criminal courts. As a result, on August, 29, 1842, Congress passed "an Act to provide further remedial justice in the courts of the United States," giving district court judges and the Supreme Court justices authority to return habeas corpus writs for foreign nationals held in state courts for acts committed under the order of foreign powers. A hearing before the federal tribunal would determine whether the act was, in fact, ordered by a foreign government. If so, the individual would be discharged from confinement and set free. In this sense, the law of nations became the statute law of the United States. It was not wholly of Webster's doing, but it was a noteworthy event.[16]

A parting shot on the *Caroline* incident appeared in a formal note from Webster to Lord Ashburton during the resolution of the northeastern boundary (discussed below). The two men had developed a friendship when Webster was in England, and they genuinely respected one another. Formality was mixed with a stiff cordiality in their correspondence over the *Caroline*, as it had been over the McLeod affair. Webster wrote that the acts in which the *Caroline* was engaged (allegedly bringing guns and ammunition to Canadian rebels) notwithstanding, the fact that Canadian forces burned the ship while it was moored in American waters was "of itself a wrong, and an offense to the sovereignty and the dignity of the United States, being a violation of their soil and territory." The British government had not, at the time of the letter to Ashburton, offered "atonement or apology." The honor of the American nation and its "sensitiveness" thus remained a subject for Ashburton's "grave consideration."[17]

This stiff-necked nationalism of portions of the correspondence in the two cases was not mere patriotic fustian or punctilious formula. Webster's ideal American nation was conceived in law. It was a law-abiding nation and expected the same from other nations. The true Constitution was to be rooted in law, not self-dealing or political advantage. For example, when it came to international law of slavery, consider Webster's handling of the highly charged *Creole* case in 1842. The brig had left Hampton Roads in Virginia bound for New Orleans with a crew, two of the owners, and 135 slaves. On November 7, 1841, within sight of the British colony of the Bahamas, nineteen of the slaves rebelled, killing one of the owners and wounding several of the crew. When, two days later, the ship docked in Nassau, the British authorities, at the urging of the colony's black population, freed all but the nineteen, and after five months of their confinement, decided not to prosecute them. (In 1833, Parliament had passed the Emancipation Act, ending slavery in all British territories.) True, slavers bound for the United States, in violation of international treaties and federal law, often posed as domestic coastal shipping. Still, the southern Democratic outcry against the British in Congress was loud and long. President Tyler was himself a slave owner and defender of slavery (he would, in retirement, support secession), and he bid Webster scold Ashburton.[18]

Webster's views of the slave trade were well known from his 1820 Pilgrim Landing speech. They had not changed. As he told Justice Story, "We have not considered as fugitives from justice either the slaves who were concerned in the mutiny nor those who were not, and therefore have made no demand for the delivery of either (from the British authorities)." In fact, he concealed in his formal note to Ashburton something of these very sentiments in a kind of code. He cited the rule of law, the comity of nations, and the customary law of the sea, as well as the differences between slave law in the United States and the law of freedom in Britain, to insist that American property be returned to its rightful owners. Webster then inserted the following somewhat awkwardly placed passage in the middle of a paragraph on interrupted voyages of American ships: "If slaves, the property of citizens of the United States, escape into the British territories, it is not expected that they will be restored. In that case, the territorial jurisdiction of England will have become exclusive over them and must decide their condition." This was an entirely new view of the British carrying off slaves during the Revolutionary War and the War of 1812. Webster was flying here under false colors; that is, he was not representing the established American position, but his own. Story's opinion for the Court in the *Amistad* case was not precedent, as the slaves of that ship were brought ashore on American soil.[19]

Ashburton's reply was shorter and just as formal, explaining that he had no brief to settle the matter, nor had Her Majesty's government decided on the question of reparations. A payment of $110,000 would eventually arrive in 1853, but more important was Ashburton's response to Webster's coded passage: "You admit that if slaves, the property of American citizens, escape into British territories, it is not expected that they will be restored." Ashburton then misstated American law: "nor need I remind you that it is exactly the same with the laws of every part of the United States where a state of slavery is not recognized." At the time, only a handful of northern states had passed what would later be called personal liberty laws, protecting to some extent the freedom of black residents. In the main, however, runaway slaves were still subject to capture in free territory and returned to their masters or mistresses. To be sure, Ashburton might simply have gotten slave law in the United States wrong, but why include the passage at all in a note explaining why he could do nothing about the matter? It seems more likely that Ashburton was signaling his reception and approval of Webster's views.[20]

Webster reveled in the accolades that followed the boundary dispute settlement, but they were short lived. Clay's friends were targeting Webster, and their arrows were starting to hit the mark. They accused him of adultery, though he denied it, and pandering to the Democrats, which was at least partly true. It was "a dreadful pounding" in public, accentuated by his personal problems. His debts were accumulating and his credit was disappearing. Even his preeminence in Massachusetts politics was faltering, as advocates of Clay's program of internal improvements saw Webster as a liability. His loyalty to Tyler was the last straw. He was now a man without a party. He hung on in the administration, making a botch of Mexican policy but playing a useful part in what would become the open door to the China trade. This was part of the "Tyler Doctrine" that Webster crafted in the closing days of 1842—an expansionist plan for American interests in the Pacific and for Hawai'i in particular. There was more to do—about the Turks and the Greeks, a subject that had interested him twenty years previously; about Oregon; and the boundary from the Great Lakes to the Pacific; about so many things—but he was tired, and Marshfield and the sea called to him. He resigned, under fire, on May 8, 1843.[21]

His first two-and-one-half years as secretary of state had proven Webster capable of true statesmanship, but lurking in the corners were his taste for high living and his almost pathetic need for approval. As he grew older, this need began to overshadow his talents and shade his achievements. Looking to put behind him both partisanship and corruption, Webster faced the prospect of the dissolution of the Union over the slavery question with genuine horror. Only through the sacrifices of someone of his stature, so he believed, could there be some way to avert this peril.

8. "Union Now and Forever": The Calhoun-Webster Exchange in the Senate, March 4–7, 1850

After many years of unfulfilled yearning for the White House, a multitude of sessions in the Senate watching the rise of the hated Democratic Party, and a stint as Tyler's secretary of state ending with his undeserved departure, Webster physically was little more than a shell of his once robust self. The goal of wealth had proved an illusion. Years of spending more than he earned had left him saddled with debt. The right to private property had been his guiding light. Now that was fading, along with his aspirations to national, as opposed to regional, leadership. A return to the Senate in 1845 gave him a forum, but the light of ambition that had burned so brightly in his career was flickering. In 1848 the death of son Edward from typhoid fever while serving in the Mexican American War, and the passing, three days later, of daughter Julia from tuberculosis so depressed Webster that all thoughts of political advancement faded. The Whig Party had turned to other men with a military rather than a legal background. His hopes flickered, then died, when the hero of the Mexican American War, Zachary Taylor, was nominated.[1]

Webster had never compartmentalized his legal and his political careers. Like many of his senatorial cohorts in the Supreme Court bar, he would finish his arguments before the Court in the basement and walk up the stairs to the Senate chamber to hear debate or conduct business at his desk. In private correspondence he revealed disappointment and, sometimes, rancor. In public, he wore a more politic face.[2]

Nevertheless, the long campaign to save the charter of the Charles River Bridge took something from Webster that political defeats and growing indebtedness had not—it proved that a new generation had little use for Webster's constitutional jurisprudence. The attempt to fill the gaps in the Constitution, to draw the boundaries between politics and law, public use and private rights, that Webster and a friendly Supreme Court had earlier assayed, were now discarded or recast by the Jacksonian Democracy. Whigs in Congress and the White House had to adopt many of the tactics of the Democracy to win office. The new generation of politicians besotted themselves with the issue of slavery, an issue that Webster had avoided most of his career. In the maelstrom they unwisely stirred, could the relationship between federal power and state sovereignty that Webster and Marshall had labored to define be at stake as well?[3]

If the draining impact of the *Charles River Bridge* case, abetted by advancing age, was apparent on him, he could not afford to slow down. But by the 1840s, in case after case, Webster submitted incomplete or hurried briefs, argued before increasingly inhospitable benches, collected his fees, and moved on to the next case. More and more often, his argument in these cases was reported in part only or not reported at all. A great career in law was ending.[4]

In the Senate, however, his speeches remained a magnet for the very democracy he decried. Rich and poor filled the galleries and the aisles to hear him. Acoustics in the old Senate chamber were remarkably fine (compared to the terrible acoustics in the House), and Webster's big voice accommodated the throng, much as an opera performer at the Met sings to the back of the hall. His second reply to Robert Hayne had made him the spokesman of a free people. The debate over the Henry Clay compromise bills in 1850 solidified his reputation as a Union man. But could he remain faithful to the jurisprudential theory that underlay so much of his legal career and diplomacy in the face of the new and more ominous round of southern secession threats? In a speech he would later call "Union Now and Forever," he offered his answer to that challenge.[5]

At the center of the tempest in the Senate was the balance of free and slave states in Congress. Despite both John Quincy Adams's and Martin Van Buren's efforts, Congress and the outgoing president, John Tyler, offered Texas the chance to enter the Union by treaty as one state. Were it divided into multiple states, it would have upset the balance. The incoming president, James K. Polk, urged Texas to accept the terms of the absorption treaty, and in 1846 Texas formally became a state. Its annexation, matched by the admission of Iowa two years later, kept the balance between slave and free states, but it teetered with each new application for statehood.[6]

The annexation of Texas, followed by US claims to a border on the Rio Grande, brought Mexico and the United States to the brink of war. President

Polk ordered American troops to patrol the Rio Grande aggressively, and a clash with Mexican forces led to a declaration of war in Congress in 1846. It was a war that slave states wanted and free states dreaded, for all the territory that might come with victory, including the future states of New Mexico, Arizona, and California, might be slave states. John Quincy Adams had become the foremost voice opposed to the admission of Texas precisely because it would expand the domain of slavery, but a stroke crippled him for much of 1846 and he was unable to attend Congress. If he had been in his seat, he would have applauded David Wilmot, a Pennsylvania Whig, who sought to forestall that event by proposing that no territory acquired from Mexico would be open to slavery. In the House, where free states' population gave them a majority of members, the Wilmot proviso won; Wilmot made clear that his proposal was based on "viewing slavery as I do." Meanwhile, in the Senate, led by John C. Calhoun, a majority did not agree to pass the proviso. He deplored the proviso and the language accompanying it as an example of "blind fanaticism . . . daringly opposed to the Constitution."[7]

The public discourse over slavery in the debates over the admission of California to the Union as a free state and the imposition of a new federal fugitive slave law all but immobilized the Senate in late winter of 1850. By 1850 the nation could no longer avoid the slavery issue. Since 1819 it had been marching from the edge to the center of national political discourse. Like Fortinbras and the Norwegian forces in Hamlet, its approach could not be stayed. As in the play about a regime change, words became signs of coming upheaval. Congress seemed mesmerized by the topic of the expansion of slavery. Once more, fears of secession of parts of the Union so real and so pervasive in the Confederation period emerged. Faced with the threat that the South would secede if the admission of California as a free state were to upset the balance in the Senate—a threat made all too real by the escalating rhetoric in Congress—Webster's old rival Henry Clay of Kentucky pulled together a series of compromise bills. Thirty years earlier, Clay had engineered the Missouri Compromise, which included a promise that no territory north of the latitude 36°30′ (Missouri's southern boundary) would come into the Union as a slave state. California straddled the line. Its voters had decided that they did not want slavery (or the presence of free persons of color, for that matter). Clay proposed that California enter as a free state and that a powerful new federal fugitive slave law accompany its admission. The Fugitive Slave Act of 1850 provided for federal commissioners in the North to aid southern slave catchers.

Finally, a bill would have ended the slave trade in the District of Columbia—the objective of antislavery petitions to Congress since 1835.[8]

In response, two of the most famous—perhaps *the* most famous—of all speeches in the Congress came within four days of each other, on March 4 and March 7, 1850. South Carolina's Calhoun delivered the first; Webster supplied the second. Both were seemingly about the compromise legislation that Henry Clay had authored. The frankness with which they confronted the issue of disunion demonstrated how close secession loomed. Calhoun's address summarized arguments he had made as early as the exposition of 1828. Webster's address appeared to be a bombshell, departing from his private belief in the evil of slavery to plead for the survival of the Union. Both were made by very able lawyer/politicians, and both offered legalistic solutions to the problem of disunity. One may, as with the Hayne-Webster exchange, regard them as warring briefs: one for the South, and the other for the Union.[9]

Calhoun, fatally ill with tuberculosis, was carried into the Senate chamber on a couch by his Virginia colleague James Mason and South Carolina's Andrew Pickens Butler. Mason read Calhoun's speech. It warned of secession if the Congress did not go far enough to protect southern interests. All the previous fall, Calhoun had been sounding the call for secession if more concessions were not made to the South. Note that Calhoun divided the country into North and South, not pro- and antislavery or Whig versus Democrat. Party divisions, he rightly saw, had been replaced by sectional divisions.[10]

Calhoun invoked long personal experience in national politics. For much of his career in Congress he had defended the institution of slavery with fierce logic and genuine commitment. He was also a Unionist. The two now clashed. "I have, senators, believed from the first that the agitation of the subject of slavery would, if not prevented by some timely and effective measure, end in disunion." His fears of disunion were real enough. Even as he addressed the Senate, "fire-eating" politicians in the South, notably Robert Barnwell Rhett of South Carolina, were agitating for secession. They would gather shortly in Nashville, Tennessee, to debate whether to form a new nation based on the protection of slavery.

The pressure on the Whig Party in the South, a bastion of unionist sentiment, was unrelenting and almost unbearable, as politician after politician left his Whig moorings and sailed to the Democratic harbor. "The agitation has been permitted to proceed with almost no attempt to resist it, until it has reached a point when it can no longer be disguised or denied that the Union is in danger. You have thus had forced upon you the greatest and gravest question that can ever come under your consideration: How can the Union be preserved?" Calhoun thought the answer was plain. "There can be but one answer—that the immediate cause is the almost universal discontent which pervades all the States composing the Southern section of the Union." The cause of the discontent was the prospect of a northern assault on the South's peculiar institution. "This widely extended discontent is not of recent origin. It commenced with the agitation of the slavery question and has been increasing ever since."[11]

Calhoun's reasoning was as much economic as it was political. He was a believer in statistical evidence. Calhoun assumed that American economic progress rested on the export of southern staples, and the Mississippi River was the great outlet for those exports—particularly cotton and sugar—to the world. But Calhoun saw danger as well as opportunity in the Mississippi waterway, for the upper reaches of the Mississippi lay in the Midwest, the home of much of the "long-continued agitation of the slave question on the part of the North, and the many aggressions which they have made on the rights of the South." The result was that "the equilibrium between the two sections in the government as it stood when the Constitution was ratified and the government put in action has been destroyed."

Calhoun had seen the growth of the Free Soil territories, expanding to the West, and the slave territories confined, imprisoned in the existing lands of the South. Slavery so confined would consume itself, and the section with it. "The result of the whole is to give the Northern section a predominance in every department of the government, and thereby concentrate in it the two elements which constitute the federal government: a majority of States, and a majority of their population, estimated in federal numbers. Whatever section concentrates the two in itself possesses the control of the entire government." It was simply a matter of statistics—of numbers, space, and wealth.[12]

Calhoun saw the final outcome as occurring not within weeks or months but eventually:

> Unless something decisive is done, I again ask, what is to stop this agitation before the great and final object at which it aims—the abolition of slavery in the States— is consummated? Is it, then, not certain that if something is not done to arrest it,

the South will be forced to choose between abolition and secession? Indeed, as events are now moving, it will not require the South to secede in order to dissolve the Union. Agitation will of itself effect it, of which its past history furnishes abundant proof.

The movement against slavery had gone from a relative handful of reformers seeking to persuade southerners to give up slavery to a national political movement. Calhoun did not differentiate between the Free Soilers, who simply did not want slavery to expand into new territories, and the abolitionists, who wanted to end slavery where it already existed. Perhaps in his mind the two were synonymous, or perhaps he thought the Free Soil movement would eventually become abolitionism. In fact, the Free Soil movement would be folded into the new Republican Party in 1856, but that party's platform never endorsed the forcible freeing of slaves in the slave states. It was fear for the future, rather than current political realities, that drove Calhoun's thinking on this point.[13]

Calhoun had reached the peroration, the concluding portion of his address. Every ear must have been strained to the utmost to hear Mason read what Calhoun had written. This was his final hour, and his address lived up to it. "If the agitation goes on, the same force, acting with increased intensity, as has been shown, will finally snap every cord, when nothing will be left to hold the States together except force." Surely there was another way. "How can the Union be saved? To this I answer, there is but one way by which it can be, and that is by adopting such measures as will satisfy the States belonging to the Southern section that they can remain in the Union consistently with their honor and their safety."

Calhoun was a lawyer, and to his dying day he believed that the solution to disunion must be found in law rather than in partisanship. "There is but one way by which it can with any certainty; and that is by a full and final settlement, on the principle of justice, of all the questions at issue between the two sections. The South asks for justice, simple justice, and less she ought not to take. She has no compromise to offer but the Constitution, and no concession or surrender to make." Legislation protecting slave property was the answer, including the new fugitive slave bill. "But will the North agree to this? It is for her to answer the question. But, I will say, she cannot refuse if she has half the love of the Union which she professes to have, or without justly exposing herself to the charge that her love of power and aggrandizement is far greater than her love of the Union." Calhoun was pleading with free-state senators to accept a comprehensive and binding fugitive slave law, little realizing, or perhaps fully realizing but refusing to credit, that such a law would become only another irritant between free and slave states.[14]

Three days later Webster joined the debate. His now shopworn blue frock coat hung on his bowed shoulders. He stood, as he always had, with one hand on the clerk's desk, no longer a gesture; now for support. His voice had lost some of its strength but none of its vibrancy. He must have known that his would not be the Senate's final word, but perhaps his own. "I wish to speak to-day, not as a Massachusetts man, nor as a Northern man, but as an American, and a member of the Senate of the United States." The Senate, to which he had devoted the better part of his public life when not in court, was always the nation's deliberative body. It had, thus, some of the trappings of a court, and Webster this day brought to it all of his court-honed powers. He even regarded it as a court. "It is fortunate that there is a Senate of the United States; a body not yet moved from its propriety, not lost to a just sense of its own dignity and its own high responsibilities, and a body to which the country looks, with confidence, for wise, moderate, patriotic, and healing counsels."

On this day the Senate was the nation's highest court for Webster. The analogy to the House of Lords, which was the highest court in England, is instructive. The crown high courts, including common pleas, exchequer, and king's bench, were the models for the US Supreme Court, but the Lords, including the law lords, had long exercised a kind of national jurisdiction, hearing all appeals from the other courts. Its rulings were final. So, too, the US Senate, with its long tradition of deliberation, its members' long terms in office (something like life tenure in many cases), and its legislative duties, including ratification of treaties, was something like the Lords.

Would not his Senate colleagues allow him a little fustian, as Marshall had permitted Webster for so many years? "It is not to be denied that we live in the midst of strong agitations, and are surrounded by very considerable dangers to our institutions and our government. The imprisoned winds are let loose. The East, the North, and the stormy South combine to throw the whole sea into commotion, to toss its billows to the skies, and disclose its profoundest depths." But Webster denied that he spoke this day as a politician. He spoke to the nation, for the nation, of the nation.

Read as a legal brief, the oratorical flourishes take on new shades of meaning. "I have a part to act, not for my own security or safety, for I am looking out for no fragment upon which to float away from the wreck, if wreck there must be, but for the good of the whole, and the preservation of all." He was today the voice of *we the people* "for the preservation of the Union." That was his client, and in zealous advocacy for his client he used all the tools of his trade, even if it meant leaving behind his political and moral attachments. One did not win a legal case on moral grounds then any more than today.[15]

Webster's call for moderation was not in the nature of ordinary legal argument. It was the advocacy expected of a statesman, and by now that is what he was. He had served his country with honor, discretion, and ability as its secretary of state, a post then far more esteemed than it is today. In a way, the California agitation called for statesmanship, in the shape of interstate diplomacy. Webster consciously adopted the role of international lawyer, a role requiring him to put aside regional and party identifications and advocacy. What his auditory may have missed, and historians did not restore, was adoption of this pose. Again, he sought to lay out the relationship between the public interest and individual rights and to police the boundary between law and politics. Public interest might favor the end of slavery, but the individual rights of property holders trumped a majoritarian Free Soil. The fugitive slave bill was a legal solution to the nation's woes; political allegiances, including his own, must not be allowed to undo what law proposed to accomplish. Perhaps even more important, his defense of the fugitive slave bill, though it seemed to favor the slave interest, was but another attempt to elevate federal law making over states' rights.

As was often a lawyer's tactic in pleading a lawsuit, Webster stated both sides of a case as though they had equal weight—or at least could be accorded equal weight:

> Upon the general nature and influence of slavery there exists a wide difference of opinion between the northern portion of this country and the southern. It is said on the one side, that . . . slavery is a wrong; that it is founded merely in the right of the strongest; and that is an oppression, like unjust wars, like all those conflicts by which a powerful nation subjects a weaker to its will; and that, in its nature, whatever may be said of it in the modifications which have taken place, it is not according to the meek spirit of the Gospel. It is not "kindly affectioned"; it does not "seek another's, and not its own"; it does not "let the oppressed go free."

These are the sentiments that are cherished, and of late with greatly augmented force, among the people of the Northern States.

Then, with juristic license, as a judge might, he turned to "the South, upon the other side, having been accustomed to this relation between two races all their lives, from their birth, having been taught, in general, to treat the subjects of this bondage with care and kindness, and I believe, in general, feeling great kindness for them, have not taken the view of the subject which I have mentioned." Did he believe any of that? He had written privately that he too thought that slavery was a "great evil." He had publicly condemned the slave trade. He opposed the admission of additional slave states to the Union, starting with Missouri and continuing with Texas. In the debate with Hayne, he favorably contrasted the free Northwest Territory with the South. He had begun to trim those sails in 1833, when he was quoted in *Niles Register* as believing that slavery was a matter for individual states to decide, undoubtedly hoping for southern Whig support for a presidential bid. Yet his personal views had not changed. In 1844 he told a correspondent, "I regard slavery in itself as a great moral, social and political evil."[16]

How then could he repeat the litany of defenses that southern slaveholders provided for their conduct, even in his concessions to the slavery-is-a-positive-good argument? The answer is a complex one. He must save the sphere of law, here congressional law making, from politics; and the individual right to property legally obtained and held from the lawlessness of extreme abolitionism. Perhaps he could still save the federal union from extreme states' rights (aka secession); and the hardest, how to concede, to some small extent, that the law protected the slave owners' private property rights against public outcry. Making concessions was the only way Webster could envision to cling to a fragment of his lifelong jurisprudential contribution.

The March 7 speech was a courtroom performance in which Webster, counsel for the Union, made the case for its survival. With the Union as his client, he could offer as evidence southern views of slavery. Those views, which he briefly and somewhat stiffly recited, were admissible in court, if not in his heart or in his politics. A lawyer can do for his client what he would feel morally obnoxious in his personal life. Webster never owned a slave, traded a slave, or invested in the slave trade. But nearly half of the white population of the Union lived in slave states, and over two million slaves were bought, sold, and transported within the South before 1850. How else could the Union be defended if the South's peculiar institution were not given a temporary pass?[17]

Again, a speculation about Webster's tactical motives presents itself. A cunning counsel may concede a little in a present case hoping to save his client from future calamity. In the second half of the 1840s, immigration from Ireland and Germany to the United States became a flood. The floodwaters poured into northern cities and the upper Midwestern countryside. The free population of the North grew by over 4.5 million from immigration alone. Cities in the North tripled in size. Webster knew all this, indeed had seen it firsthand. He had argued the Passenger Cases himself. Overall free population in the North was outstripping the growth of the free population in the South. New York had grown from 2.4 million to 3.1 million, Pennsylvania from 1.7 million to 2.3 million, Ohio from 1.5 million to 2 million, and Illinois from 480 thousand to 850 thousand. Virginia's population, by contrast, had remained almost stagnant. The so-called black bottom states (for their rich soil) of Georgia, Alabama, and Mississippi had grown in population, but the overall numbers were smaller, and much of the increase was unfree. The balance between free and slave states' representatives in the House already favored the former. The imbalance would grow in coming years. That meant a growing imbalance in the Electoral College as well as in Congress. Perhaps a temporizing strategy would save the Union for free labor—simply compromise now and wait until the weight of numbers overwhelmed the slaveocracy?[18]

Webster had always been a supporter of the expansive federal government. The fugitive slave bill proposed by Clay and demanded by Calhoun and the rest of the slave South was a measure resting on the Rendition Clause of the Constitution. That clause, part of Article IV, read, "No person held to service or labour in one state, under the laws thereof, escaping into another, shall, in consequence of any law or regulation therein, be discharged from such service or labor, but shall be delivered up on claim of the party to whom such service or labour may be due." The clause was the basis of the Fugitive Slave Act of 1793, the enforcement portion of which read, "The person to whom such labor or service may be due, his agent or attorney, is hereby empowered to seize or arrest such fugitive from labor, and to take him or her before any Judge of the Circuit or District Courts of the United States, residing or being within the State, or before any magistrate of a county, city, or town corporate, wherein such seizure or arrest shall be made." The new bill expanded the federal bureaucracy, adding commissioners and expanding the budget. A future federal government no longer in southern hands might use that bureaucracy and budget for other purposes.[19]

Or the law might galvanize antislavery sentiment in the North. Webster was never an abolitionist. Later in his speech he would inveigh against that movement. Could he have been playing a deep game, denouncing abolitionism while anticipating that northern resistance to slavery would coalesce around the idea of due process for suspected runaway slaves? The notion was simple and was already present in piecemeal form throughout the Free Soil states. State law would mandate jury trials for suspected bondsmen, on the presumption that they were freemen until proven otherwise. New England, New York, and Pennsylvania had led the way with this version of "interposition," and later a stronger form of "nullification" became popular among some jurists in the North. Was Webster, covertly, among them—the concessions to the slave South a temporizing measure?[20]

Webster's diplomatic correspondence over and over cited "rule of law." Webster was hardly an expert on the law of nations, and much of his writing on international law was boilerplate, but when he wrote that the rule of law required him to do or say something, he meant it. Set aside the politics of Free Soil and proslavery, and the law was clear. To have argued that the proposed new law was a violation of the Constitution or unprecedented or simply political was itself a political stance. Fidelity to settled law constrained Webster. Runaway slaves were the property of their masters even though the master no longer had possession. This was the Court's decision in *Jones v. Van Zandt* (1847). True, under the new bill, the suspected runaway was not given the presumption of freedom and was not accorded due process of law under the federal statute by allowing slave catchers to bring their quarry before federal commissioners and gain the necessary certificate to remove the suspected runaway from the state with little more than a perfunctory hearing.[21]

Was the new fugitive slave bill political? Of course it was, a concession to the slaveholding states necessary to compromise on the admission of California as a free state. Was it only political? No. It was that noxious alchemy that Webster had so long resisted. But surely the Constitution had explicitly provided for such measures? At least that is what the Rendition Clause seemed to imply. Was it necessary to save the Union? It seemed on its face to fit the mold set by *McCulloch* and consistently defended by Webster. In fact, it was much farther reaching than the BUS II cases, thrusting slave catching and federal commissioners to aid the slave catchers in every free state. Nothing quite matched it until Congress sanctioned the blockade of southern coastlines in the Civil War. "In the excited times in which we live, there is found to exist a state of crimination and recrimination between the North and South. There are lists of grievances produced by each; and those grievances, real or supposed, alienate the minds of one portion of the country from the other, exasperate the feelings, and subdue the sense of fraternal affection, patriotic love, and mutual regard."[22]

The northern states' assistance to runaway slaves was the chief among these lawless acts for slaveholders. Webster recognized as much. But how to frame his displeasure? Here he went for a robust rule-of-law stance.

> There has been found at the North, among individuals and among legislators, a disinclination to perform fully their constitutional duties in regard to the return of persons bound to service who have escaped into the free States. In that respect, the South, in my judgment, is right, and the North is wrong. Every member of every Northern legislature is bound by oath, like every other officer in the country, to support the Constitution of the United States; and the article of the Constitution which says to these States that they shall deliver up fugitives from service is as binding in honor and conscience as any other article.

Webster offered a commentary on *Prigg v. Pennsylvania* (1842) that must have been personally difficult. He was as close to Justice Story as to any man, and was not eager to criticize Story's dictum in *Prigg*. Webster thought that the duty to render lay with the states under the 1793 act, but in *Prigg v. Pennsylvania*, a decision by Justice Story, the state was not obliged to assist in the recapture or the rendition of a suspected runaway. Hence the necessity of a new law creating federal officialdom to perform this function. In effect, it was Story's aversion to slavery that put Webster, and the nation, in the awkward plight of needing the 1850 Fugitive Slave Act.

> I repeat, therefore, Sir, that here is a well-founded ground of complaint against the North, which ought to be removed, which it is now in the power of the different departments of this government to remove; which calls for the enactment of proper laws authorizing the judicature of this government, in the several States, to do all that is necessary for the recapture of fugitive slaves and for their restoration to those who claim them.[23]

Here Webster could have stopped. He had agonized over how much of his older strictures on politics and law he could abandon without giving up everything he had once held so dear and that had been so clear to him. Again he offered his understanding of the difference between the political and legal in the Constitution and characterized the fugitive slave bill as one more proof of federal supremacy over the states under the Constitution. He had not, however, explained how his views rested on a plausible distinction between public interest and private rights. He believed that liberty was a private right; but so was property. Northern antislavery agitation was already upsetting that balance—that is, in the abolitionist demand that the larger good required the end of slavery and the slave interest's reply that southern interests required the protection of slavery Webster saw the seeds of chaos. Thus the passage of the bill would not save the Union. It would merely provide further disruption and discontent in the North. Abolitionists would continue to aid runaways in flagrant disobedience to the law.

As disobedience to the law was abhorrent to him, he continued onto the dark and bloody ground of abolitionism, admonishing the reformers to behave themselves. Of the abolition societies, "I do not think them useful. I think their operations for the last twenty years have produced nothing good or valuable. At the same time, I believe thousands of their members to be honest and good men, perfectly well-meaning men." If only these good men would see the light as Webster saw it, that is, put the law ahead of their agitation for the freedom of the slave. Instead, "they sent incendiary publications into the slave States; at any rate, they attempted to arouse, and did arouse, a very strong feeling; in other words, they created great agitation in the North against Southern slavery. Well, what was the result? The bonds of the slave were bound more firmly than before, their rivets were more strongly fastened." Let the better nature of men take its course, and slavery would gradually disappear. Press too hard against the South, and it would "bind faster the slave population of the South."[24]

What was left of the public/private divide? There had never been much of a division in the slave South, where public law guaranteed the private right to another person's labor and private rights rested on the state slave law. Perhaps the solution to the present lawlessness was more and better law. There was always hope. The alternative was the demise of the Union, accompanied by civil war. "I hear with distress and anguish the word 'secession,' especially when it falls from the lips of those who are patriotic, and known to the country, and known all over the world, for their political services." For any attempt to secede would be met with violence. "Secession! Peaceable secession! Sir, your eyes and mine are never destined to see that miracle. The dismemberment of this vast country without convulsion! The breaking up of the fountains of the great deep without ruffing the surface! Who is so foolish, I beg every body's pardon, as to expect to see any such thing?"

It was grandiose thinking for Webster to hope that an oration could save the Union, but no more grandiose than his oral argument in the Supreme Court chamber downstairs. For Webster, so often looking back with longing, had now seen the future. Though it be through a glass darkly, he envisioned a nation rent by treason. The rest of the speech was peroration, increasingly overwrought predictions of hosts of evils. Webster grew impatient, repeating himself in metaphor after metaphor, as if he were afraid to finish, his words alone holding the Union together. His final passage became legend: "No monarchical throne presses these States together, no iron chain of military power encircles them; they live and stand under a government popular in its form, representative in its character, founded upon principles of equality, and so constructed, we hope, as to last for ever."

Webster understood, as few others did, that the foremost and most pressing question of March 7, 1850, was not merely a political one. It was a constitutional one. Could the Constitution countenance, much less counsel, secession, or was it only meaningful if the Union were indissoluble? Did the "liquidation" of the Constitution have a literal as well as a figurative meaning? Once again, the question for the lawyers—for Calhoun was a lawyer like Webster—was who had the last word when it came to constitutional interpretation. Was it the elected officials of the federal government—the members of Congress and the president? Was it only the judges? This was the political/legal conundrum left silent by the framers. If one accepted a strong version of states' sovereignty, could leaders of the respective states lead those states out of the Union on their own authority? Did the states have the final say in interpretation of the Constitution? The Constitution spoke clearly on matters of adding land to the national domain, severing states into pieces, and organizing new territories.

On the question of secession, the Constitution was silent. One could, as Webster had in previous times, cite the preamble's "We the People," but Justice Story's *Commentaries on the Constitution* (1834) had stated that the preamble was purposive, not self-effectuating. Shortly after Webster spoke, William Henry Seward would revive the preamble in his higher law Senate speech. Marshall and Hamilton, in different places, had thought the preamble self-effectuating, but their legacy—a strong nationalism—was imperiled. The Jacksonian Democracy leaned toward states' rights. Webster was a Whig, not a Democrat, but he too finally seemed to bend in the strong wind of southern secession threats—or had he?[25]

Look again at the speech as a legal argument instead of a political manifesto. See how the three concerns than ran through his jurisprudence converge in the speech. The fugitive slave bill had taken the issue of slave recapture out of politics and made it a matter of law. Process for recapture and return was now clear. Opponents would decry its lack of due process, but the process was to be followed in all cases. The bill removed the issue from the state legislatures and put it in the hands of federal commissions, marshals, and judges. Finally, the supremacy of federal over state government was clear. In all three of these ways, the bill satisfied the criteria that Webster had first proposed in the *Dartmouth College* case. The outcome was morally abhorrent, but to Webster's mind it was necessary if the Union was to be preserved.[26]

Webster's speech was well received, albeit with politeness rather than genuine warmth by some in the South, and with somewhat more acclaim among conservatives in the North. In public, Webster preferred to acknowledge the compliments and minimize the insults. As he told a group of Boston citizens who wrote to commend him, he was gratified to learn that his remarks were "not altogether disapproved by the people of Massachusetts." After all, "the country needs pacification." He thought "there are no essential differences" that "are irreconcilable or incapable of adjustment." As for slavery in the new territories, well, it "cannot be," and that was an end to it. As for the fugitive slave question, "We must return to our old feelings of conciliation and regard." The Union and the Constitution would be safe against "serious dangers." Webster, writing from Marshfield, conceded to Isaac Hill, the former Democratic governor and US senator from New Hampshire, that the new generation seemed less attached to the patriotism of their generation, but he thought his words would endure. Hill, as it happened, had died in Washington, DC, a month before Webster sent the letter. One wonders if Webster had lost touch with more than the new realities of sectionalism. Although he told anyone who would listen that "I have made an effort to ally the spirit of sectional strife," words of balm were not going to calm the waters.[27]

Webster wanted the speech widely reprinted, and it was, titled a "Plea for the Union." He was still in demand as a public speaker, although the Massachusetts state legislature chose lawyer and abolitionist Charles Sumner rather than return Webster to his old Senate seat. His consolation prize was service as president Millard Fillmore's secretary of state, replacing John M. Clayton of Delaware. Webster had seven more Supreme Court cases in 1850, then three in 1851, and two in the year of his death, 1852. The new generation had indeed replaced the old defender of the Constitution in the courthouse. For him, "gloom" and despair" marked these years.[28]

Webster's foremost modern biographer judged that the country had moved ahead but "Webster stayed behind." That is more than a little unfair. Most of the country remained rural or small towns with the same values of private rights and the same dour view of politics as Webster. But Webster was now face-to-face with the contradiction in his constitutional schema: If the protection of private property was the foundational premise of the federal system, did it not include the protection of slave owners' property in their bondmen and women? If many in the free states decided, with Abraham Lincoln, that a house dividing against itself could not stand, could the Union survive in its present state? The sword would decide the issue, but lawyers on both sides of the quarrel, from its inception through its resolution, had as much to do with the shape of constitutional thinking after the war as the politicians and the generals.[29]

Conclusion: The Constitution According to Mr. Webster

Some historians regard the successor generation to the founding fathers as a failure, an age of brass following the gold of the founders. Accused of blundering into a Civil War, they were supposedly besotted by ambition and avarice. Other historians associate the generation of Clay, Webster, and Calhoun with the genocide of the native peoples and the spread of slavery. Under their stewardship the nation fell behind England and France in failing to end human bondage. Seeing these men as politicians lends some support to these judgments. Certainly, Webster's declining years overlapped with what one historian has called "the big barbeque." In an age when politicians' buying and selling influence was almost normal, Webster's avarice was almost legendary.[1]

Various historical critics of Webster, echoing some of his contemporaries, decried Webster's trimming, his deficiency in "moral energy" according to his rival, New Hampshire's William Plumer. In his now famous 1849 "Civil Disobedience" essay, a disappointed Henry David Thoreau offered that Webster "never goes behind government," meaning that Webster never contemplated "essential reform." Later scholars echoed these criticisms. Historian Richard Current found that "conflicting loyalties" that "reflected economic interest" along with "personal ambition" too often dictated Webster's political choices. Other chroniclers found that godlike Daniel was actually "profligate: with his talents, his time, his earnings." In our own time, when virtue is examined and reexamined in the thousand mutually reflecting mirrors of social media, Webster's peculation in and out of government would surely have led to his public shaming. When all that is left of reputation is public image, intellectual contributions like Webster's will easily be shoved aside.[2]

Were Webster with us today, he would recognize these harsh judgments as familiar ones. They speak to the politics of his age, and to its politicians, of which he was both. He heard them all. Then, as now, however, they do not address his attempt to complete the Constitution, an effort one can find all through his legal practice and his political oratory. It was, to be sure, a limited effort, for Webster saw mapping constitutional terrain as a legal, rather than a political, task. To recognize this, one must try to do what he could not: separate his political career from his legal thinking. Webster was not a systematic or particularly original political thinker. Still, he cited the Constitution as his authority in legal matters whenever he could, and the citations were not just patriotic bombast. Look more closely, and the threads that knit them together appear. Bear in mind that there were not then law review essays, whose thousands of pages now supply us with constitutional theory. Though he lived in the great age of literary magazines on both sides of the Atlantic, Webster did not use their pages to promote his ideas. Instead, they were embedded in his speeches and oral arguments.[3]

Return to the 1850 speech in the Senate, his greatest failure. Webster was asking members of the Senate to vote for the fugitive slave bill and both sections of the country to obey the new law. The politics of the speech rested on a legal foundation. Even abolitionists were to bow to the law. The omnibus compromise bill failed, but the Fugitive Slave Act passed. Despite his pleas, it was widely contravened in the free states. He wanted law and order. What happened was civil disobedience and secession.

As a jurisprudential intervention, however, the speech was not a failure. It brought together answers to the three unfinished constitutional questions, mapping out the landscape, in a plea for the rule of law. Webster argued that only through the process of making law and obeying it could the nation be saved from partisanship. Webster had seen this convergence long before Henry Clay proposed his compromise bills on the admission of California. For example, in the course of objecting to Andrew Jackson's refusal to agree to Congress's recharter of the BUS II, in 1832, Webster told the Senate,

> We have arrived at a new epoch. We are entering on experiments, with the government and the Constitution of the country, hitherto untried, and of fearful and appalling aspect. . . . The President is as much bound by the law as any private citizen, and can no more contest its validity than any private citizen. He may refuse to obey the law, and so may a private citizen; but both do it at their own peril, and neither of them can settle the question of its validity.

Thus Webster dealt with the politics/law divide; next he turned to the key role of the judiciary: "The President may say a law is unconstitutional, but he is not the judge. Who is to decide that question? The judiciary alone possesses this unquestionable and hitherto unquestioned right." In our own time of presidential abuse of the judiciary and the Congress, along with the president's refusal to obey the law, Webster's words, as they should, hold significance for extremists on both sides of the modern political spectrum; if only they would listen.[4]

The same point as Webster made about Jackson's conduct emerged in a missive secretary of state Webster transmitted to Waddy Thompson, US minister to Mexico, regarding a letter that Francisco Gonzalez Bocanegra, Mexico's secretary of state, had sent. Bocanegra objected to Thompson regarding American provocations on the Texas-Mexican border. Webster explained where his own, and he believed US, constitutional integrity lay. "Every provision of law, every principle of neutral obligation, will be sedulously enforced in relation to Mexico, as in relation to other powers, and to the same extent and with the same integrity of purpose. All this belongs to the constitutional power and duty of the [US] *government*, and it will all be fulfilled . . . [in the] constitutional orbit in which it revolves."[5]

Where could one find this rule of law? Though Webster served for many years in both houses of Congress, he did not see the rule of law in the rough and tumble of democracy. Only when Congress took politics out of the law would private interest truly bow to public good. As he wrote to Isaac Hill on April 20, 1850, "My effort has been, and will be, to the full extent of my power, to cause the billows of useless and dangerous domestic controversy to sleep, and be still." Then, and only then, would individual rights be protected. He said as much when he replied to Robert Hayne. The presidency was similarly bent by partisanship and party strife, as he said of Jackson. Instead, the source of the rule of law must be the courts. On September 1, 1841, in a civil but somewhat testy note, Webster replied to the Spanish ambassador Pedro Alcantara Argaïz's demand that the slaves of the ship *Amistad* be returned to their putative Spanish owners. The Supreme Court, in an opinion by Webster's close friend Joseph Story, following a brilliant oral argument by Webster's Massachusetts colleague John Quincy Adams, had ruled that the African men aboard the ship were never part of its cargo. They were free and had been taken illegally (according to a US-Spanish accord on the slave trade) from their African home. Webster told the Spanish legate that the Supreme Court had spoken, and its judgments on the Constitution were final. "The president had no power to review or alter any of the judgements of that court, it being a tribunal wholly independent of the executive, and one whose decisions must be regarded as final and conclusive upon all questions brought before it." Although the Spanish had been assured by outgoing president Martin Van Buren that the Africans would be returned to slavery, no president could gainsay a Supreme Court decision. When Argaïz again wrote to Webster to protest that interpretation of an international treaty was not in the purview of the US Supreme Court, Webster lectured the Spanish diplomat: "The Supreme Court is a part of [our] government . . . and its decision, in matters lawfully within its jurisdiction, is the final decision of United States upon such matters."[6]

Webster bid his countrymen look for the rule of law in the considered, deliberative, responsible judgments of the Court. That is why, though he despised Roger Taney, Webster did not publicly attack the Taney Court's jurisprudence. Consider Webster's notes for the defense of the state of Rhode Island in its miniature war with the Dorrites. The latter had sought, by force, to change the state constitution to provide universal manhood suffrage. That reform eventually came through the normal processes of constitutional amendment, but in the meantime, a band of militiamen had entered one of the rebels' homes and arrested the denizens. In *Luther v. Borden* (1849), wherein the plaintiff sought a federal court's aid against the militiamen, Webster was prepared to argue, "There is another principle of American liberty of the highest importance and directly applicable to this case, when in the course of events, it becomes necessary, to ascertain the Will of the people . . . the legislative power provides for that ascertainment . . . the old constitutions have been so changed." The Dorr party did not succeed in the normal course of proceeding and so undertook to oust the existing government. But "men cannot get together, count themselves say they are hundreds or thousands, judge of their own qualification, call themselves the people, and then proclaim alterations of the fundamental law, or any other law." They must act according to law to change law. If the state government will not allow this, they may turn to Congress or the courts. They may not use self-help. Webster might as well have been speaking to the abolitionists and certainly to John Brown and his insurrectionists at Harpers Ferry in 1859, but by that time, Webster had gone to his reward.[7]

Consider as well his brief stint as Millard Fillmore's secretary of state. Webster supported the vigorous enforcement of the Fugitive Slave Act, both in his official role and out of doors. His mantra, *Union now and Forever*, went along with his insistence that northern courts and state governments could not be allowed to disdain federal law. As he told the committee of Tarrytown, New York, on January 27, 1851, which had asked that he appear and address them on George Washington's birthday, "hold on with unflinching firmness to the Constitution and to the union of the states," for to breach the Union and defy the Constitution was "treason." The message was thus two-faced: the one that looked upon the South warned that secession was treason. In the case of the runaway slave Anthony Burns, Webster demanded that Massachusetts not interfere with his recapture and return him to his masters. Webster's critics decried his insistence on the rule of law as an attempt to win southern Whig support for his presidency in 1852. But Webster had so antagonized Free Soil opinion in the North that, if anything, his stance sabotaged any chance he would be chosen.[8]

Webster's legacy was just not his voice or his rhetorical tropes, not his politics or his ambition, not his youthful defense of the right of private property, not his repeated invocation of the Constitution, not the greatness or the failure of his generation in the face of the Indian and slavery questions, but his commitment to the rule of law. Traced through his arguments in court and his senatorial addresses, the rule of law becomes his answer to the three great questions of the incomplete Constitution. The public will cannot be allowed to crush private rights, even when these belong to a minority. Politics may not dictate law, and legislatures may not overawe courts. The federal government must remain supreme over the states, and the Union of the states is inseparable. These, his attempts to survey the three open questions in the Constitution, together constituted the foundations of rule of law in his eyes.

Perhaps Webster's constitutionalism will be regarded as conservative, or even antidemocratic. That too is unfair. His ideas of reform—the moral, educational, and economic ideals of the former Federalists and later the Whigs—began as paeans to a society of family farms, small commercial ventures, and local schools and colleges. But Webster's views evolved. He saw the future in the "diffusion" of property, a kind of natural redistribution based, as he explained in his second reply to Hayne, on the opportunity to enjoy the fruits of one's labor. He saw the danger to this in the dissolution of the Union.[9]

Like Nietzsche's owl of wisdom, Webster's rule of law jurisprudence came too late to save the nation. In his analysis of both the political/legal and the public/private questions Webster worried that the power of the courts was continually eroded by the legislative branches. As the Jacksonian Democracy grew in influence in both state and national elections, the check the courts posed to the representative branches diminished. The omens predated Webster's demise. In cases like *Worcester v. Georgia* (1832), a state simply ignored that check upon its wanton disregard of federal treaty and the High Court's decision. Under the leadership of Chief Justice Taney, the federal courts became handmaidens to states' rights, with only a few exceptions at the same time as politics immobilized Congress, its deliberations coming to an abrupt halt over the question of admitting Kansas as a slave state. With the Kansas territory bleeding, the Court tried and failed in *Dred Scott v. Sandford* (1857) to provide a foundation for lasting rule of law. Taney, as Webster might have predicted, had gone too far in his dicta that persons of African ancestry could never be citizens and Congress could never bar slavery from territories. The slave South applauded, but the free North recoiled in horror. The chief justice's opinion in *Dred Scott* was truly a "self-inflicted wound." The political party system, operating through presidential elections, became a provocation rather than an occasion for mediation in 1860. Webster's effort to separate politics from law went for naught. There was no dividing line between public and private. States' rights had won the day.[10]

When Abraham Lincoln was legally elected president, South Carolina, whose politicians Webster had challenged so often, rejected the rule of law. They refused to accept the results of a presidential poll and announced that they were withdrawing from the Union. Secession took with it eleven states, and the rule of law was not reestablished until hundreds of thousands of men had died and billions of dollars of property was destroyed in a Civil War. The tragedy of Webster's life—and it was tragic—was not the fall of the great man through his own hubris, but the descent of the nation into lawlessness and violence.[11]

Where then did Webster's legal legacy survive? Ironically, given his own views, the answer is not in the case law. In the aftermath of the Civil War, theoreticians like judge and law professor Thomas Cooley of Michigan preached a doctrine very similar to Webster's. Cooley's *A Treatise on the Constitutional Limitations Which Rest Upon the Legislative Power of States of the American Union* (1871) cited the *Dartmouth College* case as fully establishing the proof of state grants to private individuals from further state interference and *McCulloch* for the rule that the power to tax is the power to destroy. Contracts that conferred private property rights must be safe from state interference. Missing from the text and the analysis therein, however, was Webster. The source of the rule may have been counsel's briefs or oral argument, but the citations of the rule in later treatise and case law is the Court. In lists of lawyers, Webster is classed as an orator and statesman, but not a theorist. When Webster's great cases are cited in judges' opinions and casebooks, Webster has no place. Felix Frankfurter's *The Commerce Clause under Marshall, Taney and Waite* (1923) gives a brief nod to Webster's involvement in *Gibbons*. Nothing more. In such fashion, the contributions of the lawyers like Webster were forgotten, but in law and legal history, nothing is really lost. Webster is there in the pages of the *U.S. Reports* and in the *Congressional Globe*. Perhaps even more important in these modern days of rage and protest, the value of the rule of law is never lost.[12]

Did his labors at least map the boundaries of the unfinished Constitution? Webster could no more finish it than anyone in his generation, as he found. Despite his lifelong effort to answer the three questions, even the convergence of his answers on the concept of rule of law, the Constitution remained unfinished. Asking courts to do what cannot be done is a vain enterprise. What Webster perhaps did not realize is that the incompleteness of the Constitution is its guarantor of continued capacity for growth. A completed Constitution cannot change. It is fixed in time. But the times change, values change, and the needs of a nation and people change. A vibrant Constitution accommodates these changes. There is always the amending process, and amendments have changed the Constitution greatly, but seeing the need for an amendment and implementing it is much like reinterpreting the document as it stands—they require a recognition that the Constitution is incomplete. Amendment and reinterpretation are the lifeblood of our constitutionalism. The unfinished Constitution ensures the rule of law.[13]

Notes

INTRODUCTION

1. Jay Parini, "The American Mythos," *Daedalus* 141 (2012): 54; Emily Bazelon, "We the People," *New York Times Magazine*, March 1, 2020, 27–33, 46–47; Thomas Jefferson to John Adams, August 30, 1787, in Julian P. Boyd, ed., *Papers of Thomas Jefferson* (Princeton, NJ: Princeton University Press, 1955), 12:69.

2. Edmund Randolph to the Constitutional Convention, July 26, 1787, in Max Farrand, ed., *Records of the Constitutional Convention of 1787*, rev. ed. (New Haven, CT: Yale University Press, 1937), 4:37; [James Madison,] *Federalist*, no. 37, *New York Daily Advertiser*, January 11, 1788; Jonathan Gienapp, *The Second Creation: Fixing the American Constitution in the Founding Era* (Cambridge, MA: Harvard University Press, 2018), 78; Paul G. Ream, "Liquidation of Constitutional Meaning Through Use," *Duke Law Journal* 66 (2017): 1650–1652; but see William Baude, "Constitutional Liquidation," *Stanford Law Review* 71 (2019): 1–70. Note that nothing in the body of the Constitution tells federal officers, elected officials, or jurists how to interpret its language.

3. Henry Baldwin, *A General View of the Origin and Nature of the Constitution and Government of the United States* (Philadelphia: John C. Clark, 1837), 1; Joseph Story, *Commentaries on the Constitution of the United States* (1833), 3:267; R. Kent Newmyer, *Supreme Court Justice Joseph Story, Statesman of the Old Republic* (Chapel Hill: University of North Carolina Press, 1983), 310–311. I do not intend to weigh in on the controversy over originalism here (but see the final pages of this work). It seems clear to me that the danger of supposing that constitutional language today means what it meant to the framers is obvious. See Jonathan Gienapp, "The Foreign Founding: Rights, Fixity, and the Original Constitution," *Texas Law Review* 97 (2019): 115–116.

4. Story, *Commentaries*, 3:267.

5. The Tenth Amendment is dear to advocates of "new federalism"; Kurt T. Lash, "James Madison's Celebrated Report of 1800: The Transformation of the Tenth Amendment," *George Washington Law Review* 74 (2006): 165–199. But see Mark R. Killenbeck, "No Harm in Such a Declaration," in Killenbeck, ed., *The Tenth Amendment and State Sovereignty* (Lanham, MD: Rowman & Littlefield, 2002), 14 and after (the Tenth Amendment remains unclear). Also, John H. Clough, "Federalism: the Imprecise Calculus of Dual Sovereignty," *John Marshall Law Review* 35 (2001): 1–44. The revival of the Tenth Amendment has its critics. See, e.g., Akhil Amar, *America's Unwritten Constitution: The Precedents and Principles We Live By* (New York: Basic Books, 2012), 52, 61; Larry Kramer, *The People Themselves: Popular Constitutionalism and Judicial Review* (New York: Oxford University Press, 2004), 12, 29, 45; Mark Tushnet, *Taking the Constitution Away from the Courts* (Princeton, NJ: Princeton University Press, 1999), 127. All of these, and the rest of the genre, argue for the legislative branch as the best suited to determine constitutional meanings, a position that Webster rejected.

6. P. J. Marshall, "Parliament and Property Rights in the Eighteenth Century British Empire," in John Brewer and Susan Staves, eds., *Early Modern Conceptions of Property* (London: Routledge, 1995), 530–544; Richard L. Bushman, *King and People in Provincial Massachusetts* (Chapel Hill: University of North Carolina Press, 1992), 93; Morton Horwitz, *The Transformation of American Law, 1780–1860* (Cambridge, MA: Harvard University Press, 1977), 64.

7. [James Madison,] *Federalist*, no. 10, in J. R. Pole, ed., *The Federalist* (Indianapolis: Hackett, 2005), 49.

8. James Madison to Edmund Pendleton, September 23, 1789, in Maeva Marcus et al., eds., *Documentary History of the Supreme Court of the United States, 1789–1800* (New York: Columbia University Press, 1995), 4:517; Charlene Bangs Bickford et al., eds., *Documentary History of the First Federal Congress* (Baltimore: Johns Hopkins University Press, 1992), 11:825–836.

9. Or rather, it could have been drawn in very different places: see, e.g., Daniel A. Farber, *Retained by the People: The "Silent" Ninth Amendment and the Constitutional Rights Americans Don't Know They Have* (New York: Basic Books, 2007), x. The Ninth Amendment should have a "pivotal role" in defining rights of privacy and such. However, there are those who are convinced that a bright-line distinction had been drawn in 1787; see, e.g., Justice Sandra Day O'Connor's dissent in *Kelo v. City of New London*, 545 U.S. 469, 494 (2005) (O'Connor, J.): "Today the Court abandons this long-held, basic limitation on government power. Under the banner of economic development, all private property is now vulnerable to being taken and transferred to another private owner, so long as it might be upgraded—*i.e.*, given to an owner who will use it in a way that the legislature deems more beneficial to the public—in the process. To reason, as the Court does, that the incidental public benefits resulting from the subsequent ordinary use of private property render economic development takings 'for public use' is to wash out any distinction between private and public use of property—and thereby effectively to delete the words 'for public use' from the Takings Clause of the Fifth Amendment. Accordingly I respectfully dissent."

10. Jack N. Rakove, *Original Meanings: Politics and Ideas in the Making of the Constitution* (New York: Knopf, 1996), xvi.

11. See, e.g., Committee on the Judiciary of the US House of Representatives v. Donald F. McGahn II, US Court of Appeals for the District of Columbia Circuit, No. 19-5331 (2020) (courts should not interfere in interbranch "political" tussles); Stephen Breyer, *The Court and the World: American Law and the New Global Realities* (New York: Knopf, 2015), 12.

12. Wendell Bird, *Criminal Dissent: Prosecutions under the Alien and Sedition Acts of 1798* (Cambridge, MA: Harvard University Press, 2020), 361–362; Peter Charles Hoffer, Williamjames Hull Hoffer, and N. E. H. Hull, *The Supreme Court: An Essential History* (Lawrence: University Press of Kansas, 2007), 6–7; Jed H. Shugerman, *The People's Courts: Pursuing Judicial Independence in America* (Cambridge, MA: Harvard University Press, 2012), 76–77 (state high court judges face political pressure in antebellum era).

13. Robert A. Dahl, *How Democratic Is the American Constitution?*, 2nd ed. (New Haven, CT: Yale University Press, 2003), 30.

14. Stanley Elkins and Eric McKitrick, *Age of Federalism: The Early American Republic, 1788–1800* (New York: Oxford University Press, 1993), 257–294; Peter Charles Hoffer, *The Free Press Crisis of 1800: Thomas Cooper's Trial for Seditious Libel* (Lawrence: University Press of Kansas, 2011), 27–72; Andrew Burstein and Nancy Isenberg, *The Problem of Democracy: The Presidents Adams Confront the Cult of Personality* (New York: Viking, 2019), 241–242, 252–254, 266–267.

15. Richard E. Ellis, *The Jeffersonian Crisis: Courts and Politics in the Young Republic* (New York: Oxford University Press, 1971), 36–108. Greg Weiner, in *The Political Constitution: The Case against Judicial Supremacy* (Lawrence: University Press of Kansas, 2019), 175, argues that republican constitutionalism requires courts to bow to popular and representative political means to settle many socially and culturally divisive issues, rather than invent compulsory legal rules. It is "people's indifference to constitutionalism" that "opened the field to judges." Actually, the field was opened by litigation—people went to the courts to seek relief from the decisions or acts of legislative or executive branches that Weiner extols. Weiner's work fits in a corner of the popular constitutionalism literature on the same book shelf with Akhil Amar, *America's Unwritten Constitution: The Precedents and Principles We Live By* (New York: Basic Books, 2015); Larry D. Kramer, *The People Themselves*; and Mark Tushnet, *Taking the Constitution Away from the Courts*, among others.

16. This seems to be a popular view among political scientists who study the courts. The danger lies in conflating *political*, meaning having or using power, and *partisan*, meaning attached to a particular party or faction's interests. See, e.g., Justin Crowe, *Building the Judiciary: Law, Courts and the Politics of Institutional Development* (Princeton, NJ: Princeton University Press, 2012), 3–4 and the accompanying notes, 272–273; Terri Jennings Peretti, *In Defense of a Political Court* (Princeton, NJ: Princeton University Press, 2011), 180–181; David W. Neubauer and Stephen S. Meinhold, *Judicial Process*, 5th ed. (Boston: Wadsworth, 2010), 13–15.

17. John Jay to John Adams, January 2, 1801, in Henry P. Johnson, ed., *Correspondence of John Jay* (New York: G. P. Putnam, 1893), 4:285. Adams, having been voted out of the presidency, wished Jay to return to the chief justiceship he had left in 1795. Both men were Federalists. Thomas Jefferson to James Madison, December 28, 1794, in Paul L. Ford, ed., *Works of Thomas Jefferson* (New York: G. P. Putnam, 1904), 8:156. The more modern formulation, most often associated with the Critical Legal Studies movement, "denies the distinction between law and politics." Legal history becomes a subfield of political history. Roy Kreitner, "Legal History as Political History," in Markus D. Dubber and Christopher Tomlins, eds., *The Oxford Handbook of Legal History* (Oxford: Oxford University Press, 2018), 137. Webster, to be sure, would never have conceded this.

18. Jack Rakove, "Constitutional Problematics, circa 1787," in Rakove et al., eds., *Constitutional Culture and Democratic Rule* (Cambridge: Cambridge University Press, 2001), 59; Gienapp, *Second Creation*, 334; Gienapp, "The Foreign Founding," 116.

19. Lino Graglia, "The Growth of National Judicial Power," *Nova Law Review* 14 (1989): 53.

20. Rufus Choate, Eulogy of Daniel Webster, October 28, 1852, in Thomas E. Woods Jr., *The Political Writings of Rufus Choate* (Washington, DC: Henry Regnery, 2002), 237; Charles Caverno, *Reminiscences of the Eulogy of Rufus Choate on Daniel Webster . . .* (Boston: Serman and French, 1914), 8; Suzanna Sherry, "The Founders' Unwritten Constitution," *Chicago Law Review* 54 (1987): 1136–1137 n42; Maurice G. Baxter, *Daniel Webster and the Supreme Court* (Amherst: University of Massachusetts Press, 1966), 35.

21. Quotes in Gienapp, *Creation*, 96, 374nn44–45.

22. Rather than recognizing the novelty and power of Webster's approach to contractual private rights, students of the Court emphasize Marshall's and Story's views of the subject. See, e.g., Morgan D. Dowd, "Justice Story, the Supreme Court, and the Obligation of Contract," *Case Western Reserve Law Review* 19 (1968): 525 ("the heavy hand of Marshall and Story in Dartmouth); Christopher M. Joseph, "Joseph Story and the Dartmouth College Case," *Fairmont Folio: Journal of History* 1 (1996): 17–29 (Story expands Contracts Clause); James W. Ely Jr., *The Contracts Clause: A Constitutional History* (Lawrence: University Press of Kansas, 2016), 3, 51 ("under the guidance of Marshall," "the Marshall court was instrumental"); Charles F. Hobson, *The Great Chief Justice: John Marshall and the Rule of Law* (Lawrence: University Press of Kansas, 1996), 103 (Marshall defines "the true principle" of contract). Whether one takes a formalist or a realistic view of precedent, it is conventionally understood as the rule laid down in prior case by a court of appeal in the same jurisdiction on the same point of law as the later court faces. Melvin A. Eisenberg, *The Nature of the Common Law* (Cambridge, MA: Harvard University Press, 1991), 50–52 (precedent restrains); but see Karl Llewellyn, *The Common Law Tradition: Deciding Appeals* (Boston: Little, Brown, 1960), 71–73 (precedent often overturned).

23. Breaches, fissures, cracks, cavities, holes—all alternatives to the "gaps" terminology are open to the same interrogation. What was a "gap" in a document? It is missing text? There was no missing text in the Constitution, save for when an amendment altered the original. Instead, here and after, the "gap" is the failure to address a significant issue in the interpretation of the documents. It is a metaphor, just as the surveyor seeking to draw boundary lines in the constitutional landscape is metaphorical language.

24. "Death of Daniel Webster," October 25, *New York Daily Times*, 5.

25. George Ticknor Curtis, *Life of Daniel Webster* (New York: Appleton, 1893), 1:53, 57.

26. Mark M. Smith, *Listening to Nineteenth-Century America* (Chapel Hill: University of North Carolina Press, 2001), 2.

CHAPTER 1: A NEW ENGLAND MAN

1. Robert V. Remini, *Daniel Webster: The Man and His Time* (New York: Norton: 1997), 311. Caroline was a loving stepmother and a social asset to Webster, as well as a financial liability.

2. Remini, *Daniel Webster*, 146–147, 353.

3. Remini, 58 (attachment to *Dartmouth*). Remini's work is thoroughly researched and accessibly written, truly a "life and times" biography, but very old fashioned in the sense that it, like Thomas Carlyle or Ralph Waldo Emerson, understood the historical impact of great men. "The mighty pillars of the state are swept away" (762) with the passing of Webster, Clay, and Calhoun, Remini concluded his work. There is a grandeur in this, the focus on personality, and personal relationships, in one anecdote after another, but little in the way of analysis of legal ideas. For example, "Attorney general William Wirt sighed" (196) begins the account of *Gibbons v. Ogden*. Richard N. Current's *Daniel Webster and the Rise of National Conservatism* (Boston: Little, Brown, 1955) is more concise, and still more sensitive to ideas, but not particularly interested in law. Like Remini's Webster, Current's is a politician first and foremost. Other biographies include Irving H. Bartlett, *Daniel Webster* (New York: Norton, 1978), offering a psychological portrait of a flawed man who did not examine those flaws. The focus is on politics in Norman D. Brown, *Daniel Webster and the Politics of Availability* (Athens: University of Georgia Press, 1969); Robert F. Dalzell Jr., *Daniel Webster and the Trial of American Nationalism, 1843–1852* (Boston: Houghton Mifflin, 1973); and Sydney Nathans, *Daniel Webster and Jacksonian Democracy* (Baltimore: Johns Hopkins University Press, 1973), all of whom agree on Webster's qualifications for the top office and his vaulting ambition for it.

4. Nan Johnson, "The Popularization of Nineteenth-Century Rhetoric: Elocution and the Private Learner," in Gregory Clark and S. Michael Halloran, eds., *Oratorical Culture in Nineteenth-Century America: Transformation in the Theory and Practice of Rhetoric* (Carbondale: University of Southern Illinois, 1993), 139–140; Christopher Grasso, *A Speaking Aristocracy: Transforming Public Discourse in Eighteenth-Century Connecticut* (Chapel Hill: University of North Carolina Press, 1999), 406, 407. "Black Dan," in S. J. Lyman, *Life of Daniel Webster* (New York: Appleton, 1855), 220.

5. Description from Remini, *Daniel Webster*, 27–28; Current, *Webster*, 26; Robert C. Byrd, *The Senate, 1789–1989: Classic Speeches, 1830–1993* (Washington, DC: Government Printing Office, 1994), 3. The Golem comparison is mine.

6. Gary Remer, *Ethics and the Orator: The Ciceronian Tradition of Political Morality* (Chicago: University of Chicago Press, 2017), 144. But in nineteenth-century collections of speeches of orator-statesmen and in modern communications studies, Webster was not included.

7. Daniel Boorstin, *The Americans: The National Experience* (New York: Random House, 1965), 307, 311; Craig R. Smith, *Daniel Webster and the Oratory of Civil Religion* (Columbia: University of Missouri Press, 2005), 13. See also Kimberly K. Smith, *The Dominion of Voice: Riot, Reason, and Romance in Antebellum Politics* (Lawrence: University Press of Kansas, 1999), 92; James Perrin Warren, *Culture of Eloquence: Oratory and Reform in Antebellum America* (State College: Pennsylvania State University Press, 2010), 6; and Timothy J. Williams, *Intellectual Manhood: University, Self, and Society in the Antebellum South* (Chapel Hill: University of North Carolina Press, 2010), 75–77.

8. Peter Charles Hoffer, *The Free Press Crisis of 1800: Thomas Cooper's Trial for Seditious Libel* (Lawrence: University Press of Kansas, 2011), 27–50; Wendell Bird, *Criminal*

Dissent: Prosecutions under the Alien and Sedition Acts of 1798 (Cambridge, MA: Harvard University Press), 10–30.

9. Edward Larson, *A Magnificent Catastrophe: The Tumultuous Election of 1800, America's First Presidential Campaign* (New York: Free Press, 2007), 268.

10. The Judiciary Act of 1801 was short lived, repealed by the Republican majority in Congress in February 1802. Under a new Judiciary Act, the federal courts went back to the 1792 system of circuit courts held by a traveling Supreme Court justice and the district court judge, but the number of circuits was enlarged to six and the number of Supreme Court sessions was reduced from two to one. Peter Charles Hoffer, Williamjames Hull Hoffer, and N. E. H. Hull, *The Federal Courts: An Essential History* (New York: Oxford University Press, 2016), 79–85.

11. Webster to Cook, January 14, 1803, in Fletcher Webster, ed., *Private Correspondence of Daniel Webster* (Boston: Little, Brown, 1875), 1:131; Alfred S. Konefsky and Andrew J. King, "Legal Education in Early Nineteenth Century New England," in Konefsky and King, eds., *Webster, Legal Papers, The New Hampshire Practice* (Hanover, NH: University Press of New England, 1982), 1:1–8, 10, 19; G. Edward White, *Law in American History, Volume 1: From the Colonial Years through the Civil War* (New York: Oxford University Press, 2012), 281–282.

12. John M. Shirley, *The Dartmouth College Causes and the Supreme Court of the United States* (Chicago: Jones, 1895), 83–84.

13. Webster's reported argument in La Jeune Eugènie, 26 F. Cas. 832 (1822). In *Smith v. Turner* (1847) in Andrew J. King, ed., *The Papers of Daniel Webster, Legal Papers: Volume 3, Federal Practice*, part 1 (Hanover, NH: University Press of New England, 1989), 718, Webster did not argue against the domestic slave trade. Remini, *Daniel Webster*, 68, 169, 183, 186: Webster did not celebrate white supremacy, as did southern leaders, and had advanced views of the rights of free blacks and Indians. Daniel Walker Howe, *The Political Culture of American Whigs* (Chicago: University of Chicago Press, 1979), 38; James Brewer Stewart, *Abolitionist Politics and the Coming of the Civil War* (Amherst: University of Massachusetts Press, 2008), 50. Aaron R. Hall, "'Plant Yourselves on Its Primal Granite': Slavery, History and the Antebellum Roots of Originalism," *Law and History Review* 37 (2019): 746: "Through a discussion of the Founding and examples drawn from a larger body of constitutional cases involving slavery, this article charts how lawyers and judges used vernacular constitutionalism to litigate and govern the most volatile of subjects. *It was overwhelmingly that body of cases that ushered Founding narratives into courts during the Early Republic*" [italics added]. Daniel Webster invariably ushered founding narratives into his oral arguments, and they neither rested on nor supported slavery.

14. William I. Schaffer, "Daniel Webster—The Lawyer," *Temple Law Quarterly* 7 (1932): 9; "Fell into," quoted in Remini, *Daniel Webster*, 59.

15. Konefsky and King, *Webster, Legal Papers, New Hampshire Practice*, 1:72; William Plumer to George Ticknor, April 2, 1863, quoted in Current, *Webster*, 10; Webster quoted in Shirley, *The Dartmouth College Causes*, 76.

16. *Lewis v. McGregor*, 1807, in Konefsky and King, *Webster, Legal Papers, New Hampshire Practice*, 1:138–149; Webster to Ezekiel Webster, December 12, 1807, ibid., 190.

17. Douglas A. Irwin, *Clashing over Commerce: A History of U.S. Trade Policy* (Chicago: University of Chicago Press, 2017), 103–109.

18. Donald R. Hickey, *The War of 1812: A Forgotten Conflict, Bicentennial Edition* (Urbana: University of Illinois Press, 2012), 48–51.

19. Webster, July 4, 1812, Address to Washington Benevolent Society, quoted in George Ticknor Curtis, *Life of Daniel Webster* (Boston: Appleton, 1893), 1:105. These ideas anticipated Whig Party ideology, but if Webster elucidated them before there was a Whig Party, why would he then be called a Whig? Perhaps because the Whig Party of 1832 was the Webster party?

20. Konefsky and King, *Webster, Legal Papers, New Hampshire Practice*, 1:166.

21. Remini, *Daniel Webster*, 117–118; Leonard Baker, *John Marshall, A Life in Law* (New York: McMillan, 1974), 520; Webster to Joseph Story, August 6, 1822, in Fletcher Webster, ed., *Writings and Speeches of Daniel Webster: Private Correspondence* (Boston: Little, Brown, 1903), 17:320.

22. R. Kent Newmyer, *Supreme Court Justice Joseph Story: Statesman of the Old Republic* (Chapel Hill: University of North Carolina Press, 2004), 176; Maurice G. Baxter, *Daniel Webster and the Supreme Court* (Amherst: University of Massachusetts Press, 1966), 23.

23. Architect of the Capitol, "Old Supreme Court Chamber," https://www.aoc.gov /explore-capitol-campus/buildings-grounds/capitol-building/senate-wing/old-su preme-court-chamber, accessed October 19, 2020. The Senate was better for oratory, its half-domed ceiling an almost perfect auditory; Remini, *Daniel Webster*, 286.

24. The St. Lawrence, 8 Cranch 434 (1814) and 9 Cranch 120 (1815); The Grotous, 8 Cranch 456 (1814) and 9 Cranch 368 (1815); The Mary, 2 Wheaton 123 (1817); The Ariadne, 2 Wheaton 143 (1817); The George, 2 Wheaton 278 (1817); The Argo, 2 Wheaton 287 (1817); The Divina Patora, 4 Wheaton 52 (1819); Inglee v. Coolidge, 15 U.S. 363; U.S. v. Rice, 17 U.S. 246 (1819); Brown v. Gilman, 17 U.S. 255 (1819). On privateers in the War of 1812, see Faye M. Kert, *Privateers: Patriots and Profits in the War of 1812* (Baltimore: Johns Hopkins University Press, 2015), 50–56.

CHAPTER 2: "IMPAIRING THE OBLIGATION OF CONTRACTS"

1. Robert L. Clinton, "The Obligation Clause of the United States Constitution: Public and/or Private Contracts," *University of Arkansas Law Review* 11 (1988): 343–346 (quotations); James W. Ely Jr., *The Contracts Clause: A Constitutional History* (Lawrence: University Press of Kansas, 2016), 12–13; Forrest MacDonald, *Novus Ordo Seclorum: The Intellectual Origins of the Constitution* (Lawrence: University Press of Kansas, 1985), 271. The Contracts Clause is variously referred to in scholarship as the Contract Clause and, as earlier, the Obligation Clause.

2. See, e.g., Julian S. Webb, "Contract, Capitalism, and the Free Market: The Changing Face of Contractual Freedom," *Law Teacher* 21 (1987): 23; Morton J. Horwitz, *The*

Transformation of American Law, 1780–1860 (Cambridge, MA: Harvard University Press, 1977), 180–185.

3. Andrew J. King, ed., *The Papers of Daniel Webster, Legal Papers: Volume 3, Federal Practice*, part 1 (Hanover, NH: University Press of New England, 1989), 17. Despite arguments like Thomas M. Shercovy, *John Marshall's Law* (Westport, CT: Greenwood, 1994), 105, Webster did not make a natural rights or Lockean defense of vested property rights. That would have been irrelevant in the *Dartmouth College* case, as the vested right arose from a corporate charter granted to the college trustees. Webster's own experience of property as a farmer's son, and his later experience in the practice of law, showed him repeatedly that private property was created not by labor or in nature, but by specific contracts, deeds, sales, grants, and other positive legal means.

4. Horwitz, *The Transformation of American Law*, 160–173; J. H. Baker, *An Introduction to English Legal History*, 3rd ed. (London: Butterworth's, 1990), 360; David Konig, "Introduction," *Plymouth County Court Records* (Wilmington, DE: Glazier, 1978), 1:149–173; Webster to Ezekiel Webster, November 5, 1807, in Alfred S. Konefsky and Andrew J. King, eds., *Webster, Legal Papers, The New Hampshire Practice* (Hanover, NH: University Press of New England, 1982), 1:188.

5. Hendrick Hartog, *Public Property and Private Power: The Corporation of the City of New York in American Law, 1730–1870* (Chapel Hill: University of North Carolina Press, 1983), 2–4 (separation of public and private corporations), 13, 260 (blurred line between the two). On objections to the unilateral alteration of the charters, see Peter Charles Hoffer and Williamjames Hull Hoffer, *The Clamor of Lawyers: The American Revolution and Crisis in the Legal Profession* (Ithaca, NY: Cornell University Press, 2018), 112–119. The distinction between a charitable corporation and business corporation was a crucial one. Webster undoubtedly knew that state legislatures were chartering businesses that had only a tangential relation to the public good. The bargains that entrepreneurs struck with the legislatures nevertheless guaranteed that the new charter would not disturb existing property rights. For this reason, many of the corporations had limited lifespans. Bruce A. Campbell, "John Marshall, the Virginia Political Economy, and the Dartmouth College Decision," *American Journal of Legal History* 19 (1975): 62.

6. Hoffer and Hoffer, *The Clamor of Lawyers*, 9, 92, 99–100.

7. James Madison to Thomas Jefferson, February 4, 1790, in William T. Hutchinson et al., eds., *Papers of James Madison* (Charlottesville: University of Virginia Press, 1977), 13:19.

8. [Alexander Hamilton,] *Federalist*, no. 78, *New York Independent Journal*, June 14, 1788; Jennifer Nedelsky, *Private Property and the Limits of American Constitutionalism: The Madisonian Framework and Its Legacy* (Chicago: University of Chicago Press, 1990), 198–199.

9. Beverly W. Bond Jr., *The Quit-Rent System in the American Colonies* (New Haven, CT: Yale University Press, 1919); Peter Karsten, *Between Law and Custom* (Cambridge: Cambridge University Press, 2002), 119–185.

10. G. E. Aylmer, "The Meaning and Definition of Property in Seventeenth Century England," *Past and Present* (1980): 87; Matthew H. Kramer, *John Locke and the Origins*

of Private Property (Cambridge: Cambridge University Press, 2004), 118; Allan Kulikoff, *From British Peasants to Colonial American Farmers* (Chapel Hill: University of North Carolina Press, 2008), 17, 71, 106, 111, 290, 291; Hoffer and Hoffer, *The Clamor of Lawyers*, 110–111, 140.

11. The facts appear in Charles Hobson, *The Great Yazoo Lands Sale: The Case of Fletcher v. Peck* (Lawrence: University Press of Kansas, 2016), 84–92, 137–139, and in Fletcher v. Peck, 10 U.S. 87 (1810), 135, 136 (Marshall, C.J.)

12. 10 U.S. at 128 (Marshall, C.J.).

13. 10 U.S. at 129 (Marshall, C.J.).

14. 10 U.S. at 129–130 (Marshall, C.J.).

15. New Jersey v. Wilson, 11 U.S. 164 (1812).

16. Robert V. Remini, *Daniel Webster: The Man and His Time* (New York: Norton: 1997), 151–152.

17. Jere R. Daniell, *Colonial New Hampshire: A History* (Hanover, NH: University Press of New England, 2015), 176, 221; Alan Taylor, *The Divided Ground: Indians, Settlers, and the Northern Borderland of the American Revolution* (New York: Random House, 2006), 62–63. The facts were stipulated. That is, neither side disputed them. The case did not turn on whose account of the facts were true, but on questions of law.

18. Charles Flynn et al., "The Contentious History of the Dartmouth Board of Trustees," *Dartmouth Law Journal* 1 (2008): 5.

19. For example, Kings College, which became Columbia College in New York City, was by an act of the legislature in 1787 "put under the care of 24 gentlemen, who are a body corporate.... This body possesses all of the powers vested in the governors of king's college, before the revolution." Jedidiah Morse, *The American Gazetteer . . .* (Boston: Thomas & Andrews, 1804), "New" entry (n.p.); but the new charter "was a much more public" one than Kings': Robert McCaughey, *Stand Columbia: A History of Columbia University in the City of New York* (New York: Columbia University, 2003), 52. The line between public and private was never entirely clear.

20. John M. Shirley, *The Dartmouth College Causes and the Supreme Court of the United States* (Chicago: Jones, 1885), 85–103, 107, 113; Reuben D. Mussey to Leverett Saltonstall, July 18, 1816, in King, ed., *Webster Papers, Legal Papers, The Federal Practice*, 3: 39.

21. Shirley, *Dartmouth*, 142–151; Trustees of Dartmouth College v. Woodward, 1 N.H. 111 (1817).

22. 1 N.H. at 114 (Richardson, C.J.).

23. 1 N.H. at 117 (Richardson, C.J.).

24. 1 N.H. at 132, 133, 136 (Richardson, C.J.); Charles Warren, "An Historical Note on the Dartmouth College Case," *American Law Review* 46 (1912): 668.

25. G. Edward White, "The Working Life of the Marshall Court, 1815–1835," *Virginia Law Review* 70 (1984): 24–25.

26. Webster to Jeremiah Smith, December 8, 1817, in King, *Webster, Legal Papers, Federal Practice*, 3:86; Webster to Francis Brown and Charles Marsh, December 8, 1817, ibid., 3:87–88; Francis N. Stites, *Private Interest and Public Gain: The Dartmouth College Case, 1819* (Amherst: University of Massachusetts Press, 1972): 68–69.

27. Notes of Mason and Smith arguments, in King, *Webster, Legal Papers, Federal Practice*, 3:50–80; Daniel Webster to William Wirt, February 1818, in ibid., 3:99.

28. Webster to Jeremiah Mason, November 27, 1817, in Fletcher Webster, ed., *Writings and Speeches: Private Correspondence* (Boston: Little, Brown, 1903), 17:266; Webster to Jeremiah Smith, December 8, ibid., 267; Maurice G. Baxter, *Daniel Webster and the Supreme Court* (Amherst: University of Massachusetts Press, 1966), 76–79; Webster to Joseph Hopkinson, January 21, 1818, in King, *Webster, Legal Papers, Federal Practice* 3:93; Alva Burton Konkle, *Joseph Hopkinson* (Philadelphia: University of Pennsylvania Press, 1931), 321–330.

29. R. Kent Newmyer, "Daniel Webster as Tocqueville's Lawyer: The Dartmouth College Case Again," *American Journal of Legal History* 11 (1967): 129; Thomas W. Thompson to Webster, January 22, 1817, in King, *Webster, Legal Papers, Federal Practice* 3:49–50; Webster to Francis Brown, March 13, 1818, in Charles M. Wiltse, ed., *The Papers of Daniel Webster: Correspondence, Volume 1, 1784–1824* (Hanover, NH: University Press of New England, 1974), 221.

30. Richard A. Posner, "From the Bench—Convincing a Federal Court of Appeals," *Litigation* 25 (1999): 4–5; William H. Rehnquist, *The Supreme Court* (New York: Knopf, 2001), 242–243; Mark R. Kravitz, "Written and Oral Persuasion in United States Courts: A District Court Judge's Perspective on Their History, Function, and Future," *Journal of Appellate Practice and Process* 10 (2009): 249–253.

31. Trustees of Dartmouth College v. Woodward, 17 U.S. 518 (1819). Wheaton took notes as Webster spoke; see King, *Webster Legal Papers, Federal Practice* 3: 117–119. Note that the reporter gave the year for the Court's decision, but Webster's argument had been made in March of the previous (1818) session.

32. Webster's oral argument has its own page numbers, although reporter Henry Wheaton appended it at the beginning of the Court's opinion in the published report, after a copy of the original trust instrument and the state enactments. The peroration of the argument was not included, as Webster delivered it without notes. Here, Webster, brief for the trustees, 48.

33. New Hampshire Constitution of 1792, Art. II, Art. VIII. On trusteeship and equity, Dudley v. Dudley, 24 ER 114 (1705) (Cowper, J.). "Equity is no part of the law, but a moral virtue, which qualifies, moderates, and reforms the rigour, hardness and edge of the law, and is a universal truth. It does also assist the law, where it is defective and weak in the constitution (which is the life of the law), and defends the law from crafty evasions, delusions and mere subtleties, invented and contrived to evade and elude the common law, whereby such as have undoubted right are made remediless. And thus is the office of equity to protect and support the common law from shifts and contrivances against the justice of the law. Equity, therefore, does not destroy the law, nor create it, but assists it." Equity of trusts came to the colonies, and then to the states, including New Hampshire. It was included in Article III, section 1 of the federal Constitution, "in law and equity." Peter Charles Hoffer, *The Law's Conscience: Equitable Constitutionalism in America* (Chapel Hill: University of North Carolina Press, 1990), 6–79.

34. Webster, brief for the trustees, 52, 53. *Slippery slope* is the modern terminology, but the argument has been around for a long time. Variants include *domino theory, the*

wedge, the tip of the iceberg, and so on. Eric Lode, "Slippery Slope Arguments and Legal Reasoning," *California Law Review* 87 (1999): 1469–1532; Douglas Walton, *Slippery Slope Arguments* (Oxford: Oxford University Press, 1992). If the slope is real, that is, even if there is no causal connection between the imagined series of events, if the first makes the second more likely, or provides a precedent for the second, and so on, then the argument may not be fallacious. In common law systems, precedent can act in this fashion. Thus, if the Court had sustained the New Hampshire position, it would have provided precedent for the alteration of other corporate grants and trusts, and so on.

35. The English constitution was not a written, set, fundamental body of law that limited and empowered government, against which all court decisions, legislative bills, and executive acts were measured. Instead, it was and remains a collection of practices and precedents that have accrued over time. Anthony King, *The British Constitution* (Oxford: Oxford University Press, 2007), 2–3.

36. White, "Marshall Court," 5–7, 39. Wheaton's notes concluded [Webster's] "Remarks on Judge Richardson's opinion in Court below." King, *Webster Legal Papers, Federal Practice* 3:119. The editor of Webster's *Federal Practice*, vol. 3, part 1, *Private Correspondence of Daniel Webster*, 80, notes that Webster "did not know the details of Richardson's opinion" as he began preparations for the appeal. The opinion was delivered on November 6, 1817, and Webster presented his argument before the Supreme Court on March 10, 1818. By the latter date, the first volume of the New Hampshire Superior Court of Judicature had been published, under the auspices of reporter Nathaniel Adams. Whether Webster had the text, or only notes of Richardson's opinion, he knew the key parts as the US Supreme Court reporter (Wheaton) noted.

37. Webster, brief for the trustees, 53.

38. Webster's own notes for his oral argument are printed in King, *Webster, Legal Papers, Federal Practice* 3:117–153. If read aloud at Webster's usual pace, they would be considerably longer than he was reported to have spoken. I have thus used the printed version of Webster's own corrected version.

39. Webster, brief for the trustees, 53. The literature on rights arguments in the American Revolution, and the way that revolutionary lawyers reformatted older ideas to defend the new states' constitutions, is traced in Peter Charles Hoffer and Williamjames Hull Hoffer, *"The Clamor of Lawyers": The Coming of the Revolution and Crisis in the Legal Profession* (Ithaca, NY: Cornell University Press, 2018).

40. Webster, brief for the trustees, 54.

41. Webster, brief for the trustees, 55.

42. Webster, brief for trustees, 58.

43. Webster, brief for trustees, 60.

44. Webster, brief for trustees, 67.

45. Webster, brief for the trustees, 75.

46. Webster, brief for the trustees, 94.

47. Webster, brief for the trustees, 94, 95.

48. Webster, brief for the trustees, 96.

49. Webster, brief for the trustees, 105.

50. John C. Hogan, "Daniel Webster's Power of Oral Advocacy: The Argument in Dartmouth College Case," *Journal of the State Bar of California* 30 (1955): 266; Shirley, *Dartmouth*, 237–238; King, *Webster Legal Papers, Federal Practice* 3:153, 154.

51. Baxter, *Webster and the Supreme Court*, 86–89.

52. Newmyer, "Webster," 132, 133; Remini, *Daniel Webster*, 150–151.

53. Baxter, *Webster and the Supreme Court*, 92; King, *Webster Legal Papers, Federal Practice* 3:175–176.

54. Baxter, *Webster and the Supreme Court*, 89; Robert M. Ireland, "William Pinkney: A Revision and Re-emphasis," *American Journal of Legal History* 14 (1970): 235–246; Shirley, *Dartmouth*, 242–243.

55. 17 U.S. at 625, 629, 641, 645, 654 (Marshall, C.J.).

56. See, e.g., Charles F. Hobson, *The Great Chief Justice: John Marshall and the Rule of Law* (Lawrence: University Press of Kansas, 1996), 90–91.

57. 17 U.S. at 666–713 (Story, J.), 17 U.S. at 714 (Duvall, J). Shirley, *Dartmouth*, 205 and after finds much of the briefs for the plaintiffs irrelevant to the single point properly before the Supreme Court: whether the grant was a contract under the meaning of the Contracts Clause. He continued that the case was merely another round in the battle between Marshall and Jefferson, with the Federalist trustees a proxy for the former and the Republican-dominated government of New Hampshire a proxy for the latter.

58. Konefsky and King, *Webster, Legal Papers, The New Hampshire Practice* 1:260–289.

59. Jennifer Nedelsky, *Private Property and the Limits of American Constitutionalism: The Madisonian Framework and Its Legacy* (Chicago: University of Chicago Press, 1990), 220–221.

60. There is some disagreement about the contemporary importance of the decision and the precedent. James W. Ely, *The Contracts Clause: A Constitutional History* (Lawrence: University Press of Kansas, 2002), 39, found that the "decision aroused little public interest or newspaper comment at the time." Herbert A. Johnson, contrariwise, called it "the most important Supreme Court opinion concerning the [contract] clause and the nature of property rights in the United States." Herbert A. Johnson, *The Chief Justiceship of John Marshall, 1801–1835* (Columbia: University of South Carolina Press, 1997), 176. The legacy of *Dartmouth* for much of the nineteenth century was that corporation was an artificial creature of the state, and with that, Webster's attempt to map the contested boundary of private property v. public interest remained important. When the Supreme Court decided that corporations were artificial people, with Fourteenth Amendment rights, Webster's map of the constitutional landscape was no longer needed. See Greg Mark, "The Personification of the Business Corporation in American History," *University of Chicago Law Review* 54 (1987): 1441–1442.

CHAPTER 3: "NECESSARY AND PROPER"

1. Mark A. Killenbeck, *M'Culloch v. Maryland: Securing a Nation* (Lawrence: University Press of Kansas, 2006), 53–65; Stanley Elkins and Eric McKitrick, *The Age of*

Federalism: The Early American Republic, 1788–1800 (New York: Oxford University Press, 1993), 227, 229–230; Bray Hammond, *Banks and Politics in America* (Princeton, NJ: Princeton University Press, 1958), 223–233. An alternative account of the bank case appears in Eri Lomazoff, *Reconstruction the National Bank Controversy* (Chicago: University of Chicago Press, 2018), 11 and after, arguing that the bank case had more to do with events outside the courts than contemporaries admitted. I have not adopted Killenbeck's spelling of the plaintiff's name in the case citation, as it is recorded as McCulloch.

2. Killenbeck, *M'Culloch*, 64–71; Scott Reynolds Nelson, *A Nation of Deadbeats: An Uncommon History of American's Financial Disasters* (New York: Knopf, 2012), 68–69.

3. Killenbeck, *M'Culloch*, 91–92.

4. Killenbeck, *M'Culloch*, 102–103; Fanny Lee Jones, "Walter Jones and His Times," *Records of the Columbia Historical Society* (Washington, DC: 1902), 139–150.

5. See, e.g., David S. Schwartz, "Misreading *McCulloch v. Maryland*," *University of Pennsylvania Journal of Constitutional Law* 18 (2015): 2 ("everyone accepts McCulloch as a decision of the highest importance in American constitutional law"); Martin S. Flaherty, "*McCulloch v. Maryland* and We the People, Revisions in Need of Revising," *William and Mary Law Review* 43 (2001–2002): 1339 (one of Marshall's "great opinions").

6. McCulloch v. Maryland, 17 U.S. 316 (1819), Webster, brief for McCulloch, 10 (as in the report of the *Dartmouth College* case, reporter Wheaton had a print version of Webster's oral argument, and reprinted it at the beginning of the case report, giving it its own pagination).

7. Webster, brief for McCulloch, 11.

8. Webster, brief for McCulloch, 11.

9. Webster, brief for McCulloch, 12. On the drafting of the clause, see Robert G. Natelson, "The Framing and Adoption of the Necessary and Proper Clause," in Gary Lawson, *The Origins of the Necessary and Proper Clause* (New York: Cambridge University Press, 2013), 84–119.

10. The literature on the Necessary and Proper Clause's application is immense, as controversy over it went back to Alexander Hamilton's advocacy of the first Bank of the United States in 1791. The "necessary" part of the clause was the lightning rod for criticism of the clause in the formative period. Was a bank of the United States, or any similar corporation, necessary to "carry into execution" any of the other enumerated functions of Congress or of the federal government? Hamilton's answer was that the federal finances, in particular handling the national debt, required some form of federal bank. His view would be adopted in *McCulloch*. The Rehnquist Court would return to the "proper" part of the clause in reviewing federal regulatory provisions. See Printz v. U.S., 521 U.S. 898 (1997).

11. Webster, brief for McCulloch, 12.

12. Webster, brief for McCulloch, 13, 14; Natelson, "Framing," 89–91.

13. Webster, brief for McCulloch, 17.

14. Webster, brief for McCulloch, 18.

15. Webster, brief for McCulloch, 19.

16. Hopkinson, brief for Maryland, 32.

17. Hopkinson, brief for Maryland, 32; Martin, brief for Maryland, 43.

18. 17 U.S. at 400 (Marshall, C.J.).

19. 17 U.S. at 402 (Marshall, C.J.). For the idea that the preamble was self-enforcing, see Peter Charles Hoffer, *For Ourselves and Our Posterity: The Preamble to the Federal Constitution in American History* (New York: Oxford University Press, 2013), 111–112.

20. 17 U.S. at 407 (Marshall, C.J.).

21. 17 U.S. at 407 (Marshall, C.J.); A. I. L. Campbell, "'It Is a Constitution We Are Expounding': Chief Justice Marshall and the Necessary and Proper Clause," *Journal of Legal History* 12 (1991): 191.

22. 17 U.S. at 415 (Marshall, C.J.).

23. 17 U.S. at 415 (Marshall, C.J.). Elkins and McKitrick, *The Age of Federalism,* 678.

24. 17 U.S. at 417 (Marshall, C.J.).

25. 17 U.S. at 418, 419 (Marshall, C.J.).

26. 17 U.S. at 423 (Marshall C. J.).

27. 17 U.S. 427, 428 (Marshall, C.J.).

28. 17 U.S. at 432 (Marshall, C.J.).

29. 17 U.S. at 436 (Marshall, C.J.). Note Madison's assay of the Necessary and Proper Clause in *Federalist,* no. 44: "No axiom is more clearly established in law, or in reason, than whenever the end is required, the means are authorized; that whenever a general power to do a thing is given, every particular power necessary for doing it is included." On Madison's authorship of no. 44: Douglas Adair, "The Authorship of the Disputed Federalist Papers," *William and Mary Quarterly,* 3rd ser. 1 (1944): 101.

30. Amphictyon Essay no. 1, *Richmond Enquirer,* March 30, 1819. The best analysis of this and the other essays contra Marshall's opinion is the editor's introduction in Gerald Gunther, ed., *John Marshall's Defense of McCulloch v. Maryland* (Stanford, CA: Stanford University Press, 1969); and R. Kent Newmyer, "John Marshall, McCulloch v. Maryland, and the Southern States' Rights Tradition," *John Marshall Law Review* 33 (2000): 875–934.

31. Amphictyon, no. 1.

32. Newmyer, "States' Rights," 876.

CHAPTER 4. "COMMERCE AMONG THE SEVERAL STATES"

1. Notable among the twenty, *Cohens v. Virginia,* 19 U.S. 264 (1821), established the principle that the Court could review state court decisions in criminal matters, as long as the accused could claim that their federal constitutional rights had been violated by the state prosecution. The Cohen brothers' firm in Virginia sold federal lottery tickets, violating a Virginia criminal law forbidding such sales. In two decisions released the same day, the Court found that it had jurisdiction over these cases under Article III, sec. 2, giving the Court purview of all cases under the Constitution. A second decision upheld the conviction fine of the brothers, as the federal lottery tickets were only to be sold in the District of Columbia. Mark Graber believes that the Court protected this expansive view

of its appellate jurisdiction by upholding the criminal conviction—for the furor over *McCulloch* was still alive and Virginia politicians were furious that the Court had agreed to hear the case in the first place. See Mark A. Graber, "The Passive Aggressive Virtues: *Cohens v. Virginia* and the Problematic Establishment of Judicial Power," *Constitutional Commentary* 12 (1995): 67–92, at 75–78.

2. Herbert A. Johnson, *Gibbons v. Ogden, John Marshall, Steamboats, and the Commerce Clause* (Lawrence: University Press of Kansas, 2010), 21–30. See also Maurice G. Baxter, *The Steamboat Monopoly: Gibbons v. Ogden, 1824* (New York: Knopf, 1972); and Thomas H. Cox, *Gibbons v. Ogden: Law and Society in the Early Republic* (Athens, OH: Ohio University Press, 2009). Note for here and hereafter—monopoly did not have the stigma in the popular mind that it gained after the railroad era and into the twentieth century. Charles R. Geisst, *Monopolies in America: Empire Builders and Their Enemies from Jay Gould to Bill Gates* (New York: Oxford University Press, 2000), 2–3. In Darcy v. Allein, 74 ER 1131, the Court of Kings Bench declared a monopoly in the production of goods (here playing cards) was a violation of the common law provisions for freedom of trade. The exceptions were monopolies created for the common good and patents for a term of years. B. Zorina Khan, *The Democratization of Invention: Patents and Copyrights in American Economic Development, 1790–1920* (New York: Cambridge University Press, 2005), 82–84.

3. Hendrik Hartog, *The Trouble with Minna: A Case of Slavery and Emancipation in the Antebellum North* (Chapel Hill: University of North Carolina Press, 2018), 113–114.

4. Johnson, *Gibbons*, 30–31.

5. Livingston v. Van Ingen, 9 Johnson 507, 573, 574 (1812) (Kent, C.J.).

6. Johnson, *Gibbons*, 16–20, 32–34. On Kent's opinion, see Thomas P. Campbell Jr., "Chancellor Kent, Chief Justice Marshall, and the Steamboat Cases," *Syracuse Law Review* 25 (1974): 506–512.

7. Johnson, *Gibbons*, 31–47, 60–61, 72–73.

8. Cox, *Gibbons*, 122–123, 131.

9. Gibbons v. Ogden, 22 U.S. 1 (1824); Webster, brief for Gibbons, 4. Actually, because the Kent injunction had not become a final order, the Court declined jurisdiction in 1821, when the appeal was first filed.

10. Webster, brief for Gibbons, 4.

11. Webster, brief for Gibbons, 5–6.

12. Webster, brief for Gibbons, 7–8; Brian Phillips Murphy, *Building the Empire State: Political Economy in the Early Republic* (Philadelphia: University of Pennsylvania Press, 2015), 115–116.

13. Webster, brief for Gibbons, 9; Peter Charles Hoffer, *Litigation Nation* (Lanham, MD: Rowman & Littlefield, 2019), 3–10.

14. Webster, brief for Gibbons, 11–12.

15. Webster, brief for Gibbons, 13–14; Randy E. Barnett, *Restoring the Lost Constitution*, rev. ed. (Princeton, NJ: Princeton University Press, 2013), 282–290.

16. Webster, brief for Gibbons, 13; Richard N. Current, *Daniel Webster and the Rise of National Conservatism* (Boston: Little, Brown, 1955), 39–40.

17. Webster, brief for Gibbons. 13. Webster's history relied on what would later be called "the critical period" of American finances and commerce immediately following independence. See, e.g., George Van Cleve, *We Have Not a Government: The Articles of Confederation and the Road to the Constitution* (Chicago: University of Chicago Press, 2017), 102–132.

18. Webster, brief for Gibbons, 14, 15.

19. Webster, brief for Gibbons, 17.

20. Webster, brief for Gibbons, 18, 25, 26. The hidden issue of regulation of slaves in the interstate slave trade lay behind certain of the opinions in the "Passenger Cases." See Tony Allan Freyer, *The Passenger Cases and the Commerce Clause: Immigrants, Blacks, and States Rights in Antebellum America* (Lawrence: University Press of Kansas, 2014), 52–57 (were slaves carried from one state to another "commerce," or was it limited to things rather than persons?)

21. Webster, brief for Gibbons, 22, 24. This is the dormant version of the Commerce Clause, a version of concurrent regulatory authority that does not impede interstate commerce. Webster did not argue against all state regulations; only those that affected interstate commerce. Marshall would adopt this distinction in his opinion. Kent's reputation was such that Webster sent him the published brief in Dartmouth, and he never failed to praise the chancellor. John T. Horton, *James Kent: A Study in Conservatism, 1763–1847* (New York: Appleton, 1939), 267; Robert V. Remini, *Daniel Webster: The Man and His Time* (New York: Norton: 1997), 186–187. The roads question referred to the Bonus Bill, a federal project to fund roads and canals as internal improvements that Congress passed in 1816 and outgoing president James Madison vetoed as beyond the limited powers of Congress. In using the analogy, Webster was staking the case for internal improvements against Republican ideas of limited federal government.

22. Webster, brief for Gibbons, 26–27.

23. On retrospective versus prospective lawmaking, see, e.g., Neal Duxbury, *Elements of Legislation* (Cambridge: Cambridge University Press, 2013), 11–13. On finding law versus making law, see A. W. B. Simpson, *Legal Theory and Legal History: Essays on the Common Law* (London: Hambledon, 1987), 171. In our age of vastly complicated statute law, wherein courts spend much of their time interpreting what legislatures have intended, this distinction is often blurred. See Guido Calabresi, *Common Law for the Age of Statutes* (Cambridge, MA: Harvard University Press, 1985), 4–7.

24. Webster, brief for Gibbons, 28. Today, the literature on the Takings Clause of the Constitution in the Fifth Amendment might be applied to this discussion, along with commentary on restraint of trade. Webster's thinking was ahead of its time.

25. Webster, brief for Gibbons, 29. Here the question arises whether all courts are political organs, all judges political players, and all decisions politically motivated. It is a question that has plagued courts and court watchers as long as they have been in existence. Marshall drew a sharp distinction between law and partisan politics. R. Kent Newmyer, *John Marshall and the Heroic Age of the Supreme Court* (Baton Rouge: Louisiana State University Press, 2007), 210–212. Marshall's critics thought him thoroughly political in the most partisan sense; however, see, e.g., Paul Finkelman, *Supreme Injustice:*

Slavery in the Nation's Highest Court (Cambridge, MA: Harvard University Press, 2018), 29. In general, see, e.g., Richard A. Posner, "Forward: A Political Court," *Harvard Law Review* 119 (2004): 32–102 (Court is political but not necessarily partisan in its politics); and Lucas A. Powe Jr., *The Warren Court and American Politics* (Cambridge, MA: Harvard University Press, 2000), xiv and after.

26. Webster, brief for Gibbons, 30, 31–32.

27. Webster, brief for Gibbons, 36. Webster's first reply to Hayne in the Webster-Hayne debates, chapter 5 herein, explored this idea.

28. Gibbons v. Ogden, 22 U.S. 1, 187 (1824) (Marshall, C.J.).

29. 22 U.S. at 188 (Marshall, C. J.).

30. 22 U.S. at 189, 190 (Marshall, C.J.). On originalism, see Stephen G. Calabresi, "Introduction," in Calabresi, ed., *Originalism: A Quarter Century of Debate* (Chicago: Henry Regnery, 2007), 3–43. Criticism of this approach abounds; see, e.g., Laura Kalman, "Border Patrol: Reflections on the Turn to History in Legal Scholarship," *Fordham Law Review* 66 (1997): 87–124. Similar difficulties apply to the "public meaning" version of originalism. See Jack Rakove, "Joe the Ploughman Reads the Constitution; or, The Poverty of Public Meaning Originalism," *San Diego Law Review* 48 (2011): 575–600.

31. 22 U.S. at 192–193 (Marshall, C.J.); on textualism, see Keith E. Whittington, *Constitutional Interpretation: Textual Meaning, Original Intent, and Judicial Review* (Lawrence: University Press of Kansas, 1999), 58–59 (citing Madison's views as authority, although in other places Madison offered a different view, for which see chapter 1 herein).

32. 22 U.S. at 195 (Marshall, C.J.). On the conflict between realism and positivism, see Hendrik Hartog, "Pigs and Positivism," *Wisconsin Law Review* (1985): 899–937.

33. 22 U.S. at 198, 199, 203 (Marshall, C.J.).

34. 22 U. S. at 206, 207 (Marshall, C.J.). The internal slave trade was hugely profitable and moved some two million slaves around the country from 1820 to 1860. Robert H. Gudmestad, *A Troublesome Commerce: The Transformation of the Interstate Slave Trade* (Baton Rouge: Louisiana State University Press, 2002), figures from p. 9 and appendix on 210–211; Walter Johnson, *Soul by Soul: Life Inside the Antebellum Slave Market* (Cambridge, MA: Harvard University Press, 2000), 16–17, 104–105.

35. 22 U.S. at 209 (Marshall, C.J.). In short, exceptions do not prove a rule.

36. Emmet, brief for Ogden, 22 U.S. at 104; Johnson, *Gibbons*, 78–94. Johnson suggests that the counsel for New York knew that the Court was in favor of the implied powers doctrine, federal judicial supremacy, and was likely leaning in Webster's and Wirt's direction. On the other side, they must have known that states' rights doctrine, part of the "old Constitution," was still the dominant view of most state courts and legislatures. Their problem, thus, was how to argue that the New York courts should be allowed to process the matter without challenging the appellate authority of the Supreme Court. When Roger Taney replaced John Marshall and the majority of the Court seats went to Democrats, that task would become much easier. See the conclusion herein.

37. See, e.g., Newmyer, *John Marshall and the Heroic Age of the Supreme Court*, 61–64, 338; Johnson, *Gibbons*, 133–134.

CHAPTER 5: "TRUE PRINCIPLES OF THE CONSTITUTION"

1. Kirk v. Smith, 22 U.S. 241 (1824); Jeremiah Mason to Daniel Webster, December 29, 1823; Webster to Joseph Story, January 4, 1824, in Andrew J. King, ed., *The Papers of Daniel Webster, Legal Papers: Volume 3, Federal Practice*, part 1 (Hanover, NH: University Press of New England, 1989), 358–362.

2. The idea that Congress as well as the Court can be an interpreter of the meaning of the Constitution, and that Webster, in his debate with Hayne, was acting in this role, appears in Charles J. Reid Jr., "Highway to Hell: The Great National Highway Debate of 1830 and Congress as Constitutional Interpreter," *University of Toledo Law Review* 46 (2014): 13–16.

3. Richard N. Current, *Daniel Webster and the Rise of National Conservatism* (Boston: Little, Brown, 1955), 50–55; Robert V. Remini, *Daniel Webster: The Man and His Time* (New York: Norton: 1997), 298–299.

4. On tariff protests as a proxy for defense of slavery: William W. Freehling, *Prelude to Civil War: The Nullification Controversy in South Carolina, 1816–1836* (New York: Oxford University Press, 1965), 25–26 and after.

5. Harry L. Watson, *Liberty and Power: The Politics of Jacksonian America* (New York: Hill & Wang, 2006), 117; John Niven, *John C. Calhoun and the Price of Union* (Baton Rouge: Louisiana State University Press, 1988), 58–77, 158–159.

6. Richard E. Ellis, *The Union at Risk: Jacksonian Democracy, States' Rights, and the Nullification Controversy* (New York: Oxford University Press, 1989), 8–9; Niven, *Calhoun*, 158–161; Hermann E. Von Holst, *John C. Calhoun* (Boston: Houghton, 1882), 10; H. Lee Cheek Jr., ed., *John C. Calhoun: Selected Writings and Speeches* (Chicago: Regnery, 2003), 268–308.

7. Sean Wilentz, *The Rise of American Democracy: Jefferson to Lincoln* (New York: Norton, 2005), 321.

8. Christopher Childers, *The Webster-Hayne Debates: Defining Nationhood in the Early American Republic* (Baltimore: Johns Hopkins University Press, 2018), 31.

9. Paul Wallace Gates, *History of Public Land Law Development*, vol. 62 (Washington, DC: Government Printing Office, 1968), 9–10; Childers, *Webster-Hayne*, 68–74. John Van Atta, *Securing the West: Public Lands and the Fate of the Old Republic, 1785–1850* (Baltimore: Johns Hopkins University Press, 2014), 140–165, naturally locates the western lands question at the center of the Webster-Hayne debates.

10. Andrew H. Browning, *The Panic of 1819: The First Depression* (Columbia: University of Missouri Press, 2019), 206.

11. Childers, *Webster-Hayne*, 52–53, 92; Niven, *Calhoun*, 170–171. The standard modern reprint of the debates, with an introduction by the editor, is Herman Belz, ed., *The Webster-Hayne Debate on the Nature of the Union* (Indianapolis: Liberty Fund, 2000).

12. Childers, *Webster-Hayne*, 87.

13. Maurice G. Baxter, *One and Inseparable: Daniel Webster and the Union* (Cambridge,

MA: Harvard University Press, 1984), appendix of Webster Supreme Court cases, 249–250; Walter Johnson, *Soul by Soul: Life inside the Antebellum Slave Market* (Cambridge, MA: Harvard University Press, 1999), 3–18. The conventional wisdom is that the debate between Hayne and Webster was over state sovereignty versus national sovereignty, and the defense of New England and its industries. See, e.g., Belz, "Introduction," in *The Webster-Hayne Debate*, xi–xii; Childers, *Webster-Hayne*, 102–103.

14. John Van Atta, *Wolf by the Ears: The Missouri Crisis, 1819–1821* (Baltimore: Johns Hopkins University Press, 2015), 74–75.

15. Van Atta, *Wolf by the Ears*, 72–75; Peter Charles Hoffer, *John Quincy Adams and the Gag-Rule, 1835–1850* (Baltimore: Johns Hopkins University Press, 2018), 32–33; Williamjames Hull Hoffer, *The Caning of Charles Sumner: Honor, Idealism, and the Origins of the Civil War* (Baltimore: Johns Hopkins University Press, 2007), 11–13; Childers, *Webster-Hayne*, 78. Modern intersectionality theory argues that oppression of racial minorities is always accompanied by oppression of women and the poor. That is not quite what I mean here.

16. Robert Y. Hayne, Speech in the Senate, January 19, 1830, 21st Cong., 1st sess., reported in *Niles Weekly Register* 37, no. 25: 416.

17. Hayne, Speech in the Senate, January 19, 1830, *Weekly Register*, 417.

18. Hayne, Speech in the Senate, January 19, *Weekly Register*, 417. Fear of dependence in the South ran the gamut from the great planters to the yeomanry: John Ashworth, *The Republic in Crisis, 1848–1861* (Cambridge: Cambridge University Press, 2012), 123; Lacy K. Ford, *Deliver Us from Evil: The Slavery Question in the Old South* (New York: Oxford University Press, 2009), 512; Lacy K. Ford, *Origins of Southern Radicalism: The South Carolina Upcountry, 1800–1860* (New York: Oxford University Press, 1991), 84.

19. Webster, Speech in the Senate, January 20, 1830, 21st Cong., 1 sess., *Niles Weekly Register* 37, no. 26: 435.

20. Webster, Speech in the Senate, January 20, *Weekly Register*, 436.

21. Webster, Speech in the Senate, January 20, *Weekly Register*, 437.

22. Webster, Speech in the Senate, January 20, *Weekly Register*, 437.

23. Webster, Speech in the Senate, January 20, *Weekly Register*, 437.

24. Webster, Speech in the Senate, January 20, *Weekly Register*, 437, 438.

25. Webster, Speech in the Senate, January 20, *Weekly Register*, 438.

26. Webster, Speech in the Senate, January 20, *Weekly Register*, 440.

27. Harlow W. Sheidley, "The Webster-Hayne Debate: Recasting New England's Sectionalism," *New England Quarterly* 67 (1994): 5; Childers, *Webster-Hayne*, 107; Baxter, *One and Inseparable: Daniel Webster and the Union*, 182–183.

28. Hayne, Speech in the Senate, January 21, 1830, in *Webster and Hayne's Celebrated Speeches* (Philadelphia: T. B. Peterson, 1830), 3. On honor and the antebellum South, see Bertram Wyatt-Brown, *Southern Honor: Ethics and Behavior in the Old South* (New York: Oxford University Press, 1982), 360–361. This was even true of lawyers. Ibid., 392.

29. Hayne, Speech in the Senate, January 21, *Celebrated Speeches*, 10.

30. Hayne, Speech in the Senate, January 21, *Celebrated Speeches*, 10, 11, 12.

31. Hayne, Speech in the Senate, January 21, *Celebrated Speeches*, 15; Niven, *Calhoun*, 171.

32. Hayne, Speech in the Senate, January 21, *Celebrated Speeches*, 15, 18.

33. Hayne, Speech in the Senate, January 26, *Celebrated Speeches*, 36. That Hayne "descended" to personal vituperation is clear. Baxter, *One and Inseparable*, 182; Stefan M. Brooks, *The Webster-Hayne Debate* (Lanham, MD: University Press of America, 2009), 65, 66; but Hayne had done some quick homework, for example, finding a copy of an 1825 speech by Webster more or less opposing a protective tariff on the same grounds as Hayne. Theodore D. Jervey, *Robert Y. Hayne and His Times* (New York: Macmillan, 1909), 244; but then, the author, a vice president of the South Carolina Historical Society, thought Hayne had the better of the exchange and could not understand why Webster's speech had gained such fame.

34. Webster, Speech in the Senate, January 26–27, 1830, *Celebrated Speeches*, 37, 67.

35. Webster, Speech in the Senate, January 26–27, *Celebrated Speeches*, 42, 43

36. Webster, Speech in the Senate, January 26–27, *Celebrated Speeches*, 50; Childers, *Webster-Hayne*, 113.

37. Webster, Speech in the Senate, January 26–27, *Celebrated Speeches*, 68, 70, 71.

38. Webster, Speech in the Senate, January 26–27, *Celebrated Speeches*, 79, 83, 84.

39. Childers, *Webster-Hayne*, 113–124, 126, 132–135.

40. Webster, Remarks at Philadelphia, December 2, 1846, in James W. McIntyre, ed., *The Writings and Speeches of Daniel Webster* (Boston: Little Brown, 1903), 4: 9; Webster, Remarks Delivered at a Public Dinner in New York City, March 10, 1831, in Edwin P. Whipple, ed., *The Speeches and Orations of Daniel Webster* (Boston: Little Brown, 1914), 317.

41. Gerard N. Magliocca, *Andrew Jackson and the Constitution: The Rise and Fall of Generational Regimes* (Lawrence: University Press of Kansas, 2007), 67.

CHAPTER 6: "SECUR[ING] INDIVIDUAL
PROPERTY AGAINST LEGISLATIVE ASSUMPTION"

1. George Rogers Taylor, *The Transportation Revolution, 1815–1860* (New York: Holt, Rinehart & Winston, 1951), 100–101; Daniel Walker Howe, *What Hath God Wrought: The Transformation of America, 1815–1848* (New York: Oxford University Press, 2007), 211–242.

2. Howe, *What Hath God Wrought*, 533; Morton Horwitz, *The Transformation of American Law, 1780–1860* (Cambridge, MA: Harvard University Press, 1977), 133–134.

3. Horwitz, *Transformation*, 46–47; Robert V. Remini, *Daniel Webster: The Man and His Time* (New York: Norton: 1997), 452–461.

4. Charles River Bridge v. Warren Bridge, 7 Pickering (Massachusetts) 344, 427, 442 (1829); Stanley Kutler, *Privilege and Creative Destruction: The Charles River Bridge Case* (Philadelphia: University of Pennsylvania Press, 1971), 36–37, 44–50.

5. Clearly, at least to Webster, *Charles River Bridge* was analogous to *Dartmouth*.

Taney saw the resemblance and would strike a mortal blow at Webster's argument in the earlier case. Gerard N. Magliocca, *Andrew Jackson and the Constitution: The Rise and Fall of Generational Regimes* (Lawrence: University Press of Kansas, 2007), 79.

6. Proprietors of Charles River Bridge v. Proprietors of Warren Bridge, 36 U.S. 420 (1837); Dutton, brief for Charles River Bridge, 54, 71, 73 (again, the reporter, Richard Peters, set off counsel arguments with separate page numbers); William Wiecek, *The Lost World of Classical Legal Thought* (New York: Oxford University Press, 1998), 34. References to Warren Dutton appear in all three volumes of the *Webster Legal Papers, Federal Practice.*

7. Webster, brief for Charles River Bridge, 203.

8. Webster, brief for Charles River Bridge, 204; Kutler, *Privilege,* 79.

9. Webster, brief for Charles River Bridge, 208.

10. Webster, brief for Charles River Bridge, 205.

11. Webster, brief for Charles River Bridge, 208; Kutler, *Privilege,* 29–30.

12. Webster, brief for Charles River Bridge, 209.

13. Webster, brief for Charles River Bridge, 211.

14. Webster, brief for Charles River Bridge, 215, 216.

15. Webster, brief for Charles River Bridge, 240, 242; Greenleaf, brief for Warren Bridge, 243.

16. Webster, brief for Charles River Bridge, 247.

17. Albert Venn Dicey, *Introduction to the Study of the Constitution,* 10th ed. (London: Macmillan, 1960; orig. 1885), 202.

18. Proprietors of Charles River Bridge v. Proprietors of Warren Bridge, 36 U.S. 420 (1837); Kutler, *Privilege,* 172–179; Webster, Notes for Oral Argument, March 10, 1831, in Andrew J. King, ed., *The Papers of Daniel Webster, Legal Papers: Volume 3, Federal Practice,* part 1 (Hanover, NH: University Press of New England, 1989), 421, 457, 463–495; Webster, brief for Proprietors of Charles River Bridge, 247; Remini, *Webster,* 458.

19. R. Kent Newmyer, *John Marshall and the Heroic Age of the Supreme Court* (Baton Rouge: Louisiana State University Press, 2007), 412.

20. "Alabama Bank Cases": Bank of Augusta v. Earle, 38 U.S. 519 (1839), in which Webster argued the Bank of United States v. William Primrose; License Cases: 46 U.S. 504 (1847), three cases from Massachusetts, Rhode Island, and New Hampshire, respectively, in which Webster argued Thurlow v. Massachusetts against the Massachusetts law; and Passenger Cases, 48 U.S. 283 (1849), in which Webster argued against the Massachusetts law, in Norris v. City of Boston. The cases are covered in King, *Webster Legal Papers, Federal Practice,* part 2, 3: 647–731. Tony Allan Fryer, *The Passenger Cases and the Commerce Clause: Immigrants, Blacks, and States' Rights in Antebellum America* (Lawrence: University Press of Kansas, 2014), 64–66, argues that Webster's hopes for Whig Party nomination to the presidency hampered his argumentation in the cases, as the issue of slavery lurked behind the Commerce Clause and other arguments for federal power over state law.

21. See, e.g., Webster to Jeremiah Mason, February 23, 1837, in Fletcher Webster, ed., *Private Correspondence of Daniel Webster* (Boston: Little, Brown, 1875), 4:190; on

Taney nomination, see Remini, *Webster*, 437, 443; on Webster's efforts in Taney Court, see King, *Webster, Legal Papers, Federal Practice* part 2, 3:733. Luther v. Borden, 48 U.S. 1 (1849); Webster, brief for Borden et al., 69.

22. King, *Webster, Legal Papers, Federal Practice*, part 2, 3:937.

23. Groves v. Slaughter, 40 U.S. 449 (1841); Walter Johnson, *Soul by Soul: Life Inside the Antebellum Slave Market* (Cambridge, MA: Harvard University Press, 200), 51. The occasion was awkward for Webster because, like Clay, he had no liking for the slave trade.

24. George Ticknor Curtis, *The Life of Daniel Webster* (Boston: Little, Brown, 1872), 2:4–5.

CHAPTER 7: "THE RULE OF LAW"

1. Robert V. Remini, *Daniel Webster: The Man and His Time* (New York: Norton: 1997), 483–500.

2. Thomas A. Bailey, *A Diplomatic History of the American People* (New York: Appleton-Century-Crofts, 1958), 213–218.

3. Alien Torts Act, 28 U.S.C. 1350.

4. The Schooner Peggy 5, U.S. 103, 109 (1801) (Marshall, C.J.); Akhil Reed Amar, *America's Constitution: A Biography* (New York: Random House, 2005), 300–307; Stephen Breyer, *The Court and the World: American Law and the New Global Realities* (New York: Knopf, 2015), 213; Anthony J. Bellia Jr. and Bradford R. Clark, *The Law of Nations and the United States Constitution* (New York: Oxford University Press, 2017), 10–15, 42, 70–71. But see David M. Golove and Daniel J. Hulsebosch, "The Law of Nations and the Constitution: An Early Modern Perspective," *Georgetown Law Review* 106 (2015): 1595–1657; and Golove and Hulsebosch, "A Civilized Nation: The Early American Constitution, the Law of Nations and the Pursuit of International Recognition," *New York Law University Review* 85 (2010): 932, arguing that the federal Constitution is part of international law rather than simply adopting portions as needed.

5. Amar, *America's Constitution*, 26; Howard Jones, *To the Webster-Ashburton Treaty: A Study in Anglo-American Relations, 1783–1843* (Chapel Hill: University of North Carolina Press, 1977), 5–19; Peter Charles Hoffer, *Rutgers v. Waddington: Alexander Hamilton, the End of the War for Independence, and the Origins of Judicial Review* (Lawrence: University Press of Kansas, 2016), 20, 21, 32, 34–35, 63, 102, 108; Jon Kukla, *A Wilderness So Immense: The Louisiana Purchase and the Destiny of America* (New York: Random House, 2003), 280–282, 385–386.

6. "An Act to Provide for the Exchange of Lands with the Indians," May 28, 1830, 21st Cong., sess. 1, ch. 148 Stats.; Worcester v. Georgia 31 U.S. 515 (1832); Stuart Banner, *How the Indians Lost Their Land: Law and Power on the Frontier* (Cambridge, MA: Harvard University Press, 2005), 217–219; Remini, *Webster*, 335; Claudio Saunt, *Unworthy Republic: The Dispossession of Native Americans and the Road to Indian Territory* (New York: Norton, 2020), 35–36, 54–55, 81–82, 163.

7. Webster to Hiram Ketchum, December 18, 1840, in Fletcher Webster, ed., *Private Correspondence of Daniel Webster* (Boston: Little, Brown, 1875), 2:96.

8. Remini, *Webster*, 562–563, 566–567; Daniel Walker Howe, *The Political Culture of the American Whigs* (Chicago: University of Chicago Press, 1979), 223.

9. Howard Jones, "Daniel Webster," in Edward S. Mihalkanin, ed., *American States-men: Secretaries of State from John Jay to Colin Powell* (Westport, CT: Greenwood Press, 2004), 525; Remini, *Webster*, 512–513.

10. Alan Taylor, *The Civil War of 1812: American Citizens, British Subjects, Irish Rebels, and Indian Allies* (New York: Knopf, 2010), 413–419; Howard Jones, "Anglophobia and the Aroostook War," *New England Quarterly* 48 (1975): 519–539; Jones, *Webster-Ashburton*, 33–47.

11. Webster to Edward Everett, January 20, 1842, in *Works of Daniel Webster*, 9th ed. (Boston: Little, Brown, 1856), 6:271.

12. Webster to John Fairfield, April 11, 1842, in *Works of Webster*, 6:274–275; Daniel Walker Howe, *What Hath God Wrought: The Transformation of America, 1815–1848* (New York: Oxford University Press, 2007), 674–675; Jones, *Webster-Ashburton*, 91–94.

13. Jones, *Webster-Ashburton*, 102, 114, 118, 126–127; Keith Hamilton and Richard Langhorne, *The Practice of Diplomacy: Its Evolution, Theory and Administration*, 2nd ed. (London: Routledge, 1995), 119–120.

14. Henry Fox to Webster, March 12, 1841, in *Works of Webster*, 6:247–250; Webster to Fox, April 24, 1841, ibid., 250–262; Webster to John J. Crittenden, March 15, 1841, ibid., 262–266; Bellia and Clark, *Law of Nations*, 180–181; Walter Stahr, *Seward: Lincoln's Indispensable Man* (New York: Simon & Schuster, 2012), 78–79; Jones, *Webster-Ashburton*, 23–31.

15. Thomas Nichols, *Eve of Destruction: The Coming Age of Preventive War* (Philadelphia: University of Pennsylvania Press, 2008), 2.

16. "Act for Remedial Justice in the Courts of the United States," August 29, 1842, in *Works of Webster*, 6:267–269; Stahr, *Seward*, 76–80. "A special messenger brought the trial day's events to Seward. Finally, when he was conveniently acquitted, McLeod was accompanied to the Canadian border "under the governor's direction." Frederick W. Seward, ed., *Autobiography and Memoir of the Life of William H. Seward* (New York: Appleton, 1877), 568. Whig newspapers, to which party Seward belonged, commended him for "wisdom and firmness" and offered that he had "saved the general government from itself."

17. Webster to Lord Ashburton, July 27, 1842, in *Works of Webster*, 6:292–293; Jones, *Webster-Ashburton*, 98.

18. George Hendrick and Willene Hendrick, *The Creole Mutiny: A Tale of Revolt aboard a Slave Ship* (Chicago: Ivan Dee, 2003), 77–111.

19. Webster to Joseph Story, March 17, 1842; Edward Everett, ed., *Writings and Speeches of Daniel Webster . . . Hitherto Uncollected* (Boston: Little, Brown, 1903), 4:364; Webster to Ashburton, August 1, 1842, in *Works of Webster*, 6: 311. Webster knew that he could not rely on Story's opinion for the Court in U.S. v. Schooner Amistad, 40 U.S. 518 (1841), as the fact pattern was entirely different. The older American demand that slaves

either be returned or Britain pay cash for their value is discussed in Alan Taylor, *The Internal Enemy: Slavery and War in Virginia, 1772–1832* (New York: Norton, 2013), 430.

20. Ashburton to Webster, August 6, 1842, in *Works of Webster*, 6:315.

21. Remini, *Webster*, 565–582.

CHAPTER 8: "UNION NOW AND FOREVER"

1. Robert V. Remini, *Daniel Webster: The Man and His Time* (New York: Norton: 1997), 642–644, 648.

2. Remini, *Daniel Webster*, 420, 421, 443, 457–458.

3. Sean Wilentz, *The Rise of American Democracy: Jefferson to Lincoln* (New York: Norton, 2005), 484; Daniel Walker Howe, *What Hath God Wrought: The Transformation of America, 1815–1848* (New York: Oxford University Press, 2007), 572–573. On Webster's later practice, see, e.g., Andrew J. King, ed., *The Papers of Daniel Webster, Legal Papers: Volume 3, Federal Practice*, part 2 (Hanover, NH: University Press of New England, 1989), 732, 738. For an explanation of Jackson's constitutional theory, based on the notion of generational cycles, see Gerard N. Magliocca, *Andrew Jackson and the Constitution: The Rise and Fall of Generational Regimes* (Lawrence: University Press of Kansas, 2007), 54–56. Bear in mind that Jackson was not only a lawyer but had served on his state's highest bench. His view of the Constitution associated strong presidential powers with the will of the people—a view that one of his admirers, US president Donald J. Trump, adopted.

4. Appendix in King, *Federal Practice*, vol. 3, part 2, 1061–1066.

5. On old Senate chamber acoustics, see Donald A. Ritchie, *The U.S. Congress: A Very Short Introduction* (New York: Oxford University Press, 2016), 116.

6. Holman Hamilton, *Prologue to Conflict: The Crisis and Compromise of 1850* (New York: Norton, 1966), 34; William Freehling, *The Road to Disunion: Secessionists at Bay, 1776–1854* (New York: Oxford University Press, 1990), 494–495. See, generally, Frederick Merk, *Slavery and the Annexation of Texas* (New York: Knopf, 1972). Material in these pages has been adapted from my *John Quincy Adams and the Gag Rule, 1835–1850* (Baltimore: Johns Hopkins University Press, 2017), 64–73.

7. David Wilmot, speech in the House, February 8, 1847, *Congressional Globe*, 29th Cong., 2nd sess., appendix, 16318; Calhoun, speech in the Senate, February 19, 1847, ibid., 453, 455; Freehling, *Road to Disunion*, 495–496.

8. Robert V. Remini, *Henry Clay: Statesman for the Union* (New York: Norton, 1992), 730–761; Merrill D. Peterson, *The Great Triumvirate: Webster, Clay, and Calhoun* (New York: Oxford University Press, 1987), 449–475; Freehling, *Road to Disunion*, 495–498.

9. Peterson, *Great Triumvirate*, 452; Michael S. Green, *Politics and America in Crisis: The Coming of the Civil War* (Santa Barbara, CA: ABC-CLIO, 2010), 35.

10. Calhoun, Speech to the Senate, March 4, 1850, *Congressional Globe*, 31st Cong., 1st sess., 451.

11. Calhoun, Speech to the Senate, 451, 452.

12. Calhoun, Speech to the Senate, 455.

13. Calhoun, Speech to the Senate, 455.

14. Calhoun, Speech to the Senate, 455.

15. Daniel Webster, Speech in the Senate, March 7, 1850, *Congressional Globe*, 31st Cong., 1st sess., 476.

16. Webster, Speech in the Senate, 477; H. W. Brands, *Heirs of the Founders: The Epic Rivalry of Henry Clay, John Calhoun, and Daniel Webster, the Second Generation of American Giants* (New York: Random House, 2018). 492; Remini, *Daniel Webster*, 169, 183, 320, 434.

17. Internal slave trade figures: Robert H. Gudmestad, *A Troublesome Commerce: The Transformation of the Interstate Slave Trade* (Baton Rouge: Louisiana State University Press, 2002), figures from p. 9 and appendix on 210–211.

18. Howe, *What Hath God Wrought*, 527. "Population of States and Counties of the United States," Bureau of the Census, www.census.gov/population/www/censusdata /PopulationofStatesandCountiesoftheUnitedStates1790–1990.pdf. The speculation is mine.

19. R. J. M. Blackett, *The Captive's Quest for Freedom: Fugitive Slaves, the 1850 Fugitive Slave Law, and the Politics of Slavery* (New York: Cambridge University Press, 2018), 7–8; Andrew Delbanco, *The War before the War: Fugitive Slaves and the Struggle for America's Soul from the Revolution to the Civil War* (New York: Penguin, 2018), 8–9, 315, 317–318.

20. Thomas D. Morris, *Free Men All: The Personal Liberty Laws of the North, 1780–1861* (Baltimore: Johns Hopkins University Press, 1999), 42–43, 208.

21. Rendition Clause, Art. IV, sec. 2, cl. 3; Fugitive Slave Act of 1793, 1 Stat. 302 (1793); Jones v. Van Zandt, 46 U.S. 215 (1847). Compare Webster's stance with that of Massachusetts chief justice Lemuel Shaw in Leonard Levy, *The Law of the Commonwealth and Chief Justice Shaw* (Cambridge, MA: Harvard University Press, 1957), 77–78 and after.

22. Webster, Speech in the Senate, 477.

23. Webster, Speech in the Senate, 477; Prigg v. Pennsylvania, 41 U.S. 539 (1842).

24. Webster, Speech in the Senate, 482.

25. William Henry Seward, Speech in the Senate, March 11, 1850, in George Baker, ed., *Works of William Henry Seward* (New York: Redfield, 1853); 74; Peter Charles Hoffer, *For Ourselves and Our Posterity: The Preamble to the Federal Constitution in American History* (New York: Oxford University Press, 2013), 120, 122, 140; Peter Charles Hoffer, *Uncivil Warriors: The Lawyers' Civil War* (New York: Oxford University Press, 2018), 1. More on Seward's higher-law speech is forthcoming in Peter Charles Hoffer, "William Henry Seward: Country Lawyer and Lawyer for the Country."

26. Did Congress overstep its constitutional authority to impose on states an aspect of slave law? That is, slave law in the slave states allowed a master or his hires to pursue slaves found on other person's property and return them forcibly to their legal owners. Law in the free states had no such provisions. Then did the Fugitive Slave Act exceed the provisions of the Fugitive Slave Clause? The answer seemed plain to Webster—it did not.

27. Webster to Thomas H. Perkins, April 9, 1850, *Works of Daniel Webster*, 9th ed. (Boston: Little, Brown, 1856), 6:546, 547, 548; Webster to Isaac Hill, April 20, 1850, ibid., 6:550; Webster to R. H. Gardner, June 17, 1850, ibid., 6:566.

28. Webster, Speech in the Senate, 482; Remini, *Daniel Webster*, 673–675, 707; Maurice G. Baxter, *One and Inseparable: Daniel Webster and the Union* (Cambridge, MA: Harvard University Press, 1984), 251; Webster to the Bunker Hill Committee, June 13, 1850, *Works of Webster*, 6:565.

29. Remini, *Daniel Webster*, 461; Hoffer, *Uncivil Warriors*, 167–178; Stephen Berry, *A House Dividing: The Lincoln-Douglas Debates of 1858* (New York: Oxford University Press, 2016), 1–11; Earl M. Maltz, *Dred Scott and the Politics of Slavery* (Lawrence: University Press of Kansas, 2007), 140–156.

CONCLUSION

1. Blundering generation: J. G. Randall, "The Blundering Generation," *Mississippi Valley Historical Review* 27 (1940): 3–28; slavery: Edward Baptiste, *The Half Has Never Been Told: Slavery and the Making of American Capitalism* (New York: Basic Books, 2014), 112–114; Native peoples: John P. Bowes, *Land Too Good for Indians: Northern Indian Removal* (Norman: University of Oklahoma Press, 2016), 212–213; corruption: Mark W. Summers, *The Plundering Generation: Corruption and the Crisis of the Union, 1849–1861* (New York: Oxford University Press, 1988), 183–184, 188–189, 219–220; Kenneth Stampp, *America in 1857: A Nation on the Brink* (New York: Oxford University Press, 1992), 30.

2. Henry David Thoreau, "Resistance to Civil Government," in Elizabeth Peabody, ed., *Aesthetic Papers* (New York: Putnam, 1849), 209; Richard N. Current, *Daniel Webster and the Rise of National Conservatism* (Boston: Little, Brown, 1955), 191; Robert V. Remini, *Daniel Webster: The Man and His Time* (New York: Norton: 1997), 9; Arthur M. Schlesinger Jr., *The Age of Jackson* (Boston: Little, Brown, 1945), 84; H. W. Brands, *Heirs of the Founders: The Epic Rivalry of Henry Clay, John Calhoun, and Daniel Webster, the Second Generation of American Giants* (New York: Random House, 2018), 7.

3. We return to the question at the very beginning of this book: was Webster consciously trying to resolve the paradoxes in the Constitution? Or was he shifting and swerving through ideas to serve his clients' varying interests? The fact that he made real contributions to these issues cannot be denied. But one can still ask whether the consistency and depth of his jurisprudence is the present author's fabrication. Clearly, I have one answer to this question, but readers may adopt a different one.

4. Daniel Webster, *Speech of the Hon. Daniel Webster on the Presidential Veto of the Bank Bill, July 11, 1832* (Boston: J. E. Hinckley, 1832), 32, 19. Taney actually disagreed with removal of the deposits by seeking a writ in federal court—he knew with John Marshall sitting in the center seat, it would not work. But as attorney general, then as secretary of the treasury, he worked closely with Andrew Jackson to kill the bank. Robert V. Remini, *Andrew Jackson: The Course of American Democracy, 1833–1845* (Baltimore: Johns Hopkins University Press, 2013), 57, 95, 97, 98–103.

5. Webster to Waddy Thompson, July 8, 1842, in *Works of Daniel Webster*, 9th ed. (Boston: Little, Brown, 1856), 9:457; Fergus M. Bordewich, *America's Great Debate: Henry*

Clay, Stephen A. Douglas, and the Compromise that Preserved the Union (New York: Simon & Schuster, 2013), 170–172.

6. Webster to Isaac Hill, April 20, 1850, in *Works of Daniel Webster*, 9th ed. (Boston: Little, Brown, 1856), 6:550; Webster to Chevalier d' Argaïz, September 1, 1841, and June 21, 1842, ibid., 6:395, 399.

7. Webster, notes for Luther v. Borden (1849), in Andrew J. King, ed., *The Papers of Daniel Webster, Legal Papers: Volume 3, Federal Practice*, part 2 (Hanover, NH: University Press of New England, 1989), 756; Daniel Walker Howe, *What Hath God Wrought: The Transformation of America, 1815–1848* (New York: Oxford University Press, 2007), 603 ("a classic statement of Whig constitutional philosophy.").

8. Webster to the Citizens of Westchester County, NY, January 27, 1851, in *Works of Webster*, 6:586; Earl M. Maltz, *Fugitive Slave on Trial: The Anthony Burns Case and Abolitionist Outrage* (Lawrence: University Press of Kansas, 2010), 38–39; Remini, *Webster*, 696–697.

9. Sean Wilentz, *The Rise of American Democracy: Jefferson to Lincoln* (New York: Norton, 2005),485.

10. Dred Scott as "self-inflicted wound": Charles Evans Hughes, *The Supreme Court of the United States* (New York: Columbia University Press, 1928), 50.

11. Peter Charles Hoffer, *Uncivil Warriors: The Lawyers' Civil War* (New York: Oxford University Press, 2018), 172–178.

12. Thomas M. Cooley, *A Treatise on the Constitutional Limitations Which Rest upon the Legislative Power of States of the American Union*, 2nd ed. (Boston: Little, Brown, 1871), 126, 480; G. Edward White, *Law in American History*, vol. 1 (New York: Oxford University Press, 2012), 280; Felix Frankfurter, *The Commerce Clause under Marshall, Taney, and Waite* (Chapel Hill: University of North Carolina Press, 1937), 2: "In this wide and novel field of labor, our judges have been pioneers." Webster does not make it into Randy Barnett, *Restoring the Lost Constitution: The Presumption of Liberty* (Princeton, NJ: Princeton University Press, 2013); or Richard A. Epstein, *Takings: Private Property and the Power of Eminent Domain* (Cambridge, MA: Harvard University Press, 1985), or any of the other modern classic defenses of private property.

13. Jonathan Gienapp, "The Foreign Founding: Rights, Fixity, and the Original Constitution," *Texas Law Review* 97 (2019): 136–137. Obviously, I am arguing for a living Constitution. A bibliography on the originalism/living Constitution conversation would fill many pages. A very short version begins with Antonin Scalia, *A Matter of Interpretation: Federal Courts and the Law*, rev. ed. (Princeton, NJ: Princeton University Press, 2018); Randy Barnett, *Restoring the Lost Constitution* (Princeton, NJ: Princeton University Press, 2013); and Keith E. Whittington, *Constitutional Interpretation* (Lawrence: University Press of Kansas, 1999), which feature original intent, plain text, and other varietals of originalism, and, contra, Jack M. Balkin, *Living Originalism* (Cambridge, MA: Harvard University Press, 2011); David A. Strauss, *The Living Constitution* (New York: Oxford University Press, 2011); and Mark Tushnet, *The Constitution of the United States of America*, 2nd ed. (Portland, OR: Hart, 2015): 1: "The difference between the canonical and the efficient constitution is clear: the written constitution's words must somehow be adapted

to deal with problems of governance that have arisen since 1787." While Tushnet's observation is persuasive, it is not the basis of my argument for Webster's modern relevance. Webster saw an incomplete Constitution, not a perpetually evolving one.

Index